7/92

APR 1992

Lucky
in
Love

Also by Catherine Johnson, Ph.D.

When to Say Goodbye to Your Therapist

CATHERINE JOHNSON, PH.D.

Lucky
in
Love

The Secrets of

Happy Couples and How

Their Marriages Thrive

VIKING

VIKING
Published by the Penguin Group
Viking Penguin, a division of Penguin Books USA Inc.,
375 Hudson Street, New York, New York 10014, U.S.A.
Penguin Books Ltd, 27 Wrights Lane, London W8 5TZ, England
Penguin Books Australia Ltd, Ringwood, Victoria, Australia
Penguin Books Canada Ltd, 10 Alcorn Avenue, Suite 300,
Toronto, Ontario, Canada M4V 3B2
Penguin Books (N.Z.) Ltd, 182–190 Wairau Road,
Auckland 10, New Zealand

Penguin Books Ltd, Registered Offices:
Harmondsworth, Middlesex, England

First published in 1992 by Viking Penguin,
a division of Penguin Books USA Inc.

1 3 5 7 9 10 8 6 4 2

Names and other descriptive details of the individuals
represented in this book have been altered in most
instances.

LIBRARY OF CONGRESS CATALOGING IN PUBLICATION DATA
Johnson, Catherine.
Lucky in love : the secrets of happy couples and how their
marriages thrive / Catherine Johnson.
p. cm.
Includes bibliographical references.
ISBN 0-670-84354-7
1. Marriage—United States.   2. Interpersonal relations.
I. Title.
HQ734.J56   1992
646.7'8—dc20   91-26976

Printed in the United States of America
Set in Palatino
Designed by Kathryn Parise

*This book is dedicated to
my husband, Ed*

Acknowledgments

Throughout the months I spent traveling around the country to interview couples for this book, I learned a great deal about the importance of belonging to a strong and loyal family. As the mother of an eighteen-month-old when I began, I'm not sure how I could have completed this project without the help of my own family. So I would like to start with them. I want to thank my mother and father, Patricia and Robert Johnson; my in-laws, Dr. Norman and Claire Berenson; my sisters, Rosalyn Clement and Elizabeth Caslin, and their husbands, Neal and Keith; and my brother and his wife, Dave and Dee Johnson. All five couples gave me and my little boy a room in their homes and many hours of their time for baby-sitting, as well as their help in finding happily married couples in their own parts of the country.

I would also like to thank my editor, Mindy Werner, for her enthusiasm, support, and patience throughout the months of writing, as well as for her insight into and sensitivity toward the lives of people far away. And, apart from gratitude, I'd like to express my admiration for her sheer stamina. Editing an entire manuscript in one's ninth month of pregnancy during a Manhattan heat wave is far above and beyond. Thank you, Mindy.

As always, I owe a great deal to my agent, Geri Thoma, who always "gets it," and who is invariably a lot of fun on the telephone. Geri knew exactly what this book was about from the beginning, and could communicate her convictions forcefully to all. *Thank you*.

My husband, Ed, saw me through, and made the dream of my own happy family come true.

And finally, I thank the many wives and husbands who shared their lives with me. These strong and generous people are the unsung heroes of our day. Surrounded as we are by constant media tales of family failure—tales of incest, abuse, alcoholism, codependency, "dysfunctional" behavior of every stripe—we forget how powerful a force for good the strong family truly is. These couples reminded me that if, as a culture, we are going to blame our families for our troubles, then we must equally thank them for our success. They are the Source. Thank you.

Contents

Lucky
in
Love

Introduction

❦

I grew up believing there were no truly happy marriages. It was the era of Rock Hudson and Doris Day, and I remember my mother saying it was always the "sappy" couples on the Jack Paar show who divorced six months later. The ones who held hands on national television, who billed and cooed and nuzzled for millions to see: they were the ones who were abusing and betraying each other in private. Their marriages were destined to fail, the last embers of their love fading away as we watched them glow in the gray-and-white wash that was early television.

Invariably, my mother turned out to be right. At least as far as famous people were concerned, a fifties childhood taught you that appearances were inevitably deceiving. Happy couples were not happy, not really; they only looked that way to the wistful outsider, to the hopeful souls among us wishing to believe that a life lived happily ever after was a true possibility in the true world.

Small wonder, then, that I spent the entire decade of the 1970s, my first years of adult life, avoiding marriage. It took me until I was thirty to work up the nerve, and when I finally did get married I was none too confident that I would be able to remain so in the years to come. With demographers predicting that half of my generation would divorce at least once (a hapless 20 percent of us, I read, were slated to divorce not once but *twice*), I believed, in my heart, that my new husband and I had only a fifty-fifty chance at best. It was hubris to think otherwise. I had never stayed in a relationship longer than three years; what made me think I could now live happily with one man for the rest of my life?

For that was my hope. I was in my thirties, I was married to a man I loved, and I wanted to wake up in my seventies and see him still there beside me. I wanted my young marriage to last; more than that, I wanted our marriage to thrive.

It was somewhere around this time that I came across a classic sociological study of American marriage called *The Significant Americans*. Thirty years ago, in the early 1960s, two Midwestern sociologists, John F. Cuber and Peggy B. Harroff, set out to investigate the hidden lives of America's most successful citizens. What, they wondered, were the highly accomplished among us, the prominent doctors, lawyers, artists, and politicians, doing behind closed doors? Successful in public life, had they fared equally well in matters of the heart?

The results were, and are, fascinating. In Cuber and Harroff's sensitive prose I found the familiar marriage of suburban fiction, the marriage that has dwindled over the years into a union of quiet desperation. These were the marriages in which life and love had slipped away in the night, in which man and wife (as they thought of themselves then) now paid deference to the brittle form of the marital vows while quietly accepting the fact that the substance was lost to them forever. "He is a good provider," these long-married people offered simply, trying to explain what now held them together; "she is a good mother." Love and passion were gone; a distant and strained appreciation remained.

It was an intimate portrait of the classic 1950s marriage, the kind of union that was to give marriage such a bad name when the children of these men and women themselves reached the age of choice. "At thirty-eight you're not *old*," one wife told her interviewers, "yet you find that sex has gotten humdrum, the children fill your time with trivia—no stimulation, just fatigue. You hardly ever see your husband and when you do, he's preoccupied with other things. These all creep up on you and all of a sudden you realize you're *never* going to be a couple again—not really!"

The testimony of husbands was just as bleak. "[It's been] nothing dramatic," one said, "just a slow recognition that we didn't have much in common. . . . It wasn't only sex that we got crossed up about. Whenever we got to talking we . . . would very quickly get to the point where there was nothing to talk about anymore. We just sat and looked at each other."

And finally, a clergyman of the time offered his own perspective on the upstanding citizens of his day: "If there were more solid relationships between the husbands and wives in my congregation, we'd have a hard time keeping this church organized as well as it is. If the men and women were mated the way they ought to be, if their lives were full and their hearts full of each other, they would want to be together—and all those evening committee meetings and groups would dwindle to nothing. . . . They come here just to work out their desertions at home by these binges of altruism."

For me, reading Cuber and Harroff's book some twenty-odd years after it first appeared was a powerful exercise in the shock of recognition. I had the feeling of discovering the Source: Here it was, in an aging library book, one of the original renderings of the image of marriage with which I had grown up. Here it is, I thought, this is where it comes from: all my fellow thirtysomethings with their dread of tract houses and wood-paneled station wagons (Chrysler has the likes of Cuber and Harroff to thank for the emergence of the Jeep)—it was their book, and all the books and movies and novels like it, that so profoundly warned me and my contemporaries away from marriage. It was works like these—and the undeniable reality they represented—that made what was to follow seem so right for a time: the sexual revolution, open marriage, the institutionalization of divorce. All were ways out, or around, the cage we thought was 1950s marriage.

The trouble was, none of these strategies worked. Most famously, "open marriage" turned out to be a complete debacle; inevitably George and Nena O'Neill—the couple who had brought open marriage to the world in their book by that title—divorced, and Nena wrote a second book taking everything back. Horrifyingly, the sexual revolution brought us AIDS, and divorced people did not go on to become gay divorcés. Instead they remarried in droves, only to enter into second marriages with a slightly higher divorce rate than the mortality figures for first marriages.

If open infidelities and divorce were the 1970s response to the problems of marriage, by the 1980s a new generation, my own, had turned to the world of work. Career was the answer, we thought, for women certainly. Now the career would come first, the man second. Marriage rates for the baby-boom generation dropped precipitously; childlessness soared. The culture as a whole turned away from marriage, away from a *belief* in marriage as an important life goal. This was so much the case, in fact, that as I researched this book couples who had married during the 1970s and early 1980s often told me they remember feeling out of step with their peers, uncool. Among college-educated men and women at that time there was tremendous pressure not to marry in the first place, or, if you did marry, to maintain separate last names and separate, "independent" lives. Psychologists urged their married patients to seek individual fulfillment, and to take separate vacations. And the divorce rate continued to rise.

Having lived through the turbulent divorce-ridden years of the 1960s, '70s, and '80s, today's commentators on marriage and the family ratify the fatalistic wisdom of the 1950s. There can be stable couples, they concede; there can be couples whose marriages *survive*. But deeply, ongoingly happy couples? No. These you find only in situation comedies, they tell us, and in prime-time commercial breaks. Happy couples are not real couples. In the words of Germaine Greer, writing of her profoundly flawed father in no less significant a forum than the *New York Times Book Review*, "I think the important thing to remember is that there's no such thing as a normal family."

Few authorities would argue the point. When it comes to marriage, the media and academe are steeped in negativity. Page through Arlene S. Skolnick's premier college textbook on marriage, *The Intimate Environment: Exploring Marriage and the Family*, now in its fourth edition, and you find numerous examples of this. On the first page of her thorough and, in fact, quite useful book Skolnick tells us flatly that there is "a dark side to family life"—apparently to *all* lives, of *all* families. Later on she observes that "according to a number of recent studies force and violence may be a fundamental part of family life."

Remarkably, Skolnick is no enemy of marriage; she believes in the institution and argues that in our day marriage is alive and well. She is simply, she says, being realistic: "Conflict and ambivalence," she writes, "are as intrinsic to the family as intimacy and love. . . ." For authors like Skolnick, to say that violence is a fundamental part of family life is not to condemn marriage; it is simply to face "facts." Hers is the kind of realism that sees good and bad as two sides of the same coin; for Skolnick, as for so many other theorists of marriage, happiness and unhappiness in marriage are always linked. When we marry, these authors say, we sign on for both.

But do we? Is it *necessarily* true that happiness and unhappiness in marriage are always connected, for all couples? The problem with this kind of "realism" is that it has grown out of clinical observations of only one kind of family: the family in trouble. We hear very little from psychologists about families who are thriving. Family-systems theory, perhaps the dominant school of thinking about marriage today, originated in work with the families of schizophrenics. Not infrequently, researchers found, these highly stressed family members gave each other mixed messages that could be extremely damaging to self-esteem and the ability to make decisions and take action. But the obvious question is: Which comes first, the schizophrenic family member or the mixed messages? It is entirely possible that under these conditions frazzled parents are driven to the point that they are no longer able to say what they mean. Special-education assessors quote a wonderful line concerning this very issue: "Mental illness is genetic; you get it from your kids."

It is easy enough, of course, to imagine how a family struggling to cope with a schizophrenic parent or child might end up giving each other highly contradictory signals; no doubt their feelings are contradictory indeed. But systems theorists soon extended their findings to the rest of society, arguing that all families are fundamentally similar to families in which one member suffers from a serious mental illness. All families, they believe, engage in "paradoxical communications," telling each other one thing while saying another. Skolnick herself endorses this approach to understanding the family, observing that "violent families" and "families with mentally ill children" are no different in kind from any other family. Dysfunctional families simply display an exaggerated form of the tensions that exist in all families.

This is a remarkably dire vision of the family, given the incredible level of stress placed upon family members by a schizophrenic parent or child, or by a violent spouse. It is important to ask ourselves, before we accept this view as gospel, whether it really makes sense to argue that a peaceful family is different only in *degree* from a family in which spouses are threatening each other's very lives. The obvious problem with basing all marital theory upon dysfunctional families is that inevitably all families come to seem dysfunctional. Because scholars make little or no attempt to identify and study healthy, highly functional families, the very notion of a healthy family disappears.

Not surprisingly, journalists adopt the same approach. Here is best-selling explicator of the marital relationship, Maggie Scarf, author of *Intimate Partners:* "People *expect to be happy* once they have paired off, entered the house of marriage and closed the door behind them," she writes. The italics, a typographical eyebrow raised, tell the story: people's expectations of happiness in marriage are clearly wrongheaded, delusional. Soon enough she tells us so straight-out: "When we marry," she writes, "irrational hopes . . . run high." Later Scarf offers a scale of marital health, ranging from the least-functional marriage to the most-functional one. She carefully describes the manner in which couples relate to each other at each of the lowest four levels, but when she reaches the highest level she shifts her stance: "Level one on the scale," she writes, ". . . [is] less an interpersonal reality than it is an ideal." For Scarf, the extremely unhealthy marriage is all too real, the extremely healthy marriage only a dream. Very healthy marriages, she tells us, do not exist in reality.

Scarf's sentiments precisely capture the conventional wisdom. The "normal" marriage, nearly all psychologists believe, progresses inexorably from idealization (the "honeymoon phase") to disillusionment (when reality dawns), after which the best a couple can hope for is to achieve a mature accommodation to each other's "flaws." Strangely, most theorists seem to feel that this progression from idealization to a rather harsh form of "realism" represents the way a marriage *should be*, that there would be something wrong with a marriage in which the idealization phase continued undisturbed for many years. On this point Skolnick approvingly quotes one of her many sources, psychologist George Simpson, on the correct response to the question "Do you ever regret your marriage?" "The mature answer," Simpson observes, "is of course." He makes his prejudice clear when he observes that ". . . any person who gets very high scores [for marital happiness] may not be happy but slap-happy." For many a theorist of marriage, it would seem, genuine happiness is a highly suspect state, a sign of lingering delusion, denial, or simple foolishness.

Needless to say, this is not an enticing vision of the wedded state. Quite reasonably, my own generation soon reached a collective decision that if marriage was such a bad thing, the logical solution was to put our energies elsewhere. The problem was, neither full-throttle careerism nor separate vacations turned out to be the answer. The sad truth is that my generation has largely failed in its quest to be different—different, at least, in any way that would make us happier. What *is* different about my generation is not that we have better marriages but that we are less stable in bad ones: our divorce rate is nearly double that of our parents' generation.

Nor have we proved able to move beyond marriage to a state of happy aloneness. Defeated at last by the burdens of "liberation," many of my generation finally concluded that even a so-so marriage was better than a life in which you were still dating at forty. By the late 1980s, we were ready to settle.

So it was that, having lived through the high hopes and sad awakenings of recent family history, I recognized at once the quiescent marriages of Cuber and Harroff's "significant Americans." This much was no surprise. But what did startle me in their work was the fact that these alliances were not the universal reality. Instead, Cuber and Harroff discovered a small and largely hidden group of couples who were thriving in what the authors came to think of as the "vital" marriage: these men and women were profoundly and passionately involved with each other. They were alive to their partners; they were emotionally, intellectually, and sexually vivid and present in the other's existence. They were in love, and had been for many years. In short, they had realized the goal of happily-ever-after; for these people, the dream had come true.

Strangely, their existence was an extraordinarily well-kept secret. And, as I read the personal testimony of these people, the reasons for their invisibility became apparent: they themselves were at pains not to let friends and neighbors know how they felt about each other, how happy they were, how passionate their sexual bond remained. They kept their happiness to themselves because, as they told Cuber and Harroff, their friends neither understood nor approved: their more conventionally mated neighbors, they reported, saw them as immature, overly dependent upon their mates, selfish.

This feeling was not mere paranoia, either. Vital couples were right about the way other people felt: Cuber and Harroff found massive disapproval of vital couples among their friends and neighbors, and among the experts of the day. The famous conformism of the 1950s was part of this. Upstanding members of their communities, Cuber and Harroff's less happily wed "significant Americans" put in long days at the office, equally long nights attending to civic duties. Church committee meetings, the PTA, and ice-cream socials consumed their free hours. In sharp contrast, vital couples preferred to spend their time together. They routinely spurned the Tuesday night church fund-raising committee in order to spend time with each other—a practice read as distinctly antisocial by their fellows.

The experts of the day went further yet. One anonymously quoted psychologist, contemplating the intensely close nature of these relationships, stated authoritatively: "Any man or woman who has to live *that close* is simply *sick*. He must need a mate as a crutch! He's too dependent! There's just something unhealthy about it." And an unnamed doctor, confronted by a wife who balked at taking the vacation he had prescribed unless her husband, with whom she was very much in love, could go, too, responded: "In all these years, Mrs. Frank, that's the first neurotic symptom I've noticed in you."

In the 1950s, it seems, having a terrific marriage did not endear you to your fellows. Quite the contrary. The authorities of the day endorsed the status quo, championing the static, devitalized marriage as the ultimate standard in adult rationality, responsibility, *maturity*. And they enforced this ideology relentlessly.

So fierce were they, so unyielding, in their rejection of the passionate marriage that you come to wonder about their motivation. Do we look back at the wholesome 1950s and see an oedipal incapacity to think of husbands and wives—*mothers and fathers*—as sexy? Perhaps.

Or do we see a simple case of envy? Poignantly, Cuber and Harroff quote the pensive reaction of a sales executive, himself less happily married, who said of a vital couple he knew: "By god, they do have something though. You feel it when you're around them. You should see the hell he raises around the office when he has to go home a little late, and the way he fights a trip out of town if he has to go alone. I wonder what it is."

I wonder, too. Because you do see those couples who are alive and well, or who look to be; you see them and wonder if they really are as happy as they seem. At weddings, I like to watch the older people dancing. There is always one pair who dance extraordinarily well together; they know the steps by heart, and they radiate a kind of absolute confidence and verve. Undeniably, they are sexy together. To me, they have always looked like the real thing and now, reading Cuber and Harroff, I found dramatic evidence that they were. These marriages *exist.*

And that is the point at which this book begins. Who are these couples? How did they meet, how did they court, how did life stay so good for them? How did they survive the bad times?

I decided to find out. I had long been interested in the subject of health and happiness, in what it means, psychologically speaking, to be happy and well. My first book, *When to Say Goodbye to Your Therapist,* had wrestled with the question of when therapy is over: how does a patient in psychotherapy know when he or she is better? This is an important question because psychologists, like their counterparts in marital theory, have developed only sketchy notions of what it is to be *well;* most therapists are much better at describing and understanding mental illness than they are at describing and understanding mental health.

As to the issue of healthy relationships, I had researched dozens of articles about women and men over the years, all of which, in one way or another, tried to find answers to the question of how lovers can create lasting happiness. A book-length investigation into the nature of long-term, happy marriages was the logical next step.

As I embarked upon the interviews for this book I learned almost immediately that there do exist couples, many couples in fact, who will instantly give you a "never" when you ask if they ever regret their marriages. What is more, these couples are certainly as "mature" as are the couples who answer "of course." There are also couples who will tell you that they *have* thought of leaving each other in the past but are very glad, today, that they did not. Talk to people about their lives and you will find that there are couples who have been happy for many years, and there are couples whose very real and solid happiness is only lately and hard won. And of course there are miserable couples, bored couples, utterly confused and chaotic couples—as the saying goes, it does indeed take all kinds. But if the unhappy marriages we read so much about are all too real, the happy marriages are just as solid and *here;* the happy marriages *exist* in time, space, and living color just as truly as do the tragedies.

It is difficult to estimate their numbers. Cuber and Harroff gave no figure for the number of vital couples they found in the early 1960s. In the present you must weigh, on one hand, divorce statistics, which would certainly seem to point to a large population of very unhappy marriages, against public-opinion polls simply asking citizens, outright, how they feel about their relationships. The *Washington Post–ABC News* poll of October 1987 found that 93 percent of all women polled described their relationships as "good" or "excellent." While the pollsters did not explicitly ask, "Are you happy?" it is probably fair to assume that a woman who perceives her marriage to be excellent is also a woman who perceives her marriage to be happy. Two years later, in 1989, the Gallup Organization polled people on the subject of marital fidelity and found that, quite contrary to the usual perception of rampant adultery across the land, fewer than one in ten spouses reported ever having been unfaithful. Whether or not the 90 percent who say they have been faithful mates would also call themselves happy is an open question, but it does raise the possibility that there are many more happy husbands and wives among us than we think. If 90 percent of a random sample tell *Washington Post*/ABC their relationships are excellent, if 90 percent of a second random sample tell Gallup they have been faithful to their mates, then it is a distinct possibility that many happy marriages exist.

How do we reconcile these responses with current divorce rates? Perhaps by raising the possibility that a telephone survey is not the best of methods to get at the truth of an individual marriage. Who among us is going to confess an infidelity to a Gallup poll taker with his or her spouse present in the same house? Not surprisingly, the entirely private 1990 survey discussed in the book *The Day America Told the Truth*, by advertising executives James Patterson and Peter Kim, produced findings consistent with the divorce rate. Out of more than 2,000 randomly selected Americans almost half of the sample said that there was no reason to get married, ever! Twenty percent said that if they had it to do over they definitely would not marry the same person again, and another 25 percent said they were not sure. On the other hand, more than half said that if they had it to do over again they *would* choose the same person. How many of these couples are happily married as opposed to simply resigned to their fates we cannot know; Patterson and Kim did not ask. Nevertheless, if more than half would remarry the same person, it makes sense to assume that a good number of married people are in fact quite happy with their lives and loves.

Of the couples with whom I spoke, fifty-six were thriving. However, because my sample of one hundred couples was not randomly selected, this figure cannot give us any *statistically* significant insights into the proportion of happily married couples among us. This is a work of journalism, not of social science. Nevertheless, the couples in this book were not radically different from other people; certainly none of them saw their happy experience of marriage as being unique. They were simply people with a gift, either natural or acquired over many years' experience, for love and marriage. Their experiences have a great deal to tell the rest of us.

I went about finding these couples in a number of ways. Some I discovered by asking friends and colleagues whether they knew someone whose marriage seemed particularly good. Usually they did. I found the rest of my sample by placing a notice in several newspapers across the country: "For a book on marriage I would appreciate hearing from couples married seven years or more who would be willing to sit for a brief interview." The *Los Angeles Times* published this request as an Author's Query in the book review section, and I placed the same advertisement in the classified sections of newspapers in Chicago and Houston. I chose seven years as the cutoff not because seven years is a long time to be married, but because it would allow me to interview some couples in their twenties. This was important because the culture surrounding marriage has changed so dramatically in recent years. I thought it quite possible, rightly as it turned out, that stable couples in their twenties might have a completely different view of marriage and divorce than did stable couples in their forties and older. I wanted to see whether the experience of having married young within a culture of divorce had affected these couples' marriages.

I wanted, as well, to cover as broad a range of distinct time frames as possible. Every generation marries under a different set of historical circumstances, and the historical moment influences the course of their marriage. A couple marrying during the Great Depression faced an entirely different set of tensions and challenges than did a couple marrying at the height of the Vietnam War. And, as we will see, a young couple marrying during the period of national disillusionment following Watergate faced different problems still. The seven-year cut-off gave young couples a forum.

Ultimately I interviewed one hundred couples drawn from across the country: from the city of Los Angeles and its surrounding communities, from Sacramento, from the suburbs of Houston, from Chicago and its suburbs, and finally from the eastern cities of New York and Philadelphia. Couples spanned the entire economic range, from bankruptcy to great wealth. In age they ranged from their twenties to their eighties. The shortest marriage had lasted for seven years; the longest-married couple had celebrated their fifty-fifth anniversary. Almost all were white; only one black and one Hispanic couple volunteered.

Approximately sixty were very happily married. This percentage is obviously skewed toward the positive since many of the couples came into the group precisely because they were—or were perceived by their friends to be—happy. "Happiness" took all forms: Some couples had suffered a great deal of conflict over the years but were very happy now; some couples had been happy together from the beginning. Some couples were highly sexual; others tilted more toward the friendship end of the marital spectrum.

Of the remaining forty couples, only two were desperately unhappy. The rest could be described as suffering from "ordinary" woe: these were people who simply seemed irritated with each other, whose marriages were marked by ongoing, if usually minor, friction. Often these couples seemed not so much angry with each other as overwhelmed by life. I remember one pair who was swamped with bills and struggling to raise three young children. Even with both spouses working full-time they were still living on the financial brink, and they suffered daily conflict over who would have money to buy what. Would the husband be allowed to buy a new automotive part for his hobby of restoring old cars, or would the children be given new tennis shoes for summer even though their school shoes still fit? The constant frustration of having to share limited resources cast a pall over their marriage. Nevertheless, they were a solid couple: in a crisis they always pulled together, they told me. There had been a time, a few years back, when they had faced bankruptcy. "We never fought then," the wife told me. Real trouble brought them together, and, working together, they had managed to repay all of their creditors.

None of these marriages was violent or more than marginally destructive. Instead couples bickered, or grew distant, or suffered a mutual case of the blahs. In other cases spouses had, over time, managed to fashion sound, working relationships with mates who had turned out to be disappointing in some respects. After years of difficulties these couples were not blissfully happy; certainly they were not as happy as were couples who had continued to see each other as the near-perfect partner in life. But they were happy *enough*. All members of this group strongly appreciated what was good about their alliances; while a bad marriage may be worse than no marriage, a just–all right marriage, it seems, may be preferable to the rigors of single parenthood.

All told, then, the couples whose lives appear in these pages may be happier than the norm, but if they are, they are not in any way "abnormally" cheerful. Many of them—in fact, most of them—knew other couples just as happy as they; few of them struck me, meeting with them face to face, as leading lives utterly different from the rest of us. Their example tells us that happiness in love is a much more realistic and attainable goal than we may have been led to believe.

I do mean *love*, in its fullest sense. A significant number of these couples remained, after many years together, after children and bills and sagging flesh and thinning hair, *in love*. Romantically and physically in love. Theirs did not in many cases conform to the prevailing notion of the good marriage, in which initial passion is soon replaced by the subtler pleasures of warmth, comfort, affection. After ten years, twenty years, thirty or forty, they were still profoundly excited by each other. If, as the experts would have it, romantic love is inherently delusional—inherently an idealization of a reality that is flawed— these couples had managed to sustain remarkably idealized visions of each other for remarkable lengths of time.

Perhaps my favorite couple in this respect were Larry and Jane Weissberg. (All but one couple in this book are referred to by pseudonyms; however, no husband or wife is a composite of several people put together.) After thirty-two years of marriage Larry routinely refers to his wife as "America's most beautiful woman," an expression of his love for her that clearly delights them both. "I'll be calling my husband from an open telephone booth with people waiting in line," says Jane, "and I'll say to him, 'This is America's most beautiful woman.' And he has me believing it!" Now clearly, for most men, to be calling your wife America's most beautiful woman is to be indulging in romantic idealization—thirty-two years down the line, in Larry Weissberg's case. In many happy marriages idealization simply is not a passing phase; it is not the doomed honeymoon period that mature mates are thought to outgrow. It is, rather, an abiding and fundamental aspect of a couple's bond.

How do these couples do it? In the following pages they describe their lives and the principles by which they live. These are couples who have achieved what all married people would like to achieve; their insights can help the rest of us in our own quest to succeed in life and love. Throughout the book I have distilled their stories and insights into axioms, brief one-line summaries of hard-won experience. These amount to a working list of guidelines for creating and sustaining a good marriage.

Not all couples followed all principles; the important thing, as we will see, was for couples to agree upon the particular principles *they* would follow, in their own homes. Each couple wrote their own rules. Nevertheless, the principles in this book were the ones that happy couples mentioned most often.

Couples varied, of course, in how consciously aware they were of the rules that guided their actions. Highly verbal spouses had often formulated their own maxims that they could share with me as soon as they were asked; less verbal couples related to each other more intuitively. But verbally oriented or not, almost all happy couples could abide by their principles naturally and readily; they had become good enough at being married that they did not have to stop and *think* every time a problem arose. If a couple believed in equality between partners, for instance, they automatically conducted arguments, and made decisions, in a manner that gave both partners an equal say. It might well have taken them years of conscious effort—years of "working" at their marriages—to reach this point. But a marriage was at its peak when partners were least conscious, at the moment, of what they were doing right. Ultimately, marital axioms work best when they no longer have to be thought about, no longer have to be worked at.

While their very brevity may make these boldfaced principles seem obvious at times, it is important to remember that what seems obvious on the page of a book can prove perplexing indeed in the face of reality. The truth is that trying to apply an "obvious" principle to any particular situation can be a highly complicated proposition. Consider the basic belief happy couples gave in equality between partners. How does this principle apply to the making of decisions concerning their children? Take the situation—familiar to many a good parent—in which a teacher strongly recommends that a couple place their young son, who has been a timid child from birth, in psychotherapy. When one parent is convinced by the teacher's concerns and the other is not, how is this difference to be resolved? The considerations that go into making such a decision are remarkably complex, embracing everything from the cost of therapy to the family's view of the child to concerns over how the child will react to being sent to therapy against his will. As is so often the case when making decisions about one's children, no compromise position is possible; there is no way to "split the difference." One parent's opinion is going to end up being more "equal" than the other's simply because the child either goes into therapy or he does not.

Family life can be so complicated that when we are trying to wend our way through the decisions and choices we face, it is essential to have some simple truths to hold on to. The axioms in this book are the simple truths of these couples' happy marriages. When we find ourselves confused and torn in our own marriages, the simplicity of these principles can offer a source of clarity and strength.

Even more important, the stories here offer us a second gift: the gift of hope. There are better marriages and worse just as there are better people and worse. There is no overriding, all-encompassing, fundamental darkness haunting each and every home; each marriage is different. Some marriages are good, some are bad; some are heaven on earth and some are hell.

And in heaven you are a fifty-six-year-old woman married for thirty-two years to a man who makes you believe you are America's most beautiful woman.

1

℮

Rules of
Attraction

When two people destined to spend a lifetime in love meet, how do they know they have found the *one?* It is easy enough to understand that you are falling in love, that you want to be with a person night and day *for now.* But to project these feelings thirty years into the future? To say to yourself, This is the person I want to wake up with when I am sixty—and to be right? To know such a thing would seem to demand a level of wisdom well beyond the insight required by any ordinary choice.

Yet this is precisely what vital couples manage to do: early on in their lives, they make a profoundly right decision. When two roads diverge in a yellow wood they know which fork to take, and they take it together. The question is, how? How do they know which way to turn, which person to make the journey with?

Psychologists and sociologists alike have been trying to answer this question for many years now. And in the field of research known as "marital adjustment studies," certain factors predicting future happiness have emerged. One of the classic texts on the subject, Ernest W. Burgess and Paul Wallin's *Engagement and Marriage,* published in 1953, reported that couples who were destined for happiness were:

—similar in family background

—blessed with happy childhoods

—blessed as well with parents who were themselves happily married

—between twenty-two and thirty years of age at marriage

—associated with each other, whether romantically or as friends, for a significant period of time before marriage

—socially active with friends of both sexes

—well educated

—securely and stably employed (Interestingly, stability of employment was more important than the actual amount of money a married couple had to live on. More than one study found that the happiest marriages were those in which family income was only "moderate." During that era, when it was still possible for most families to enjoy a middle-class life-style on one income, marriages were significantly less happy at both the low *and* the high ends of the scale.)

—similar in *perception* of intelligence: in other words, married couples did not have to be equally intelligent to be happy; they just had to *think* they were. It was especially important for the man not to see himself as smarter than his wife, even if he was!

—perceived as "most likely to succeed" by friends and family; that is, before they married happy couples were expected to be happy by people who knew them

—united in confidence about their future together

—united in a strong desire to have children

For the most part, with certain crucial exceptions, Burgess and Wallin's observations held true of the happy couples with whom I spoke. In particular, a similarity in family backgrounds—especially a similarity in having been raised in happy families—was an enormous boon to couples who were trying to forge a happy life together in today's world. Also, a fundamental equality between spouses was essential.

Couples today differed from their counterparts in the first half of the century most noticeably in their confidence concerning the future.

With divorce rates standing at 50 percent, few couples in their twenties and thirties can feel as confident of their marital fates as could young marrieds in the 1940s, when divorce was still uncommon.

While Burgess and Wallin's list is certainly intriguing, and helpful as far as it goes, it is not all that easy to apply to an individual life. What does it mean, to any given man and woman newly in love, to be able to tick off the items one by one: "We've known each other for two years, we went to college, we are both Methodists, we have a lot of friends." If you and your beloved can claim four predictors in a row, does this make yours a case of Damn the torpedoes, full speed ahead?

Obviously not. Divorce rates being what they are, there are going to be large numbers of Methodist couples who have many friends and a long engagement ending up unhappy and alone. To put such findings to use in our own lives, we have to consider exactly what they mean in terms of the real couples in this book.

The good news is that the happy couples with whom I spoke confirmed Burgess and Wallin's discovery that trying to predict a lifetime of happiness is not as tall an order as it might seem. Friends and family are strikingly accurate in their assessments of a couple's chances, as are the couples themselves. It is at least somewhat possible to forecast the future, and the majority of the happily married couples with whom I spoke bore this out. Their families and friends had "approved" of their relationships; there were only three long-married couples whose families had not, and of these, two couples had in fact experienced a great deal of conflict and unhappiness although they were doing well now. This brings us to our first principle concerning vital couples:

- **If your friends and family do not think you are making the right choice, listen.**

Naturally this principle comes bearing an important caveat, which is that we should listen only to friends and family members who clearly have our own best interests at heart. Sonia Hansen, whose story is told further on, married her husband, Michael, over the strong objections of her mother, a chronically depressed woman who, having been widowed young, was loathe to lose either of her two daughters to marriage. "I was supposed to be my mom's mom," Sonia said.

"My mother told me no one could ever love me as much as she did. She hates Michael to this day." Sonia escaped into a good marriage, but her sister, never married, still lives with their mother. Sonia was right to reject her mother's advice.

How do true friends and loving family members make their predictions? In the first place, most of us, whether we are aware of it or not, carry a checklist very similar to Burgess and Wallin's in our heads. Parents and friends invariably consider such issues as the similarity of a couple's economic and educational standing, as well as of family background. Though it goes against the grain of our democratic beliefs, in fact couples do fare better, on the whole, when there is not a great disparity in terms of their socioeconomic backgrounds. This principle is far from an absolute, but it holds true often enough that families are justified in applying it.

Beyond this, friends and family pay attention to how the couple *feels* together. Lovers who are destined to form vital relationships typically seem at home with each other from the start—and this sense of a proper "fit" communicates itself to those around them. From the outside (and from the inside as well) the members of a newly forming happy couple go together the way different colors or textures can go together: they *look* good next to one another.

This rightness of fit is apparent in vital couples' memories of their first dates. Rachel, now in her early sixties and married over forty years, described the blind date on which she met her husband: "I was going to Penn State and I was dating a guy I really couldn't stand. Eventually he gave my number to John, who was going to school in Allentown, where my family lived." When Rachel came home from school for Thanksgiving, John called.

On their very first date they doubled with two of John's closest friends and their girlfriends, making Rachel the only stranger in the group. Normally this arrangement would have been difficult for Rachel, who was naturally shy. And yet in the company of her future husband she felt perfectly at ease. "We went to a club in Jersey—there were blue laws in Pennsylvania then—and what I really remember about that evening is that his two friends were incredibly funny and talky, and John and I spent the whole night laughing at their jokes. We were completely comfortable with each other, and when we got home I allowed him to kiss me good night—which was unusual in those days. His kiss was very natural; I didn't object at all. It was a very nice, friendly, sweet kiss because we enjoyed each other even though we didn't know each other."

Speaking to vital couples you hear versions of this story over and over again. And this brings us to our second principle:

• **When they meet, vital couples feel immediately at home with each other.**

This is not to say that vital couples never argue, never fall upon hard times. The point is not that people who are destined to be happy together do not experience conflict; the point is that along with whatever conflict they experience goes a profound and striking *rapport*. They feel good together at once: contradicting the notion that "mature" love develops slowly over time as a couple gets to know each other, these couples frequently feel right together before they know much about each other at all. Sometimes this sense of fit is sexual; sometimes it is emotional; frequently it is both. However it happens for a particular couple, the point is that very early on, and for whatever reasons—a strong physical or emotional attraction, shared moral, religious, or political values—they feel a sweeping sense of connection.

Recent research into the social psychology of dating bears this out. When psychologists Kelly E. Piner and John H. Berg paired sixty strangers into couples, telling them at the outset that they were very similar to each other, they discovered that these men and women fell into comfortable, intimate exchange at once. They quickly came to resemble old friends or lovers in manner, gesture, and tone. Piner and Berg conclude that the feeling and behaviors that make up "closeness" emerge very early in relationships, possibly within the first ten minutes.

In short, love at first sight is a real phenomenon, the only qualifier being that vital couples have more to go on than sight alone. For them it is more a case of love at first *exchange*. From the first moment these men and women speak, they fall into the rhythms and cadences of long familiarity.

For many, this feeling never fades. As John, Rachel's husband, said, "I really like my wife and respect her, too." This fundamental liking, this fundamental familiarity and respect, allow a couple to stay together even in the face of the passionate disagreements about children and life that can emerge as time wears on. As we will see, a very serious conflict was to develop between Rachel and John—so serious that Rachel was driven to give her husband an ultimatum. That she and John were able to emerge from this period with their marriage even stronger than before is due largely to the basic respect each has always felt for the other. Their unshakable rapport smoothed the way; resolving conflict with a person we respect is a far easier task than trying to work things out with a person we no longer admire.

First Impressions

Of course, when it comes to choosing the right person, half of the game is won in not choosing the wrong one. And here we arrive at our first *cautionary* principle:

• **When it comes to falling in love, do not dismiss your first impressions.**

In other words, trust yourself. Far too often, single people try to rationalize away the small negative moments that happen upon first meeting with the wrong person. Friends and family help them along in this, continually urging their unmarried friends to give a new date the benefit of the doubt, not to be so critical, not to make up his or her mind so fast. It is a basic truth of dating life that friends and family, wanting to see you happily settled at last, are invariably eager to make compromises on your behalf—compromises they might never make themselves!

But in fact, while loved ones mean well, the evidence from happy couples indicates that this advice is not in most people's best interests. While continuing to see someone with whom we do not immediately hit it off might indeed result in a marriage, most likely it will not result in a *vital* marriage. Such advice is intrinsically about "settling," not about finding a soulmate.

And while in theory settling might sound like a nice, cozy thing to do, in practice it may be even more difficult to settle than to hold out for what we truly want. To begin with, no one wants to be settled *for:* when we enter a relationship with the attitude that we are settling, most lovers are going to withdraw—and rightfully so. Worse yet, the person being settled for may exact a steep price once the marriage has taken place. People want to feel loved wholeheartedly, and when they do not, they retaliate.

Not surprisingly, men and women who actually do marry partners they "like" but do not "love" often find their marriages to be very rough sledding indeed. Such alliances are difficult to maintain because the same things that prevented the two from falling in love in the first place now begin to wear seriously upon each other's nerves as the months and years go by. Love and marriage may be one of the few life situations in which the "bird in the hand" maxim only tenuously applies.

At worst, of course, trying always to give the benefit of the doubt can land a person in real trouble. Jessica's story is the classic cautionary tale. A graduate student in experimental psychology, Jessica was actively looking for someone to love when she met Terry—a man who was destined to bring her many months of pain—at a party given by her roommate's boyfriend.

"I was drawn to Terry the minute I saw him," she told me. "I was talking to someone in the living room, and he was out in the kitchen, sort of leaning up against the kitchen counter, listening to someone out there. I kept finding myself staring at him—I just really felt pulled in his direction." The source of her attraction? "I think I liked the really intense way he was listening to the person he was with," Jessica reflected. "And obviously I responded physically as well. Somehow we were soon talking to each other—I can't remember exactly how we managed to get together—and as we spoke I was even more attracted."

Terry did prove to be a good listener, but nonetheless, just moments after their first conversation had begun, Jessica experienced a negative premonition. "It wasn't all 'good,' " she said, describing this first conversation. "I vividly remember a moment of feeling real misgivings, a moment where I wanted to pull back. But I didn't, because overall we were just so drawn to one another. I liked him. But I *knew* that shadow was there."

Jessica's was a case of love at first sight that turned out to be all wrong—and that could have been headed off at the pass had she chosen to heed that one presentiment of danger. "Looking back," she said, "I realized what it was that had bothered me. It was a point in our conversation where he told me he was free that weekend because the woman he had planned to spend it with had had to cancel at the last minute. Then he told me her name, and she was a very well known and respected novelist. I was immediately impressed that he could be dating her, and I only half registered the fact that his telling me this was a bad sign."

It was a bad sign because by revealing this information Terry was putting Jessica, then a graduate student, into sexual competition with a woman who was far out of her league professionally. "He told me about her in a way that implied he was *glad* she'd canceled now that he'd met me. He made me feel I was winning out over this famous writer, and he was the prize." It was a highly manipulative tack to take, and was to prove prophetic of the course their relationship would follow. And, as Jessica was to discover, Terry's need to "name-drop" a canceled date also revealed a fatal lack of self-confidence. It is a truism that a person who does not much like himself will have difficulty loving someone else, and this was to be the case with Terry.

But while Jessica did hear the faint chiming of a distant warning bell, she did not heed it. Profoundly confused about men and love at the time, she no longer trusted her perceptions. "I'd had so much trouble with men by that point, I could hardly tell which way was up," she said. "It seemed as if I was always finding some tiny, negative *thing* in every new man I met. A close friend of mine kept telling me I was too hostile to men, and I could hardly argue with her—I *was* hostile. So I was trying to correct for my negativity; I was trying to give any new man I met a chance."

Having been counseled by friends and family to keep an open mind, Jessica plunged ahead into four months of extreme highs and lows with a man who could not make up his mind: one day he would sweep her up in a whirlwind of passion and love, the next day he would not call. The affair ended painfully when Terry decided he needed to see other women in order to "keep his options open"— this after declarations of love on both sides, and talk of marriage. He did not want to break up with Jessica, he made clear, just to adopt an arrangement in which he would see her when he saw her. By this point Jessica was so overwhelmed by anxiety and pain that the friend who had been lobbying for tolerance was now urging her to cut her losses and run. She did.

Jessica's case is particularly revealing because immediately after this she went on to form a good relationship—now in its seventh year—

with her husband, Tom, a man she met while in the midst of breaking up with Terry. The differences between the two first meetings are striking: "I still vividly remember my first date with my husband," Jessica said. "He took me out to dinner and we spent the entire meal totally wrapped up in a terrific conversation. Then we went to a local singles bar and danced, and I remember being thrilled because he knew how to lead; then we went to Häagen-Dazs for ice cream. And during that whole time I didn't have one single negative perception. Not one." The complete and total absence of "bad signs" was remarkable given how finely tuned Jessica's antennae now were. She was looking for flaws, and looking hard. "I was so distrustful of men at that point—I had been dating for *years*—that Tom used to accuse me of 'dating McCarthyism.' He said my attitude toward men was, 'Are you now, or have you ever been, bad to a woman?' By then that really was my approach. I remember thinking, after Tom went home, that if he really was as perfect as he seemed, then he was definitely the one."

Tom did indeed prove to be the one, and the fact that Jessica recognized his future meaning to her life in spite of the confusion, hurt, and anger she was feeling toward men as a whole tells us a great deal about the first days of happy couples. When a man and a woman who are destined to marry happily meet, they feel right together almost at once. Certainly they experience no dark undertones—even when they are *expecting* to experience dark undertones, as Jessica was. Meeting a person you can be happy with for fifty years has nothing of the furtive or the suspicious about it; it is an experience flooded with daylight. As we will see in future chapters, not infrequently a future partner felt so right, so "normal," so *fundamentally compatible with that person's everyday world*, that people told roommates and family they had met someone "right" after just the first date.

All told, then, the first piece of practical wisdom to emerge from the experience of people who married "wisely and well" is to listen to our hearts. If, when we meet someone we are dramatically drawn to, some part of us is whispering "No," then no it should be—at least, no it should be if what we are looking for is a long and happy marriage.

None of which is to say that vital couples exist in a benign and passionless zone of perfect harmony. "Brilliant" first dates can in fact be highly charged; a strong current of sexual energy often runs through them. Jessica and Tom are a good example here as well: the two of them spent much of their first meal together vigorously arguing a philosophical point. Jessica still remembers that discussion vividly. "For some reason," she recalled, "we got into the whole issue of whether people can change. I was studying experimental psychology, and my professors believed that people can't really change, that people's characters are determined by each person's particular mix of heredity and environment. So I was taking this view, and Tom strongly disagreed. He kept saying there was such a thing as free will, that you could see it in the lives of people who had made something of themselves in spite of being born into poverty and despair. I had been taught that that view was naive, so we really went at it."

Thus Jessica and Tom *inaugurated* their enduring alliance with a debate. But in spite of the fact that they were spending their first meal together arguing, there was still no dark moment, no shadow clouding the proceedings. Jessica felt entirely "comfortable" with Tom—not comfortable in the asexual, companionable mode many experts describe as the "mature" way of mating, but comfortable in the sense of feeling *free*. Sitting there at dinner with Tom, whom she had met for the first time in her life only minutes before, Jessica felt perfectly at ease vigorously making her case against "free will."

Moreover, the *content* of their argument was highly symbolic of what the two would come to mean to each other. As Jessica said, "I was arguing with Tom, but the truth is I wanted to be convinced. I *wanted* to believe there was such a thing as free will, that people could change, that they could be in charge of their lives. Although I didn't quite realize it at the time, I was arguing that people don't change not only because that was what I believed, but also because I was in a really demoralized state myself. I had just been through two years of terrible relationships with men, each one of which was basically the same terrible relationship all over again only with a new guy. It just seemed that I was doomed to repeat myself; there was no way out. What Tom was saying represented hope to me."

In short, during their initial exchange Jessica and Tom lined themselves up as pessimist versus optimist—with advantage to the latter. Neither Jessica nor Tom remembered precisely how the discussion ended, but it did not result, as a genuinely hostile conflict normally does, in a win, lose, or draw. Instead, as the conversation shifted easily to other, less charged topics, it ended with each feeling excited about the other, each feeling that at last he had found someone he could talk to—someone who was thinking about the same issues even if he or she had come up with different answers.

And it ended with both feeling the potential for a future together. At the symbolic level each heard the other saying something important. Jessica heard Tom saying, in essence, "You can change; your life can be different. This is the beginning of a new life with me." And Tom heard Jessica saying, "I want to believe you."

This apparent conflict was in fact the beginning of a courtship; it was an invitation, and a response. As Tom remembered this first conversation: "Being in law school at the time, I loved to argue, and any woman who was willing to engage in a recreational argument was immediately appealing to me. Besides, I saw a lot of truth in what Jessica was saying. That's why it wasn't irritating to disagree with her, because I didn't *really* disagree. I *do* believe it's hard for people to change; Jessica was right. I was just more optimistic than she was. I still am."

Here you see two people who, as they engage in their spirited debate, are each feeling receptive to the other's point of view. Secretly, Jessica half agrees with Tom already; secretly, Tom mostly agrees with Jessica. *Both* of them feel that, when it comes to love, it would probably be better—better as in more productive—to see things Tom's way!

In other words, the two are not *opposed*; they are instead staking out the opposite positions from which they can move toward each other, from which they can come together. They are searching for common ground. And, at a symbolic level, they are beginning the process (which we will explore in detail in the next chapter) of creating—of negotiating—the identity they will ultimately share *as a couple*. The hidden topic under discussion here is: How optimistic, how hopeful and bold, are we going to be as a team? Already, at this first meeting, they are beginning to find out.

The essential difference, then, between an initiating conflict that foretells a happy marriage and an initiating conflict that foretells months and years of wearing, habitual conflict is that the vital argument is most adamantly *not* a throwing down of the gauntlet:

- **As they begin their relationship, neither member of a vital couple is trying to <u>win</u>.**

This is precisely what goes wrong with new couples who are destined to be unhappy together: early on in their relationships they issue each other a *challenge*. Knowingly or not, they set up a contest, a struggle for dominance. Terry's mentioning of his canceled date with the renowned woman novelist would certainly qualify as just such a challenge; in positioning himself as the consort of famous writers he was pulling rank on Jessica, who was obviously dateless for the coming weekend. For his part, Tom was all too familiar with the first-date-as-combat: "I had been separated from my first wife for about two years when I met Jessica, and during that time I had gone out a *lot*. I remember one date in particular, with a marketing executive who was highly intelligent, when we argued all through the dinner. But in that case it was a real joust; it was contentious. Rather than helping us make a connection—the way it did with Jessica and me—the arguing just showed how incompatible we were."

That is the key distinction: when an initiating argument produces a sense of competition rather than connection, trouble lies ahead.

When Opposites Attract

As is apparent in the case of Jessica and Tom, whether a new couple will be drawn together by their "differences" or pulled apart depends largely upon the extent to which each *identifies* with the other—the extent to which each feels him- or herself to be *like* the other. In short, while opposites may attract, they do not wear well over time. It is a truism in the annals of marriage and family therapy that people are drawn to their opposite number, then end up despising each other for *being* opposite; in time they grow to resent the very qualities that attracted them to each other in the first place. As a general rule people do not *like* their polar opposites—at least, not for very long.

In her illuminating book *Intimate Partners*, author Maggie Scarf explains why. Diametrically opposed couples fare badly because of a phenomenon psychologists term "projective identification." When two ill-fated opposites meet and connect, each partner is projecting some unwanted part of *himself* onto the other in order to disavow that quality—to disclaim it, to convince himself that it is not part of his own makeup. A woman who is uncomfortable feeling angry, for instance, might be drawn to openly angry men; it is her lover or husband who is such an angry person, she can then tell herself, not she. He "carries" her anger. Or, a man who is uncomfortable acting aggressively in the world might choose a highly aggressive woman. She then carries his aggression. In both cases, trouble is likely to follow.

Trouble ensues because when we dislike a quality in *ourselves,* eventually we come to dislike it in our partners—even if we may have admired it at first. Take the common case of the distant, emotionally controlled man married to the clinging and overwrought woman. In this alliance each person is relying upon the other to "carry" that part of himself he or she rejects. The distant man suppresses emotional vulnerability in himself and sees this quality as entirely a characteristic of his wife. The wife suppresses her own ambitious, "masculine" qualities, projecting these onto her husband. Inevitably, she begins to resent his calm just as he begins to resent her emotionality.

These two initially passionate lovers make their pact—caretaking husband to vulnerable wife—and then they seek to live with it. But by the very nature of a projective identification, they cannot. He reaches a point at which her emotional needs grow to be profoundly draining; she comes to experience his calm reserve as abandonment. Stymied, the two polarize, become even more radically opposite, more decisively opposed. As he withdraws he becomes ever more reserved and bloodless; as she reacts to his withdrawal she becomes ever more hysterical and desperate.

From here they face limited options. They can lock horns in a battle that cannot be resolved because whatever surface issue they fight over is not what is truly at stake; or, they can give up. They can become "conflict habituated," in the terminology of Cuber and Harroff; they can turn into the kind of couple who quarrel so continually that they can no longer imagine what it would be like to live in peace. Or they can become the passive, "devitalized" couple with whom we are all familiar. Or, finally, one of them (frequently the man) can give up, refuse to fight, while the other (frequently the woman) lives out her life in a state of unassuaged and unassuageable rage, agitating for a battle her husband refuses to give her.

The principle here:

- **<u>Polar</u> opposites are not likely to remain happy together for long.**

When Opposites Are Right

Like unhappy opposites, the happy couple may also see themselves as opposites (and many couples told me that they were indeed opposite in personality), but with a difference. Happy couples do not feel themselves to be opposite in any way that really matters. One wife offered an interesting—and in many cases accurate—explanation of the way marriage works best: "Happy marriages," she told me, "come from two people who are opposite in personality but identical in background." While she herself was a lifelong pessimist married to an incurable optimist, because she and her husband were identical in ethnic and religious background they rarely disagreed. They agreed on values; they differed in emotional makeup. And neither was engaging in projective identification; neither was projecting a quality he did not like in himself onto his partner.

For their part, Tom and Jessica were far from being polar opposites either in values or in personality. Having entered a particularly pessimistic phase of her life, Jessica was definitely drawn to Tom for his optimism. Yet at the same time she herself was hardly a committed pessimist; she did not see Tom's character as being radically different from her own. She had been more optimistic herself in the past, and she would become more optimistic again in the future. If anything, she felt that she and Tom were a great deal *alike*.

Tom may well have been drawn, in part, to Jessica's apparent vulnerability. Having recently left a marriage in which he had been required to play the perpetually strong and optimistic father to a depressed wife/daughter, he was entirely ready to own up to his own moments of weakness and fear—to his own pessimism.

Perhaps more importantly, Tom did not perceive Jessica as his polar opposite. "I was immediately attracted to Jessica's intelligence and verve and liveliness," he remembered. "She may have been making a pessimistic argument, but she was making it so energetically that she came off as confident and even exuberant. Anyone with that kind of energy isn't a pessimist. Not really."

In short, not all opposition in marriage is the result of projective identification. Marrying one's opposite can be healthy or unhealthy, depending. To the extent that Jessica and Tom were attracted to each other's difference—she to his optimistic strength and he to her more pessimistic vulnerability—for them this was a perfectly reasonable, and workable, attraction. Theirs was the kind of opposition married people are talking about when they speak of a spouse being their "other half." Neither Jessica nor Tom was in flight from that part of himself/herself the other may have represented. Jessica wanted to reclaim the optimistic, strong part of herself that she seemed to have lost during her run of bad relationships; Tom wanted the freedom to be more vulnerable. Each wanted to embrace the other's differentness; each wanted to be more like the other.

Each wanted, that is, to grow, to develop, to move forward; to become a larger person. And it is this desire to enlarge the self by connecting with an "opposite" that accounts for the curiously satisfying, even exhilarating, nature of first-date arguments when they occur between two people who are destined to become a vital couple. These debates are not arguments in the classic sense of a dispute between two parties locked into their respective positions; they are instead a form of dialogue. They are an *exchange* in the true sense of the word: both partners come away having gained, having absorbed some aspect of the other's beliefs. Neither is projecting an unwanted quality onto the other but is instead recognizing and *reclaiming*, from the other, an admirable quality that he himself would like to possess—and perhaps did, in fact, possess in the past.

This process accounts for the sense of recognition that vital couples often feel when they first meet, the sense of having known this person before—a sensation that is particularly striking when you consider how many of these couples met on blind dates. Normally blind dates are virtually guaranteed to produce extreme discomfort, and yet with vital couples even the conditions of the blind date feel natural and easy. Rachel's first date with John is an excellent example of this: a shy girl, not only did she meet her husband on a blind date, she also met him on a blind date before an audience of two of his closest friends and their girlfriends. Yet because of her instant sense of connection to John she had no difficulty spending the evening in the company of an already constituted, tightly knit group of friends: "It felt very natural."

This is the real secret behind the vital couple's initial attraction:

• **Happy couples often experience themselves as being the same <u>and</u> different.**

This delicate balance allows them to realize that elusive combination of friendship (based in sameness) and passion (based in difference) that creates and sustains the vital marriage. In many happy marriages couples manage to be friends and lovers at once, an impressive achievement given that the conditions for friendship are in some ways diametrically opposed to the conditions that promote desire.

The differing requirements for passion and friendship are easiest to see when couples discuss the balance between the two in their own relationships. Many long-married couples will tell you that it is difficult to be passionate lovers when partners are as alike as two peas in a pod. Screenwriters and novelists know this instinctively; the "chemistry" between on-screen lovers is almost always generated by creating fictional characters who are dramatically opposite in important respects. In many ways Michael and Sonia Hansen embody this dilemma. In their early forties now, they have always been very much alike in terms of personality as well as values: both have long tended to avoid conflict, both had been the classic "good" child as they grew up; both were now becoming a bit more assertive; and so on. To an outsider they are very similar in tone and manner, so much so that they could be brother and sister. They were well aware of this: "We define ourselves as being very similar," Michael said. "We have some of the same thoughts, even, and will both say the same thing at the same time." According to Sonia, this had always been true. "I've felt incredibly comfortable with Michael since the very beginning," she told me.

Unfortunately, the problem with all of this sameness is that it is not very sexy. "My sister always asks me," Sonia confided, "isn't it boring being married to Michael?" Michael added, "We don't have lots of passion. We're not tempestuous." It is not that the two were not happy together; they were. Theirs was an excellent marriage. It is simply that when two people are so alike that they could be siblings, the possibilities for unbridled passion diminish. "If we wanted excitement," Michael concluded humorously, "we shouldn't have married each other."

If too much sameness dampens desire, by the same token it is difficult for two people to be friends when they are diametrically opposed in every respect. Constant conflict makes friendship between spouses impossible. Happy marriages need both sameness *and* difference, and the majority of the happy couples with whom I spoke told me that they had both.

The truth is, most of us do not yearn for a total absence of conflict in our attachments. Some time ago a friend told me a story that perfectly captured the delicate balance between opposition and connection in the happy marriage. He had just come from the second wedding of a college friend. It was a marriage of which his friend's mother did not approve. The first wife, the mother confided in my friend, had been perfectly compatible with her son; they had always gotten along, she lamented. But this new daughter-in-law, she said, was a far more difficult person and she could not for the life of her comprehend why her son would prefer this prickly second wife to the first. "I don't know," the mother said with a sigh. "I guess this time around he wants someone he can fight with."

Finding someone we can fight with is hardly a recipe for success in marriage, but still, this story does tell us something about the nature of life and love. People, most people, need something more than comfort and reliability from their life's mate; we need stability, yes, but we also need excitement and stimulation—we need a sense of *possibility*. We need to feel, when we marry, that the future is ours.

In the next chapter, we see how hope shapes the lives of happy couples.

2

The Marriage of
True Minds

The First Stage: Becoming a Couple

Once two people who are destined to be happy fall in love, what comes next?

We begin at the beginning, with the crucial first stage of becoming a couple. The first step for any marriage, good or bad, is simply to gel. The new husband must come to think of himself as a *husband*, the new wife must come to think of herself as a *wife*. Their marriage must come to feel as natural, inevitable, and real to them as the sun in the morning and the moon at night. The marriage must "take."

For that to happen, each member of the couple must incorporate the fact of being married into his or her individual identity. When John marries Susan he must become, in his own eyes as well as in the eyes of the world, John-married-to-Susan just as she becomes, in her eyes and in the eyes of the world, Susan-married-to-John.

This brings us to an essential principle concerning the next step, after the courtship and wedding:

• **For a marriage to be strong, both partners must stop being single at heart, and come to be married at heart.**

The importance of this first stage, which many of us take for granted, is most apparent when you encounter a couple who has not been able to achieve it. Laura and Jeff McCall, a young couple living with their three small children in a beach community in San Diego, offered eloquent testimony to the destructive effects of one spouse's inability to establish a firm inner sense of, or belief in, the reality of the marriage.

Former high-school sweethearts, Laura and Jeff had been married for nearly eleven years. He was thirty-two, she thirty-one. Both recalled the unreality of their early years together. "At first it feels like you're playing house," said Laura, a slim and pretty young mother whose long brown hair brushed her waist. "We had both lived at home until we got married, and we kept expecting the game to end and we'd go home." Adjusting to marriage, coming to feel that this was *real*, was especially difficult for Laura because she had grown up in a large and noisy family of ten. Now she found the small apartment she shared with Jeff, who drove off to work each morning in their only car leaving her stranded at home, intolerably quiet. Worse yet, all of her friends were single and working; there was no one to talk to throughout the long day. The stillness of those small rooms, the solitude: such conditions might breed a painful sense of unreality for any young wife. Certainly for Laura, under these conditions the marriage could not take hold.

Because their life together felt so tenuous and provisional to her, she found herself continually provoking arguments with Jeff, the kind of argument in which neither spouse knows exactly what the quarrel is about, or what has brought it on. Laura did not know what was bothering her; she knew only that something felt wrong. Bewildered, she would conclude that somehow her marriage was the problem. Confusion, anger, and chronic turmoil reigned.

Interestingly, Laura and Jeff both agreed that their marriage finally began to come together with the arrival of an "outsider" in their midst. Having managed to save enough for a down payment on the house in which they now live, they rented one bedroom out to a friend in order to cover the mortgage. He proved to be a trying roommate, and

Laura and Jeff soon found themselves solidly united in a classic alliance of, in Laura's words, "two against one." "We saw him as our teenage son," Jeff added with a smile, a clear indication of how much their difficult tenant actually helped them to forge their marital identity. Now, at last, both were able to begin the process of experiencing themselves as *married people*.

While this may be an unusual way to cement a marriage, it nevertheless reveals the importance of other people to a marriage's solidity. Alone with her thoughts in a silent apartment, Laura did not make much headway at feeling like a wife. But in joining forces with her husband to cope with an impossible housemate, she came to feel her connection to Jeff more keenly. Together against the roommate, she and Jeff could begin the process of forming a united front. And while forging a marital identity out of a two-against-one living situation may not be the best approach, at least it was a start.

Although their marriage had stabilized at this point, Laura and Jeff were to remain stalled in this initial, reality-forming stage. While for his part Jeff felt himself to be thoroughly married, Laura continued to struggle with a pervasive sense of unreality. She was not happy with Jeff, with the marriage, or with herself, and for reasons she could not grasp. All she knew was that things did not feel right. "There was this void," she told me, trying to explain the sensation. "I blamed it on Jeff."

In truth, as Laura was to discover, the problem lay neither with Jeff nor with their marriage, but with Laura's own family history. Laura had grown up in a large Catholic clan that had long represented itself to the world as the perfect family. The two parents had impressed this image upon the children as well as upon friends and neighbors: "We were always told how lucky we were to be in this family," Laura said. It was a message that profoundly confused the children because their father was, in Laura's words, "a classic Dr. Jekyll and Mr. Hyde." He was an alcoholic who, behind closed doors, practiced incest and psychological terrorism. While Laura did not offer details of his sexual abuse of the children, she did share memories of the emotional damage that she and her siblings suffered at her father's hands. He was a man who relished the cruel joke: he would sneak up behind his small children at the dinner table and seize their chairs, shaking them violently as he roared, "Earthquake! Earthquake!" This from the man she was daily instructed to regard as perfect.

The result of this radically "mixed message" (a phrase that hardly does justice to the profound set of colliding realities with which Laura and her siblings daily lived) was for Laura a pervasive feeling of unreality in her married life with Jeff. Having lived with a split between appearance and reality as a child, she could not now bring the two together in adult life. In spite of the fact that to all appearances Jeff was a good man, and their marriage happy, she could not bring herself to feel this at heart. The result for their marriage was yet more unfocused conflict, yet more anguished confrontation between two by-now-bewildered spouses trying to figure out what was wrong.

Individual psychotherapy, which Laura finally entered some nine years into her marriage, has helped her begin the process of sorting out her childhood, of forming the crucial distinctions between what was then and what is now. Nevertheless, Laura continued to have trouble simply believing in her marriage—believing in its fundamental, solid *thereness*. "I always feel as if there must be something I'm not seeing," she said. No matter how happy her life with Jeff and the children, she suffered a chronic sense of unreality.

It was a destructive feeling. And it was a feeling that was utterly foreign to Jeff's experience. Listening to his wife trying to put her difficulties into words, he gazed at her in mild amazement. Jeff, a soft-spoken and patient man who works the night shift as a manager of a local aircraft manufacturing plant, possessed the gift of being able to take things at face value. To Jeff, if you are relaxing in your living room with your beautiful new baby and your towheaded little boys, then that is happiness; that is the way things are. Jeff could not imagine what it must be like to mistrust one's own perceptions.

In the strongest and most stable of marriages, both partners feel as Jeff did; both partners trust their perceptions. While we are often admonished, rightly, not to take our partners "for granted," it is important to be able to take *the marriage* for granted. It is crucial, if a marriage is to thrive, for both partners to be able simply to assume that the marriage is as real and solid and unchanging as the earth beneath their feet.

The Second Stage: Staying on Track

Most couples, of course, do not face the overwhelming obstacles to couplehood that Laura and Jeff have confronted. Nevertheless, all couples must go through some version of the same process. Then, once they have developed a married identity, their real challenge begins: to *remain* married at heart for the rest of their lives. A good beginning is never enough: a marriage must be daily re-created and bolstered, its reality continuously reaffirmed through the years.

It is here that we have much to learn from the long-term couples in this book. These couples, every one of them, have found ways to daily confirm the paramount reality of their marriage, to daily reinforce the absolute, unquestioned thereness of home and family. This inner sense of their marriages as rock solid is essential to weathering the hard times. When families are strained by any of the myriad problems that beset people during the course of a lifetime, it can be very difficult to maintain the sweeping currents of love and affection that first brought a couple together. It is a truism that marriages often break up in the wake of extreme stress or tragedy: after the death of a child, after the loss of a job, after the death of one partner's parent. Marriages end under these circumstances because anguish devastates the grieving partners' capacity to be *in love* with each other—or even, under extreme circumstances, to be more than dimly aware of their spouse's very existence. At the very moment in which two people most need each other they have the least to give. And, in a weak marriage, when one spouse feels unloved or forgotten, the marriage founders.

But the strong marriage survives. The strong marriage survives because of its powerful feeling of reality, its invincibility, for both partners. Even when both spouses are so overcome by private worries or trauma that they are barely communicating with each other, much less making love with passionate abandon, their identity as married people sustains them. For them, leaving the marriage is *unthinkable* in somewhat the same way that defying gravity is unthinkable. The marriage is simply *there*, and will go on. In times of duress, the sturdy marital identity of the happy couple holds their marriage together until both are ready and able to *be* happy once again, to be the loving partners they were before.

Give Us This Day:
The Importance of Family Routine

How, precisely, do married people achieve this state of unshakable reality? To begin with, in strong marriages couples understand the power of the family routine:

• **Happy couples establish and follow productive daily routines.**

Give us this day our daily bread: the stable family begins each morning with a cherished pattern of waking, rising, greeting the day. One partner always makes the coffee, one partner always walks the dog, both partners read the paper over breakfast. All of the happy couples as well as most of the not-so-happy but stable couples with whom I spoke led married lives kept on track by various daily routines.

A daily routine works by making life predictable. Family members know what they are supposed to be doing and when; life makes sense. The routine reinforces their sense of family reality, allowing people to take their families for granted, to believe without question that when they wake up in the morning the family will still be there. Routines, in short, promote confidence; they promote trust in the natural and inevitable existence of the marriage. They do not in and of themselves produce happiness, great love, or good sex, but they underlie and support these blessings; they are a necessary if far from sufficient condition for the thriving marriage.

In practice, this means that those of us who feel our marriages to be adrift would do well to set about creating routine where there has been none before. Establishing a family dinner hour, setting a time at which both partners put work papers aside to concentrate on each other, brewing each other a fresh cup of coffee every morning: all of these small, routinized gestures strengthen a marriage much more than one might think. In the happiest of marriages such small, repeated detail becomes a source of enduring pleasure and strength. Routine is also of crucial importance to children: one study of National Merit Scholarship finalists found that the only factor that these high achievers had in common was that all of them ate dinner together with their families nightly!

Beyond Routine: The Family Ritual

• **Happy couples establish and follow meaningful family rituals.**

Beyond routine lies ritual. Talk to married people and invariably you will find that throughout the year, year in and year out, stable couples observe a well-defined set of family *rituals*. Many of these rituals surround larger cultural and religious events like Christmas or Thanksgiving, with each family faithfully observing its own form of the celebration. Some families open presents on Christmas Eve, others on Christmas day; but the important thing is that whichever day it is, it is *always* that day, it *must be* that day.

A family ritual, once established as ritual, takes on the force of custom. It becomes meaningful, and important, to the family that presents be opened on that day, at that time of day, every year, year after year. Research in the field of leisure studies reveals that it is important to stick to the ritual exactly because the further we depart from custom, the less likely we are to observe any part of the ritual at all. To illustrate, if as children we eat turkey and stuffing for Thanksgiving, we need to continue the tradition of turkey and stuffing as adults in order to motivate ourselves sufficiently to observe the holiday at all. If something changes, our tendency is to skip the entire affair. Suppose, for example, that for some reason it becomes impossible one year for a family to roast a turkey. Perhaps the oven has broken and the family cannot afford to replace it at the moment (as happened to one couple I interviewed); perhaps the family cook has ruptured a disc and is not up to the task (as happened to another). When one cherished detail of the ritual disappears, inertia sets in. That family's Thanksgiving is in danger of not happening at all.

Happy couples frequently develop other, more personal rituals as well. One couple might make a rule of always going out to dinner on a spouse's birthday; another might make a rule of opening a bottle of champagne, perhaps even a particular brand of champagne. Harried parents of small children might set a standing date for the weekend. One couple told me that they had created a romantic ritual. Married for fourteen years, they rendezvoused for an at-home sex date every Friday evening. Their live-in nanny would feed the three children, and they would close themselves off in their bedroom with a bottle of wine and a generous serving of cheese and spend the evening in bed. Both found these evenings highly erotic.

These rituals confirm the importance of each partner to the other or, when it is a ritual that involves the entire family, of the family to itself. And of course, a ritual, like a routine, promotes a fundamental sense of a family's reality, of its solidity. Again, it is easy to underestimate how important such seemingly small, automatic details of married life are to happy couples. People thrive upon routine; they thrive upon ritual.

The family ritual may be even more important today when, as Atlanta psychologists Karen Schwartz and John Paddock have written in their essay "Rituals for Dual-Career Couples," many traditional family rituals, such as the evening meal together, are breaking down under the demands of the two-career household. For many years wives attended to these matters. It was the wife who set and enforced mealtimes, cooked Thanksgiving dinner, and shepherded the family off to services on Christmas Eve. In short, the traditional homemaker established the routines and rituals that held the family together; she was the keeper of the flame. When two-career couples, under pressure of time, abandon these classic functions of the wife and mother, they commit a potentially fatal error. Couples need family ritual and routine in order to feel real as a family, in order to keep themselves from spinning off in a dozen different directions. Family rituals keep a couple centered on each other.

From Surviving to Thriving: The Shared Identity

In any family the creation of established routines and rituals is a powerful force for stability; but for a marriage to be stable *and* happy, something more is required. This something I call the creation of a *shared identity*. Throughout my interviews I found that whenever a couple was genuinely, seemingly effortlessly, happy, they were almost always incredibly close—so close that they could practically read each other's thoughts. The underlying principle they revealed:

- **In the happy couple two souls become one.**

Apropos of mind reading several couples told me, often humorously, that they had developed a form of marital ESP. "I think she's sending the messages," Mark Walters told me, throwing his wife Nancy a glance, "the white witch over here." Their silent communications ran the gamut from the mundane to the utterly unique.

On the mundane side, Nancy could be thinking, "I could kill for a Carvel," and within moments Mark would say, "Let's go get an ice cream." This is a common enough form of being on the same wavelength that any pair of close friends or mates could develop, but Mark and Nancy, a Chicago couple now in their late thirties, had moved well beyond the happy state of simply being in synch. Both recall, some years ago, driving by a bar with the legend "DO DROP IN" posted out front. Gazing at the sign as he passed, Mark said "Do drop *dead*" in the very moment Nancy was thinking precisely the same words. The two are so close that the same jokes can occur to them at the same time—so close they once gave each other the same Christmas card out of all of the hundreds of cards available on the racks.

Another couple, James and Ellen Wagner of the Pacific Palisades, married for thirty years, told a singularly dramatic story of what they feel is undeniably a form of ESP functioning between the two of them. Twenty years ago James was in the hospital undergoing a gastrointestinal examination when suddenly he said to his doctor, "I have to call Ellen." He insisted the doctor interrupt the procedure—an action that, he said, was entirely uncharacteristic of him—called his wife, and said, "Do you need me?"

The answer was a resounding yes. A photographer from a national magazine that had been planning a feature article on the house they had built together had just appeared at her door unannounced to begin photography, and Ellen, a perfectionist, was in a state of near-panic. She needed her husband home at once. Somehow he had received the message.

Ellen had summoned her husband to her side in this fashion more than once over the years; James said he has never missed an urgent psychic message sent by his wife, though he had missed lesser communications. He had even pulled off the freeway at times to call her when she was wanting him badly. Somehow, he knew.

Many couples described a similar if less dramatic phenomenon, offering a new twist to the notion of good "communication" within a marriage. Where it is axiomatic among couples' counselors that no spouse can be a "mind reader," these couples do precisely that: they read each other's minds, and on a regular basis. It may well be that people's "fantasies" of what a good relationship would be—fantasies of "perfect" understanding, of needs being met without the need to *ask*—are not so far off the mark. The kind of good communication these thriving couples share goes far beyond the careful laying out of emotional needs that troubled couples learn in couples' counseling. Happy couples often *are* good at expressing their feelings, but the ultimate goal of good communication is to reach the point at which they no longer *have* to be continually sitting down for formal reports on each other's state of mind. As far as the long-term thriving couple is concerned, the messages are getting across—with words or without.

The *oneness* of the happy couple will doubtless be met with a sense of dismay on the part of some. We have just emerged from a period during which the notion of the "two become one" has been roundly rejected. Feminists in particular—certainly those of us who came of age during the 1970s—have seen the marital union as destructive, with the wife losing all sense of self as she becomes a mere appendage to her husband. Other commentators have focused upon the seeming loss of individuality in both husband and wife. But whatever one's philosophical orientation, nowadays people tend to look askance at an institution in which it was once considered a good thing for one person to refer to the other as his "better half." In a culture in which a fully individuated identity is seen as the hallmark of the healthy adult, what can such a sentiment mean? For many it can mean only one thing: that the speaker has lost himself/herself in marriage, surrendered ego and will to the beloved. (Or, worse, that the speaker has demanded such surrender of his mate!) Collectively, we do not approve.

While such criticism may be all too true of the destructive marriage, the happy couple is not well served by this way of seeing the world. Happy couples are indeed each other's better "half," and they profit in so being. What is more, to term this shared identity a state of "fusion" or "boundary confusion" does not do justice to the very real achievement that it represents.

For a more positive understanding of the marital identity happy couples share, we must turn to society at large. A transcendent, shared identity is hardly a sinister thing: in much the same way that Americans experience themselves as *Americans*, the Smiths experience themselves as *Smiths*. Just as being an American permeates the individual identity of an American citizen, being a Smith comes to permeate the identities of each Smith.

What being a Smith means will vary, of course, with the family involved. Families define themselves by values, by goals, by material possessions and social standing, perhaps by certain physical characteristics and inherited abilities. ("The Smith women have always been teachers". "The Smith family has never had a divorce.") The content of the marital or familial identity does not matter so much as the sheer fact of simply possessing an identity. The Levys might take pride in sending every child to college; the Bentons might see themselves as pillars of the church. Whatever their point of view, strong couples possess a united set of values, beliefs, and goals. A shared identity.

Moreover, this identity has been forged over time, by two people who gradually come to give over more and more of their separate identities *to the marriage*. In other words, the shared identity of the thriving marriage is not made up of two entirely separate beings who happen to want the same things from life. Over time, in a happy marriage, separateness decreases. In a thriving marriage, two individuals come to think as one.

This heightened form of togetherness was striking among the couples with whom I spoke. Couple after couple told me that they did nearly everything together; the "separate vacations" approach to marriage was voted down with a resounding *No*.

This was so true that the two couples who had experimented with infidelity, an action that would seem to represent the outside interest par excellence, had actually done so as a joint project. These couples had mutually decided to see other people, had reported back to each other after each date, and had then mutually decided to return to monogamy. For most of us this would be stretching the concept of togetherness far beyond the limit, but there you have it. The degree to which happy couples could share experience was quite remarkable.

It was not that separate interests were threatening to these marriages, and indeed some spouses (though these were in the minority) had maintained a number of separate interests. Instead, what I found was that within these marriages separate interests had a tendency to become joint interests.

Separate interests merged because happy couples are good friends, and good friends share interests:

• **Happy couples usually describe each other as their best friend.**

Every happy couple with whom I spoke spontaneously used this phrase, "best friends," to describe their relationship. By "best friend" they meant much what the rest of us mean when we speak of a best friend of the same sex: husbands and wives who were best friends simply *liked* each other, very, very much. More than that: they liked each other best, above all others. They spent large amounts of time together, talking, working on their houses, traveling, pursuing joint hobbies; whatever it was that they wanted to do with their lives, they wanted to do together.

This preference for joint activity led to some surprising results. I remember being struck by Linda and Bob Martin, a working-class couple living in northern California who spent a large number of weekends attending crafts fairs together. Their house was filled with Linda's handiwork: handwoven wreaths with bows, hand-painted mother geese marching beneath the entryway mirror followed by their flocks, hand-stenciled hearts above the bookshelves in the family room. At the fairs she offered her framed cross-stitch patterns, baskets, and padded photo albums for sale. Bob traveled with her always, toting her things and setting up the booth, then keeping her company throughout the day.

Hearing this, I could not help feeling slightly amazed: how many men do any of us know who want anything whatsoever to do with women's handicrafts? Bob's active interest in his wife's hobby was particularly disorienting to me, given how stereotypically masculine he was in all respects. He sat before me wearing a handlebar moustache and cowboy boots, a rugged man's man, a fireman by trade. Raised on a ranch, he told me it was his dream to return to the land, and he and his wife had just taken their first step toward realizing that dream. They had bought an acre of land and a house across the canyon, as an equity bridge toward eventually being able to afford their own ranch. They would be moving within the month. This image, a rancher in cowboy boots sitting patiently beside his wife's booth at a crafts fair, *surprises;* it conflicts with the usually accurate enough sexual stereotypes concerning women and men and their respective interests. And yet this kind of cross-sex connecting, this best friendship between entirely heterosexual husbands and wives, was typical of the happy couples I met.

Husbands and wives could also involve each other in interests that were highly idiosyncratic to say the least. My favorite couple in this respect were Nancy and Mark. A few years back Nancy, seemingly out of the blue, had conceived a sudden interest in snakes—a hobby Mark was inexorably drawn into, to the point where he found himself one day force-feeding live newborn mice to a tiny baby snake when his wife was in bed with the flu. Although the nurturing of live infant snakes in his free time had originally been, as Mark humorously put it, the "furthest thing from my mind," ultimately he "got into it," just as he had ultimately "gotten into" each and every one of his wife's many enthusiasms. "We just feed off one another," he told me. It is a natural process, this "feeding off" the other's interests; neither demands that the other come along for the ride. What typically would happen instead was that each would develop an interest separately, and then after a while the other becomes involved, finds himself *drawn in*. As Mark said, trying to explain this process: "You see the other person having enjoyment, and you want to, too. At first I humor her, then I start to like it."

This capacity to be drawn into an activity that he would never have initiated on his own speaks as well to a certain openness on Mark's part, a flexibility: over the years, following his wife's lead, he had developed interests not only in snakes but in cat breeding (when I met them, the small duplex harbored ten cats in addition to the five snakes) and in collecting antiques (they owned a large collection of Depression glass) and stuffed bears. For her part, under her husband's influence, Nancy had become a runner. Mark was an excellent competitive runner who averaged six to eight miles a day, and Nancy, following his lead, had run for many years now as well, a discipline she knew she would not have developed without him.

Happily married couples can become so close that one wife actually told me that she had found herself one day unable to remember whether a certain opinion belonged to her husband or herself. She had gone to the movies with a friend and had been asked by a theater employee to sign a petition against a proposed city tax on movie tickets—an issue over which she and her husband had had a mild disagreement just days before. It was one of those nonessential, bickery sorts of arguments even the happiest of couples can have—as we will see in chapter three. They had been arguing over the ticket tax not because either held deep feelings on the subject of ticket taxes, but because one or both of them was in a bad mood and that was the topic that had happened to come up.

Now, as she considered whether or not to sign the petition, she realized with a shock that she could not remember whether she had been for the tax or against it during the argument! Her husband had become so much a part of her, and she of him, that for the moment she could not remember which of them had argued for the tax (saying that the city needed money) and which had argued against it (saying that the tax was regressive and unfair). Either could just as easily have argued either position, because both positions were, in their shared perception of the world, true.

Connecting

It is important to understand that this merging of two separate beings does *not* involve a loss of self. The happiest of couples frequently possessed distinctly different personalities and habits (he is an optimist, I am a pessimist; he is a night owl, I am a lark). Moreover, the happiest of couples gave each partner an equal, and separate, say in how married life was to be run. They were quite willing to argue a topic vigorously when conflict arose; difference held no threat. In short, within the shared identity there are still two people living, breathing, and moving forward in life.

Two different people (in some cases two *very* different people) can continue to exist within the shared identity of the happy marriage because the shared identity does *not* result from a process of fusion. It develops instead through a process of *internalization* similar to that which takes place within a child's mind as he grows. Just as the child internalizes his parents' voice and values, the happily married person internalizes his or her spouse's voice and values. As the child grows within the family, the adult grows within his or her marriage. Husband and wife become part of each other by virtue of having incorporated each other's being. They can think each other's thoughts because they have taken those thoughts within, made them their own. Theirs is not a loss of self, but a gain.

Thus, in the healthy marriage both partners bring the sum of what they are to the union, and each partner is enriched by the other. When marriage is taken to mean the erasure of the wife to the greater glorification of her husband, this is demonstrably not good for the wife. When marriage is taken to mean the utter defeat of individual egos by a crippling and destructive family system, this is demonstrably not good for anyone. But when marriage is taken to mean a union in which each person enlarges the other's horizons, bringing with him or her experiences, perceptions, and feelings neither would have had without the other, this is an unequivocal good.

As a practical matter, in order to achieve this union, each spouse must be open to the other. This was invariably true of the couples I met: they were accessible to each other, readily influenced by whatever the other might have to say. They listened to each other, they watched each other, they took each other in. Often they seemed to listen intently to their partners even when hearing a story told many times before.

An innately sociable nature, then, would seem to make an excellent starting place for a happy and long-lived marriage. And in fact, Burgess and Wallin's 1953 book reported that one of the factors best predicting a couple's future happiness was an active social life prior to marriage, with the couple seeing friends of both sexes. My own interviews reveal the same pattern; I found that happy couples tended to be quite sociable *as a couple*, possessing numerous treasured couples as friends. (Nora Ephron's witty observation—when you are married you date other couples—is quite right, the corollary being that if you don't date other couples there may be something wrong. The insular, intensely private alliance can all too often be a marriage with something to hide.) Nevertheless, while the natural extrovert may have a leg up on marriage, even the shyest of spouses can be profoundly happy if he or she is open to his mate.

- **Happy couples drink each other in.**

An internalized, shared identity is essential to marital happiness because it drastically reduces the opportunities for conflict. Friction decreases for the simple reason that it is not easy to sustain an ongoing battle with your spouse when you cannot remember who thinks what—at least on the nonessential issues. And on the profound issues that can wrench a couple apart—the universal issues of love, family, money—a unity of heart and soul may be essential.

Beyond this, a shared marital identity offers a method for two people who, after all, must at some level remain two separate beings no matter how close they grow, to weather the winds of change. As so many wives and husbands have discovered to their chagrin, people, and circumstances, do change. What we see happening within the happy couple is that the two partners change *together*. When one partner "branches out," develops a new interest, perhaps, or a new set of friends, or a new career, the other partner comes along. Their union, their fundamental connectedness, ensures that when one spouse is caught up in something new the other finds himself influenced and pulled in that direction as well. Thus within the thriving marriage the forces of change and innovation feed into the union, becoming part of it, rather than acting as external forces pulling it apart.

Also, a thriving union with the beloved is good for a spouse because it allays the potentially deadly force of too much solitude. (The research literature is filled with data on the shortened life spans of the lonely; James J. Lynch's book, *The Broken Heart: The Medical Consequences of Loneliness,* is a particularly good source on this subject.) The healthy union grants its partners liberation from the confines of the self, release from the prison of ego. In the words of psychoanalyst Ethel Person, love is a form of self-transcendence, a "religion of two." It is possible to have too much of the self; when we are wholly and happily united with another, self-consciousness fades. When we become part of something larger than ourselves, we can be released from the need to worry constantly about our own needs and failings.

The Dream

Finally we come to the ultimate secret of the truly thriving couple: the Dream.

• **The happiest of couples share a life Dream.**

These couples, the ones who seemed truly to glow, had moved beyond the day-to-day comforts of the shared routine and ritual, the shared identity, to the deeper realm of the shared dream. They were striving to be more than just the "Wilsons"; they were working together, shoulder to shoulder, to become some *kind* of Wilsons. The Wilsons-with-the-three-beautiful-children, or the Wilsons-who-bought-their-own-ranch, or the Wilsons-who-worked-their-way-up. The content of the dream might be virtually universal (the dream of home and family, or of worldly success and a position in society) or it might be entirely personal and idiosyncratic. It could be religious, or political. One very happy wife, sociologist Ruth Sidel, author of *On Her Own: Growing Up in the Shadow of the American Dream*, told me that in her experience politically active marriages were frequently joyful. This she had concluded from her experience with members of the antinuclear group Physicians for Social Responsibility, many of whom she felt enjoyed remarkably happy marriages—much happier than most. Whatever the content, it is the creation of the dream, the sharing of the dream, and the working together to make the dream come true that makes a couple glow.

The Sustaining Vision

The lives of Sarah and Norman Cohen reveal the power and importance of a shared dream.

Sarah and Norman met in 1933, when Sarah walked into a classroom in one of the new tuition-free junior colleges Franklin Delano Roosevelt had created to educate the young people of the Depression. Her father, once a successful restaurateur in upstate New York, had invested everything the family had in a Florida hotel in the year 1929. Now, bankrupt, he was starting over and the family could not afford to pay tuition.

Norman was there, sitting near the front of the classroom. Sarah's attraction to him was immediate. She took one look at her husband-to-be and said to herself, "By God, I'm going to marry someone who's not even out of college yet"—a momentous step for a girl who had witnessed so much financial distress within her own family. Strangely, the prospect of signing on for yet more economic uncertainty did not faze her. "We're going to have to struggle together," she thought. All this within moments of seeing her future husband for the first time, before even speaking to him.

Struggle they did, in spite of the fact that Norman proved to be the teacher of the class, and not a fellow student. Norman was intelligent and ambitious, but, as a young Jew whose deepest wish was to attend medical school, his options were severely limited. In those days of Jewish quotas it was to take him eleven years to realize his ambition.

Sarah threw herself fervently into Norman's dream, making it her own. Each year they would blanket the country's medical schools with Norman's applications for admission. At ten dollars apiece, this came to a sum they could ill afford. And each year they would wait as the mail brought the thin white envelopes bearing their form rejections within. It was not easy. For his part, Norman knew that he could not have persevered without his wife. He would certainly have given up, he told me, if Sarah had not insisted he go on. He took the rejections, dozens of them by the end of that long decade, personally; he felt constantly unworthy of his wished-for profession.

Finally, on the tenth anniversary of his efforts to win acceptance, at age thirty-one, he told Sarah that it was time to stop. Instead of investing all her time and energy into his career, he said, she should pursue her Ph.D.—a course she had set for herself years before but had abandoned when no less an eminence than the famous anthropologist Ruth Benedict had persuaded her that, being Jewish and a woman, Sarah would find her advanced degree unmarketable. It was pointless to go on, Benedict had said. Sarah listened.

Now Sarah rejected Norman's suggestion outright. "My mother was a feminist," she told me, trying to explain her persistence on behalf of his career rather than her own, "and her mother before her was a feminist. But *I* wanted my husband to have the superior craft." While many today would see this formulation as a recipe for disaster, for Sarah, in 1936, it proved to be an abiding source of strength.

Sarah's profound feelings on this score were no doubt shaped by the Depression, by that period during which so many fathers were visited with devastating professional and financial failure. Sarah had seen her father fail with disastrous consequences for his family, and she had been deeply moved by Norman's father's futile struggle to win acceptance to medical school in his early years. "My father-in-law's life had been virtually ruined by not getting into medical school," Sarah said. "It made a tremendous impression on me."

Sarah became utterly determined that her own husband should succeed where their beloved fathers had not. This was not a sacrifice of the self. It is neither accurate nor fair to view Sarah's determination that her husband succeed through the lens of contemporary feminism. Instead, Sarah was driven by the motivations of the second-generation American struggling to stay afloat during times of economic hardship: she was determined that her small family would overcome the obstacles that beset Jewish immigrants to the New World.

She was also driven by a strong attachment to Norman's family, a complicated bond that is difficult for a middle-class American of the 1990s to apprehend. "I was very strongly invested in my status with his parents," she explained. If she could help her husband become the doctor they all wanted him to be, her standing within the family would be established beyond question. "I wanted his parents to know that [Norman's becoming a doctor] was *going to be*," she said.

And it was going to be because of *her*. That a wife could be responsible for her husband's going to medical school was thinkable then in a way it is not thinkable now. Today we give credit for becoming a doctor entirely to the person who becomes the doctor; we no longer applaud the spouses and parents who provide the necessary support. But back then, a set of new in-laws would be fully aware, and fully appreciative, of how essential a wife's support, both emotional and financial, would be to her husband's achievements.

Sarah gave Norman both. She worked hard, bringing in the money to support them while he pursued an advanced degree in biology. This endeavor, too, was to bring yet more disappointment when Norman's graduate thesis was rejected by his advisors. Sarah remained resolutely optimistic for years. "Norman had wanted to be a doctor ever since he was a little boy," she said. "And he's not really so upbeat. But I was. I kept saying things like, 'I'll sleep with the dean.' " Throughout those years, Sarah never, ever, took her husband's setbacks as any reflection upon his abilities. She was right: when he was finally accepted into a medical school, at age thirty-two, he ranked in the top 1 percent of the applicants.

Their struggle did not end with the letter of acceptance, however. Medical school was costly, the hours spent interning long and hard. To pay for his schooling, Sarah and Norman borrowed thirty thousand dollars from an aunt and uncle, an extraordinary sum in those days. They managed to repay every cent through many more years of hard work and strain after Norman's graduation from medical school— years during which they faced as well the long illness of Sarah's father and the trauma of an infertility that was to prove untreatable. Life was not easy.

In their seventies when I met them, they were an extraordinarily vital and engaging couple. Both were slim, fit, and healthy; they were in love. There is no other term that captures their connection so completely. And while their happiness clearly flowed from many sources, the realized dream was an important part of it. As young Jews setting out in life, reaching adulthood in the midst of the Depression, Sarah and Norman were two people together against the world. Their union, forged in adversity, still binds them today as they reflect upon the success they have at long last won. They are like soldiers in time of war: they have been in the trenches together, have confronted an intense reality that they can share with no one else. This togetherness unites them, and—even more—the shared struggle that is now behind them makes them happy.

It is not difficult to see how this animating dream helped the marriage of Sarah and Norman to grow and flourish. When two people are utterly focused upon one goal, other issues, issues that might create conflict, dwindle in significance. With a dream to absorb one's time and emotional energy, the sheer space available for anger and discord is bound to shrink.

And, too, the animating dream is a fundamental source of optimism, of hope. In fact, to some extent the terms "optimism" and "dream" are simply different ways of saying the same thing; the dream is the expression of a couple's shared hope.

- **If the dream is good for the dreamer, the shared dream is good for the marriage.**

When Families Do Not Dream

We can see how crucial the animating dream is when we look at the lives of a couple who have not always shared a dream. Matt and Margaret Hyde, now ages forty-three and forty-one, had been together for nineteen years when we met. They met in college: she was eighteen, he was twenty. It was the height of the sixties, and, in a scenario that could only have unfolded at that time and place, they met in the midst of an impromptu party at which Matt was handing out tablets of LSD. Matt had seen Margaret around the campus; he had been attracted to her at once, but had figured she was too pretty for him. On this night he discovered that the attraction was mutual, and intense. The two walked around together all night, "clicking," in Matt's word. Finally he dropped her off at a friend's apartment the next morning.

Three days later, when they had again met by chance, Matt suggested to Margaret that they take a bath together. In the casual atmosphere of the 1960s no further preliminaries were necessary. Margaret said, "Hop to it!" and they have been together ever since.

But for all the ease with which they met and married, the course of their marriage had not been smooth. They had suffered serious problems, running the gamut from drug use to bankruptcy. And while the causes underlying these problems were complex, one important reason for their troubles, both of them now felt, was their failure to sign on for a shared dream.

For many years neither felt the need for a dream: they were too much in love to require a sustaining vision of their future to hold them together. As Matt said, "It took fifteen years for the honeymoon to end." Both felt powerfully, and continue to feel to this day, that it was their destiny to be together. A sense of destiny is, of course, an effective force for stability, but it is not an *active* force; a sense of destiny alone does not demand that either partner actually be focused, directed, on track. If it is simply your destiny to be together, there is no pressing need to be active in the service of your marriage.

That was the case with Matt and Margaret. There was no question of their being thoroughly mated. Their marriage gelled early on, and they easily formed a shared marital identity. One could almost see how connected they were just by looking at them—they were one of those couples who look alike: both stocky and dark, both with thoughtful expressions in their eyes. Being a couple, being married at heart, was not their problem. Sharing a dream was.

Without an animating dream, the two drifted, moving from New Mexico to Wyoming, from job to job, bearing three children along the way. Matt became a heroin addict, perhaps the final word in passive withdrawal from life. He was a quiet addict, a functional junkie: he went to work, and he saw their friends. But that was the extent of his involvement with life. As Margaret put it, "He was becoming a piece of furniture."

Margaret did not have a drug problem, but she, too, suffered her own form of passivity in the face of life, a passivity that stood out in relief once Matt had overcome his addiction. Having emerged from his drug years Matt began for the first time to form a serious ambition: he set his sights upon one day owning his own business. But Margaret, in the face of her husband's blossoming ambition, could not, as she said, "get on board."

In practice this meant that she could not motivate herself to accept the sacrifices they would have to make in order to realize Matt's dream. She hated the savings campaign upon which he now embarked in order to put away the necessary start-up money, and she hated the low-status job he took as a short-order cook in order to learn the restaurant business once he had settled upon that as his goal. She resisted him, quietly, at every turn.

But Matt persisted without his wife's support, and when his cousin, a wealthy talent agent from Los Angeles, offered to go in with him on a family restaurant in L.A. his dream was realized. He and Margaret and the children moved to California where, Margaret said, they promptly "fell for the glamour" of it all. Matt's cousin kept company with the rich and famous; he traveled by limousine. Even though every member of Matt's family warned him against going into business with his cousin, Matt and Margaret were swept away.

For a time, all went well, and the restaurant took off. But success bred trouble: Matt began to use cocaine with his cousin, and visions of grandeur took over. The two men drastically overextended the business, opening a chain of restaurants much too soon, too fast. Inevitably the crash came. Matt and Margaret lost everything—their money, their house, even their car. When I met them they were starting over.

Both had reflected a great deal upon what happened to them. Matt believed, and Margaret largely agreed, that for reasons having to do with her childhood she could not fully commit herself to his dream of succeeding in a business. "Her family was always poor," he said, "and I think she didn't want us to be any different." Matt remembered one occasion, many years back, when Margaret quashed his plans to take a responsible, career-track position with a computer company. Looking back, her negative reaction seemed significant to both. When he expressed an impulse to move forward with his life, to begin a career, she resisted, a reaction that was to become a pattern.

For her part, Margaret felt she had played a role in the most destructive element of Matt's life: his drug addiction. Without blaming herself, she nonetheless did shoulder part of the responsibility. "I would start an argument and push him to drugs," she told me, "when he was okay otherwise. I knew what chords to strike." While no wife can be ultimately responsible for her husband's drug use, Margaret did know her husband well enough to understand how badly he reacted to conflict. "My chemistry," said Matt, "is to do anything I can to get rid of it." Heroin was his way out.

Why Margaret should have wished unconsciously to push her husband to drugs while consciously objecting to his habit now seemed clear to both: theirs was a case of maternal feeling gone awry. Margaret was highly maternal; in her own words, she was "very good at nesting." And Matt arrived in her life much in need of mothering. His childhood had been devastating. His mother died before he entered grade school, and within two years his father remarried a woman who was to abuse Matt emotionally and physically for the remainder of his years at home. Matt's story touched Margaret deeply. "When I first met him and he told me about it," she remembered, "I just became very maternal. It was like, 'Welcome home. My arms are open to you.'" Very likely both colluded to maintain the relationship on these terms. So long as Matt remained underemployed and passive, Margaret remained the strong mother.

It is easy to see how a shared dream could have made things different. To begin, a dream might have helped Matt control his drug use. While an addiction is of course a medical and biological problem, it is also a problem of motivation. Had Matt been focused, bound, *guided* by a dream he shared with his wife, he certainly would have had more reason to leave the drugs behind earlier than he did.

Later on life might have progressed more smoothly for the two of them had Margaret been able to throw herself unequivocally into Matt's dream of opening his own business. This she could have done by directing her caring, maternal impulses toward the nurturing of a shared ambition and, later, of a young and growing business. The dream, had they been able to form one together, would have focused both upon the future. It might even have given them more resistance to the seductions of Matt's cousin by diminishing their passivity in the face of life. By her own admission Margaret never really became *active* in the effort to create a successful restaurant, she simply succumbed to the glamour of the city.

When we spoke they had made major changes in their lives. Matt had joined Alcoholics Anonymous; Margaret had attended Al-Anon, the organization for partners of alcohol and drug abusers. Together they had begun the process of forging a shared dream. They were clearly focused on the future, and on what they would work together to make it be. The two were at the start of a new venture selling insurance and financial services for a large corporation in California. Both were committed to this goal; each was ready to support the other in the daily struggles that lay ahead.

It was not that their entire dynamic would change. Instead their dynamic would now be focused outward, onto the world. Margaret would continue to be a good mother to her children, and Matt would continue to rely upon his wife's caring nature. What would be different was that her caring and his dependence upon her caring would now be bent to the service of their dream rather than to the assuaging of childhood wounds. From here on Margaret would be nurturing, and Matt would be asking her to nurture, a man who has had the proverbial "hard day at the office," rather than a boy left motherless at age three.

The Dream of Family

Beyond career and wealth and success in the eyes of the world, there is the dream of family. Many couples share this dream; it may be the most primal dream that a couple does share. Here I think of Joan and Kevin Richmond.

Joan and Kevin met in high school some forty years ago. "We were all part of the same group," Joan told me. "We used to go skating together, and then out for hamburgers." The two soon fell in together. Because both had been brought up in strict working-class Catholic households there was no question of an impassioned teen romance; they were friends and then, in time, they were husband and wife. It was all very natural, the pace and progress of their relationship from high-school sweethearts to man and wife decreed by the time and place. "Marriage just came up in conversation one day," said Joan, a slender and direct person with a husky smoker's voice. "One of us just said in passing, 'When we get married . . .' "

After their marriage, the children came quickly; Joan and Kevin knew nothing of birth control. But they liked children and were happy to begin their lives as parents.

Thus, during the first years they took life as it came; they met, they fell in love, they married, they had children. But they had not yet formed the dream. That was to grow out of hardship, out of the problems created by too little money and too little space.

Unable to afford their own place, they lived with Joan's father—an arrangement Kevin soon found intolerable. He had no control over his life there; it was not his *home*. Then, when the first baby came he felt even more left out of his own marriage and family. Things worsened steadily until Kevin finally went home to his mother for three days. "That got my point across," Kevin told me, grinning. When he returned to his wife and baby they moved upstairs, to their own tiny apartment.

It was the first, crucial step toward forming their own goals as a married couple and their own plans to realize them. Theirs was the dream, fervently shared, of a growing family securely established in a happy home. For them the dream, and with it the will to make it come true, grew out of hardship.

Forty years down the line, Kevin and Joan now shared the profound satisfaction of having realized their dream. Theirs was a happy and thriving family; a palpable atmosphere of contentment and pride pervaded the small living room as we spoke. Two of their ten grown children—as well as one much-adored grandchild—were present, injecting wisecracks and words of affection into the conversation as they listened to their parents speak. They had had as many as twenty-four family members present at one time, Kevin told me; he had counted. "The door," he said proudly, "is never locked."

An even greater source of pride was the fact that every one of their ten children was doing well. Not one had a brush with the law, Kevin reported (a fairly amazing record when you consider the troubled environment faced by young people today), nor had any suffered from a serious health problem.

Moreover, whenever one of the children had stumbled Joan and Kevin had known what to do to help. When daughter Debbie's marriage broke up she was so devastated, they were worried that she might do harm to herself, and they welcomed her and her children back into their small two-bedroom home at once. But when daughter Mary's marriage broke up and she, too, asked to come home to recover, they said no. Mary, they knew, needed to be on her own, and they forced the issue. Now she lived on the East Coast with her second husband, enjoying an income well into six figures. She told her parents that she owed it all to them, to their insistence that she spread her own wings. Together Joan and Kevin had become the wise and caring parents they had set out to be.

The animating dream lies at the heart of the thriving couple. If routine and ritual cement the bond, it is the dream that imbues a marriage with joy and meaning. The dream is the embodiment of hope. And hope lies at the heart of the happy marriage.

3

_℘_

Fighting the
Good Fight

When they faced conflict, as all couples must at some point in their lives, happy couples drew upon their shared identities to keep the peace. Having absorbed each other's perceptions of the world, they could see an argument from both perspectives, their own and their mate's: if they sounded hysterical and out of control to their partners (and they might) they knew full well that they were sounding this way. And, hearing themselves as their spouses heard them, they could turn the volume down. Also, their fundamental empathy for each other made apologies possible, when apologies were due, because happy couples understood how their angry words could affect their mates. They did not have to be told when they had gone over the line; they knew.

The result of this self-awareness was a dramatic decline in the number and intensity of arguments that happily married couples experienced. While it has become a truism that all married people argue, in fact some argue more often—and more fiercely—than others. Happy couples do argue well when they argue at all, but the real secret to their happiness lies more in their ability to avoid becoming mired in conflict in the first place.

Thus many happy couples, I discovered, rarely quarrel at all. In the beginning I was surprised by this revelation. Working my way down my list of questions I would arrive at the general topic of marital conflict. How did they handle disagreements, I would ask. Suddenly, what had been a lively and engaging discussion of a marriage would drop off into vague responses and shrugged shoulders. Trying to rekindle interest, I would press for specifics, asking a couple to describe their most recent argument. But even this direct approach was of little use for, to my amazement, large numbers of couples simply could not recall the last time they had quarreled.

I wondered. Did these couples simply not remember yesterday's spat—and if so, why not? Or, alternatively, had it been so long since they had quarreled that they genuinely could not bring the most recent occasion to mind? Could it be possible that they did not quarrel at all?

The answer proved to be yes on all counts. Beginning with the most peaceful of couples, there truly do exist marriages in which spouses rarely, if ever, quarrel. What is more, this lack of conflict cannot be explained away as a result of "avoidance" or "repression." It was not that these couples "bottled up" their anger; it was that they simply were not angry. They did not argue with each other because they had little or nothing to argue about.

These peaceable couples fell into one of three groups. Some were older people who had so successfully resolved their conflicts over the years that they were now on permanently good terms with each other. They may have been quite contentious in their younger years but were now at peace. Albeit belatedly, they were happy, and in love.

The second group who rarely quarreled were those who had made primarily companionable marriages. From the start these spouses had been more friends than lovers and, like friends more than lovers, they rarely argued. Their relationships being lower-key to begin with, these couples reported that their anger seldom grew beyond the level of minor irritation.

The third group overlapped the second: these couples did not quarrel because one or both partners was by nature disinclined to quarrel, with anyone. If they did not argue with their spouses, neither did they argue with friends, family, or colleagues. They were blessed with long fuses; they often seemed to be constitutionally cheerful. Although some of these couples were calm, companionable mates whose boiling point was set high, many belonged to the "vital" category of marriage and were quite passionate in temperament. Such couples had brought off the impressive feat of creating marriages that were animated and intense without being tempestuous.

My favorite spouse in this category was Marjorie Williams, a petite and twinkly (it is the only word that will do) great-grandmother in her eighties. She and her husband, Henry, did not seem to argue at all, though they did disagree on the subject of travel. She wanted to do more of it, he wanted to do less. Their compromise was to venture out upon one major journey a year (major, to Marjorie, being their most recent passage on a freight ship to China, about which Henry, a restless man who needs to keep himself busy, grumbled, "All that water").

Marjorie was, I believe, blessed with an innately cheerful temperament. At heart she was a happy person. All who knew her saw her this way, she told me. A few years back she had enrolled in a psychology course at her local community college and at semester's end the instructor took her aside and said, "You're always so happy. I've been wanting to ask you all term, what's your secret?" Marjorie laughed telling this story, remembering the scene of the professor asking the student her secret to life. Her secret was: that was the way she was wired.

It was not that Marjorie had suffered no hardship. She married during the Depression; she and Henry were poor. During their early years, Henry gambled away much of what little money he was able to earn each week as a street vendor. After he had conquered this problem his income was insufficient to support Marjorie and their two daughters, and Marjorie was forced to continue working even though she longed to stay home. She could not find any reliable day care at all. She and Henry went through forty housekeepers in seven years; once a sitter went out to mail a letter and did not come back. Marjorie remembered her hair going gray almost overnight from the terrible anxiety she suffered worrying about her children.

Obviously, Marjorie has suffered real problems, but it was her nature to bounce back. For her, things did not escalate. Even her husband's gambling did not provoke raging arguments, and she bore him no grudge at all. In fact, she saw him, and said so freely, as having been a wonderful husband and provider.

Not surprisingly, Marjorie and Henry were on excellent terms with their two daughters, as with their grown grandchildren, all of whom were doing well in life both personally and professionally. The family was close; the daughters and the grandchildren came often to visit. Theirs was a highly functional, and highly successful, family relationship.

Clearly, a sunny temperament helps in maintaining a happy marriage, which provides the unmarried among us with an excellent "selection" principle:

• **A marriage stands an excellent chance of succeeding when one or both partners are <u>naturally</u> cheerful people.**

Universally, the couples in which one or both partners possessed Marjorie's sanguine view of life were very happy. And almost universally their children appeared to be both productive and on good terms with their families. It is not difficult to see why. Good-natured spouses tend to shrug off the problems that can destroy a marriage. When they do quarrel, they do not draw blood.

Back in the days, so many years ago now, when Henry used to arrive home with his paycheck short, Marjorie *would* become angry. But, said Henry, "She never stayed mad at me overnight. There was always a good-night kiss." How many of us, taking care of two small girls aged one and two on an inadequate income, could muster a good-night kiss for a husband who had come home with half his paycheck squandered on card playing?

It is important to emphasize, too, that Marjorie was no martyr. Henry was a good man, "as honest as the day is long," said Marjorie, an "excellent father who was always generous with his girls"—both of whom continued to admire their father unreservedly. In short, he was a good man with one critical failing; Marjorie's faith in him was not misplaced. And her capacity to overcome her anger swiftly doubtless helped him change into the reliable and hardworking husband and father he was to become in his early thirties.

This is the ultimate "secret" of the good-natured spouse:

• **Happy couples expect each other to do their best.**

As psychologists have known for many years, positive expectations exert a tremendous force toward achieving positive results. For the darker souls among us, this is key: couples thrive when spouses focus upon what is good and true in the other. This does not mean that one needs to be a born optimist in order to thrive in marriage; I interviewed many happy couples in which one partner had been or was now chronically anxious, quick-tempered, or seriously depressed. Their marriages held strong in the face of these flaws in temperament because they did not focus their dark thoughts upon their husbands or wives. In spite of all the anxiety, anger, or sadness a troubled spouse might harbor within, he believed in his partner.

The Rules of the Game

Not all happy couples were so harmonious, of course. There were also a number who did quarrel often enough, but who so thoroughly resolved their arguments that they quickly forgot whatever the flare-up had been about. The reason they could not easily recall their most recent argument was simply that they did not hold a grudge. When a conflict arose they became angry, blew up, stormed about (or, alternatively, got mad, stopped talking, and withdrew into stony silence)—and then moved on. Their quarrels did not drag on from one day to the next; their hours together were not shadowed by unfinished business.

This capacity for resolution was the common thread running throughout all of these couples' lives. But how they resolved arguments varied enormously depending on who was involved. Some couples set a policy of never going to bed angry; one couple told me they always went to bed angry, in order to "sleep it off." Some couples shouted, some couples sulked; some couples dealt with issues as they arose, while others would let a problem go unresolved for days until they felt that the time was right to address it. In short, fighting, perhaps like making love, is highly personal. Couples must follow whatever rules and principles work best for them.

And follow rules they did: husband after husband, wife after wife, could tell me exactly what they typically argued about, exactly when they argued, precisely what could and could not be said during a quarrel, and how they made up afterwards. It was almost as if they were describing a form of intricately worked-out marital *protocol*; for these couples, an argument did not degenerate into a free-for-all. This was perhaps the most important principle to emerge from happily married people's discussion of conflict:

- **When they argue, happy couples follow the rules.**

Happy couples, in short, knew the rules, and they did not cheat. They "fought fairly."

There is one important caveat here: each couple wrote their own rules. A form of arguing that one couple might consider fair another couple might consider completely over the line. Moreover, some of the rules governing conflict could be remarkably complex. James and Ellen Wagner, whom we met in chapter two, have invented perhaps the most elaborate program for conducting an argument that I encountered. They fought frequently and energetically; they were classic yellers. Finally troubled by all the arguing, Ellen noticed a pattern: they were fighting each and every Saturday and Sunday night, evenings they customarily spent catching up on work that they had not finished during the week. As Ellen thought about their arguments, they began to make sense. "I realized our fights were 'instead of' fights," she said. "We were getting into arguments because the arguments were more stimulating and more interesting than doing our work."

Having made this connection Ellen and James acted promptly to thwart their unconscious selves. Because the fights always took place in bed, never at the living-room table, they moved all the work papers off the bed and into the living room. And they instituted a system according to which if either one said anything provocative the other would exclaim, "Derail!" The offending party then had to pay the other a quarter. This worked beautifully for them; in fact, I was able to see it in action during our interview. At one point, as Ellen was trying to explain her problems with overwork (she was spending as much as twelve to fifteen hours a day, seven days a week, poring over her various financial projects—this during the supposed retirement years of her sixties) she remarked that home computers actually add to a person's workload, rather than subtracting from it. James objected; a computer does not make work, he said. His comment instantly provoked a mini-debate between the two of them over the nature of computers and whether they do or do not ultimately create more work for their owners than they save—clearly a digression from the subject at hand, which was their marriage and why it was so happy. Suddenly recognition dawned, and with a wave of the hand Ellen exclaimed, "Derail!" And that was that. Both dropped the subject at once and returned to what they had been discussing—which was their method of resolving an argument. The rule worked perfectly.

While few of us would feel comfortable halting an argument by calling out "Derail!" to our mates, the principles underlying Ellen and James's approach to marital conflict are ones all of us can emulate. Troubled by the frequency and intensity of their arguments, they looked for a hidden pattern. Then, finding it, they set about breaking the pattern by whatever means would work. And, finally, they adopted a policy of cutting off their arguments before they escalated. Both James and Ellen recognized a bid for an argument when they hear it, as do most of us, no doubt. Not rising to the bait—more, a *conscious policy* of not rising to the bait—is a highly effective means of heading a battle off at the pass.

When they did end up in full-scale battle in spite of all their efforts to avoid it, James and Ellen learned simply to walk out of the room. This, too, was Ellen's inspiration. "It came to me one day," she said, "that our fights were totally self-contained. If one of us walked out of the room, we were back together in five minutes. We didn't even have to say 'I'm sorry,' we were so glad just to be with each other again." Knowing this about themselves, they began to walk out on arguments on purpose.

Many couples ended quarrels by using some version of this strategy. Rather than talk (or shout) a subject through, they simply brought the curtain down, called it halt. They had devised various ways of going about this. Many followed the rule of not going to bed angry. (Some told me that their parents had firmly impressed this precept upon them, and had lived by it themselves.) These couples always, whenever there was a fight, managed to kiss and make up before dropping off to sleep. As I mentioned earlier, another couple, both partners highly volatile people, purposely *did* go to bed angry. Knowing themselves as they did, knowing how easy it was for both to let their anger escalate far out of control, they purposely used sleep as a natural cooling-off period. When they awoke in the morning their heads were clear. They would rendezvous in the kitchen, a new day ahead, and kiss.

The strategy of setting an arbitrary deadline for the end of an argument frequently worked even when couples had not managed to reach an agreement by that point. Often, stable couples simply let matters drop. One wife in her mid-thirties, married for thirteen years and overwhelmed by the obligations endemic in the lives of so many women her age—two children, two jobs, and three cats in one family—recalled a Monday Memorial Day that began with a round of marital sniping that showed no sign of winding down. "It was depressing," she said, "because this was our one day off. Finally I just said, 'Let's not do this.' " Her husband agreed at once, and the two enjoyed their holiday with the children—a day that would otherwise have been ruined by anger.

Thus happily married spouses were distinguished by a capacity *not* to have to "win" an argument. By the same token, marital unhappiness and divorce are clearly associated with a strong need, on either partner's side, to be right. In his job as a postal manager Mark Walters, whom we met in the last chapter, was surrounded by divorced and divorcing men. Invariably, he said, these men were domineering, arrogant sorts who always had to be right. "You can see why their marriages are breaking up," he said, "just talking to them at work." As the years went on, then, strong couples followed the same principle of argument with which they had begun:

• **Happy couples care more about the health of their relationships than about winning arguments.**

Interestingly, happy couples were able to back away from disagreements far more serious than a tiff over Memorial Day housework. One couple who had been at odds over the husband's drinking for nearly twenty years reported that they had religiously followed the rule of not going to bed angry. The husband would come home drunk from a business dinner (this was during the 1960s when business executives were expected to drink when entertaining other executives), she would angrily object, and somehow they would manage to make up in the little time remaining before bed. Nor did she spend the next day fuming over the previous night's transgression. Again, this was not a case of wifely martyrdom. As is so often true in long marriages, her tolerance has been well justified: in his sixties today, her husband drinks only in moderation and the two are thoroughly enjoying their retirement. Both are in excellent health and very happy together.

Obviously, the capacity to resist the lure of an extended argument requires a great deal of forbearance. Whenever couples told me that marriage requires "work" (and most—though not all—did offer this observation sooner or later), what they were actually talking about was the capacity to bite one's tongue. Though it was not easy, happy spouses in long-lasting marriages had learned to choose their battles.

• **When an argument is not worth having, happy couples force themselves to walk away.**

It was the happy couple's highly developed sense of empathy for each other that helped them to avoid gratuitous conflict. All happy couples possessed a mature capacity to stand back and assess their own behavior. They were remarkably self-aware; over the years they had developed strong "observer selves," as the Japanese call this watching part of our beings. They did not "lose themselves" in battle; they knew what they were saying and how their comments were being received. They could hear themselves through the ears of their partner.

Thus happy couples followed the rules they had set for themselves. It is essential to point out, however, that simply formulating some rules for constructive argument is not enough. What made it possible for happy couples to follow their rules in the first place was a fundamental equality between partners. This sense of equal standing allowed happy couples to argue without crossing the line into all-out warfare. Marital arguments become ugly and brutal when either partner (or both) feels genuinely threatened. When a spouse feels belittled or despised by his mate he or she *must* fight back with all he or she has as a matter of sheer self-defense. In effect, an unequal pairing reduces one partner (or sometimes both) to the position of the helpless child—which is why couples' counselors speak of *"infantile* rage." Many of the most violent arguments that take place between unhappy spouses grow out of a feeling of impotent rage.

In sharp contrast, happy couples do not experience *impotent* rage. If pushed far enough—by their partners or simply by life itself—they might feel fiercely angry, but they never feel helpless. Because they know they have equal standing in the relationship, they always feel, even at their most furious, that they have some say in how things will turn out. This feeling of "empowerment," as psychologists would call it, keeps an argument within bounds. When they argue, happy couples are not symbolically fighting for their very lives, as unhappy couples frequently are. This explains, too, why a happy childhood is good for one's marriage. A married man or woman who was respected and beloved as a child just naturally assumes that he or she *counts*— no matter how incensed his or her spouse may be at the moment.

This is one of the most important principles to emerge from conversations with happy couples, a principle Burgess and Wallin identified many years ago:

• **If a couple is to be happy, it is essential that the partners see each other, <u>and see themselves</u>, as equals—regardless of how the world may see them.**

This is why simply learning the principles of "fighting fair" will not bring peace to a desperately unhappy couple, as a study from Texas A & M University reveals. Researchers there found that troubled couples who underwent training in good communication and negotiation techniques were far more likely to divorce than were couples whose therapy had addressed the psychological roots of their problems. Knowing how to fight fairly only helps when the motivation to do so is there. The first requirement in any troubled marriage, or even in any serious conflict between happily married spouses, is to recover our feeling of *respect* for our partners, and for ourselves.

Anger, Bad and Good

While each couple differed slightly in how far they were willing to let a quarrel go before taking steps to end it, and how exactly they did set about bringing it to a close, they universally shared the belief that conflicts must be ended, and sooner rather than later. In short, the common thread running through all couples' married lives was the existence of an agreed-upon plan for assuaging anger, and a capacity to put that plan into action. No one subscribed to the belief that the free expression of anger was a good thing for a marriage, as we are sometimes told; while couples universally agreed that "good communication" was essential to a happy marriage, all felt that outbursts of anger were to be closely monitored. Their overriding principle:

- **Happy couples do <u>not</u> "let it all hang out."**

Many felt that anger was profoundly destructive. One young couple just turning thirty, Elaine and Jason Stassen of Chicago, told of deciding to end their pitched battles when they saw the distress it was causing their new baby. Theirs were true blowouts, "not quite thermonuclear," Jason told me, "but almost." Both Elaine and Jason are by nature intense and stubborn; as soon as an argument broke out each would say the most hurtful things he or she could think of, about each other and even about each other's families. Doors would slam, threats would be leveled. "We were still having these screaming fights when Jamie was six months old," said Elaine. "He would cry every time. I thought to myself, 'We can't live this way.' "

Jason agreed. Their marriage had been happier, and far healthier for their little boy, since they set clear limits on their disputes. Still, both Elaine and Jason confessed that they had experienced a loss of intensity once their battles royal ended. "It would go in cycles," Jason said. "We'd have the most intense fight and then we'd get very close and say 'I'm sorry.' We'd do everything to show how much the other meant to us." Their relationship was the classic emotional roller coaster, and roller coasters exist because they are enormously pleasurable. At some level Jason and Elaine enjoyed the intensity of their fights: "I'm not really quick-tempered," said Jason, describing how a typical argument could escalate so quickly. "I would know I was getting mad, but I *wanted* to." While both were happier now, they agreed that stopping the arguments did tamp down the passion between them. Only recently had the intensity of their relationship begun to return without a need for periodic explosions to sustain it.

Still other couples told me that they rather valued their quarrels, not because they whipped up passion, but because they *released* it. These were couples who quarreled to "let off steam," couples who told me that sometimes they simply "needed" to fight. The world being what it is, they said, no one can maintain calm twenty-four hours a day. For these long, stably, and for the most part happily married couples it was a relief to be able to take their troubles home in the form of a good old-fashioned joust. As one couple, married for fifty years, told me, "We have fought religiously once a week for our entire lives."

Here again we encounter the remarkably individual nature of the happy marriage. While it is practically axiomatic among couples' counselors that partners must not "take out" their work and daily-life frustrations on one another, a number of couples did just that without causing undue harm to their marriages. Listening to these couples describe their tension-relieving spats, I came to the conclusion that the reason they could "get away" with this was that they tended not to make these arguments personal—one of the basic tenets of fighting fairly. When a happily married man who in truth was angry with his boss came home and picked an argument with his wife, he did not do it by launching an attack upon her character. Instead, a fight would erupt over something completely irrelevant—the proper pronunciation of a word, for instance. Ellen and James Wagner told me that they frequently had pitched battles over the correct way to arrive at a certain calculation, even though both had in fact arrived at the same calculation—albeit by different means. When couples needed to fight for the sake of fighting, no subject was too trivial to serve as grounds for vehement disagreement; in fact, it almost seemed the more trivial the better. In other words: as these couples understood, feathers simply do not get irretrievably ruffled when what is at stake is the proper pronunciation of the word "macabre."

When an Issue Must Be Faced

Not every issue, of course, can simply be allowed to drop. Disagreements about children (perhaps the most common source of strife among the couples in this book), money, in-laws, drinking, drugs: such problems tend not to vanish with a good night's sleep. Even the smaller, yet potentially paralyzing conflicts over what kind of new car to buy, or where to go on the summer vacation, must be resolved in order for a couple to make decisions.

When it came to smaller matters, happy couples showed themselves to be adept and generally swift at finding a way to split the difference. If one partner hated to travel and the other yearned to visit China (a common-enough pairing) they came up with a plan that allowed for *just enough* travel abroad to satisfy the adventurer, with the rest of the year spent cozily at home for the homebody. The homebody came along willingly on the yearly trip and did not complain; the traveler stayed home happily the rest of the year. They arrived at a compromise and lived with it cheerfully.

For long-married couples these were the easy questions, naturally enough. It was on the thornier issues that strong couples truly showed their mettle. Here their major strategy was diplomacy. Even in the midst of a major disagreement happy couples found a way to say an honest "yes" to each other when most of what they were feeling was "no."

In practice this meant that even if they could not actually resolve a problem between the two of them, they did manage to agree, at least, on what the problem was—and, sometimes, who was at fault. As an example of how this might work in action, take the issue of a spouse's drinking. In an unhappy marriage the spouse who does not drink sees the drinking as the problem; the spouse who does drink sees the abstinent spouse's nagging as the problem. Not only is there no resolution of the drinking issue; there is also no agreement even as to what the problem is, or where it is coming from. Absolute disagreement of this order brings many a marriage to its knees.

But in the stronger marriage these two spouses would feel more sympathy for the other's position. The alcoholic would understand, at least to some degree, that his drinking was hurting his spouse; his partner would understand that continual complaints about his or her drinking were distressing to the alcoholic. Even if neither could or would change his behavior at that time, neither would feel as if he were talking to a blank wall. Both could maintain hope for change in the future. The principle that sustained them through ongoing conflict was this:

• **When they cannot agree on how to <u>solve</u> a conflict, happy couples manage to agree, at least in part, on what the problem <u>is</u>.**

In short, happy couples were remarkably able to agree upon the nature of their problems—and not infrequently even upon their own role in creating a problem. Here again, their empathy for each other sustained the connection. They knew what their partners were thinking because they already fully understood their partner's worldview. If a wife was saying "black" while her husband was saying "white," *both* knew, usually, that in the other person's shoes they'd probably be saying the same thing. I was struck, time and again, by how fluently and sympathetically a spouse could lay out exactly what he or she was doing to provoke his spouse. I remember, in particular, Sharon and Fred Hartford, a couple in their forties who lived in northern California. Married for twenty-three years, they had been struggling through some very hard times. Fred, a natural pessimist prone to depression, had seen his livelihood as a telephone-line repairman very nearly dealt a death blow with the breakup of AT&T. All around him, people were losing their jobs; he had stood by and watched as close friends were fired after twenty years with the company. The survivors, like Fred, now held on to their jobs by the slenderest of threads. Overnight, job security had vanished, and life had become precarious. It was unlikely that Fred would ever again enjoy the same level of income and security that he had in the past.

For Fred these events had precipitated a deep, and persistent, depression. He felt that he was a failure as a father and provider; he suffered terrible guilt over his family's declining standard of living. He was haunted by the choice he made: faced with a decision of whether to stay with AT&T or move on to one of the subsidiary companies, he chose to stay. To his horror, he came to believe over the next months that he had chosen the wrong path. "I realized," he said, "I had taken food out of my children's mouths."

Gripped by these wounding thoughts, Fred was at loggerheads with his wife. Sharon, who described herself as a natural optimist, understood that her husband's lost wages were not his fault, and, what was more, she did not feel that his worth as a man was inextricably bound to his capacity to earn a good living. She told him that she was just not that interested in money.

This clash of outlook created a painful amount of friction between the two of them. She disagreed with his view of the world; he disagreed with hers. They argued. It had been an unhappy time for both of them. But what held them together was their capacity to see the other's point of view, even though neither of them had thus far changed. Within moments of my raising the subject of conflict, Sharon said simply, "He feels bad that he isn't making enough money for all of us. I tell him that I don't care about money, but that makes him feel as if I don't take his problems seriously."

That was it in a nutshell; in two sentences Sharon had laid out exactly what about her attitude was provoking her husband's anger. For his part, Fred understood the strain that his depression was creating for his wife. He was not able to shake his powerful feelings of guilt and unworthiness, he could not will himself out of depression, but he nevertheless understood that his constant unhappiness was hard on her. While neither could change his outlook, both were in complete agreement as to how exactly the difference in outlook was causing them to quarrel. They understood the source of the quarrel, even though they could not see their way clear to a solution.

Even this degree of understanding is enormously helpful to a marriage. People need to feel understood; being understood is the essence of human connection. A marriage can survive on this much alone when differences cannot be resolved. And differences are not always resolvable. Fundamental differences in temperament, the problem dividing Fred and Sharon, do not yield readily to the dictates of reason. A seriously depressed spouse cannot cheer up simply because his spouse wants him to.

But the seriously depressed spouse *can* empathize with the effects his depression is having upon his spouse. Though when I met them Fred and Sharon were not living happily ever after, theirs was a tough and resilient union—a union sustained by a meeting of the minds even across their vast differences in character and need. They may yet break through to the happiness lying just beyond their grasp.

In one way or another most happy couples laid out, and lived by, this fundamental creed:

- **When it is impossible to agree, it is important to try to <u>understand</u>.**

Reframing a Disagreement: Anatomy of a Conflict

Although strong couples find ways to cope, the harsh truth is that, over time, long-standing differences can erode the love they feel for each other. Couples were happiest, they told me, when they found some way truly to resolve the issue that was coming between them.

When a simple compromise was not possible, people in a happy relationship frequently reached agreement by *reframing* an issue in terms congenial to both. Susan and Steve James offer an example of how this works. A very happy couple who rarely argued, they found themselves coming into sharp conflict over the issue of money when

Steve, an attorney who taught law at a large university in Chicago, was offered a much more lucrative position in a Chicago law firm.

Even with two children to support, they did not absolutely need the money. Susan earned a substantial income as a sales executive for a large clothing chain in the Midwest; for most of their marriage she had substantially outearned her husband. Nevertheless, Susan wanted Steve to take the job. With two children and a demanding career she felt chronically exhausted and overwhelmed; she longed to be able to cut back to part-time work, or even leave the work force altogether for a few years, in order to spend time with her children. If Steve *could* make this possible for her, she felt, he should.

For his part, Steve was ambivalent. Knowing that the added income would make an enormous difference to Susan, his first impulse was to accept the offer. But when he spoke to some of the younger members of the firm he began to back away. They were overworked; a sixty-hour week was routine and much of the work involved corporate law, which was not Steve's primary interest. The pressure to produce was constant.

Discouraged, Steve called his wife and told her he did not think he would take the job. The hours were too long, he said, the work too boring.

Susan was furious. While Steve's hours as a professor were as long as or longer than hers, much of that time he could spend at home in his study, writing articles and briefs. The result was that Steve saw far more of their children during the week than she did, a situation that upset her a great deal. Susan felt she was missing her children's young lives.

Thus when Steve called with the news that he was turning the job down, she reacted angrily. "Even though I knew it was unfair of me, the whole idea that he had to have a job that was *interesting* made me want to scream," Susan recalled. "How interesting did he think it was for me, out there servicing the same department store accounts year in, year out? So the thought that he would just unilaterally turn down a big offer without my even having a say—it made me furious."

This was a dangerous moment in their marriage, one that could have left bad feelings behind whichever path Steve chose. Their dilemma had evolved into a classic no-win proposition: if Steve turned down the job at that point, Susan would have felt betrayed; had he accepted the job under pressure from his wife, he would have felt resentful. No compromise was possible on this particular issue: Steve either took the job or he did not.

How the two negotiated this passage in their marriage is highly instructive. To begin with, both held their tongues. "I couldn't say *too* much about how I was feeling," Susan explained, "because I didn't believe in sixty-hour work weeks myself." Nevertheless, Steve got the message; her displeasure was unmistakable in her tone and extended silences on the telephone. What she was not willing to put into words, she was putting into "nonverbals." Steve, too, exercised forbearance. He knew Susan was angry, and even though he thought she was being unfair he said nothing. Soon they hung up, Steve saying that the two of them would have to "think about it."

Nearly all happily married couples employ this delaying tactic from time to time, and its effectiveness clearly demonstrates why an open communication policy is not always the wisest choice. If Susan had blurted out all she was feeling, the consequences could have been disastrous. She would have said things she did not really believe, and she would have hurt and infuriated her husband who might have turned the job down in reaction. Instead of pushing each other to the limit, they bought time—allowing tempers to cool before tackling the issue head-on.

For the next week or so, they let the matter ride. During this period Steve began to feel guilty about Susan's having to work so hard; he began to feel that he *should* take the job whether he wanted to or not. And he began to "sell" himself on the job; even if much of the work would not be to his liking, he told himself, this would be a chance to witness the law in action. Finally he told Susan he was thinking of accepting the offer.

Now it was Susan's turn to feel guilty. She knew her husband had little interest in corporate law, and she did not like to think of his spending twelve hours a day doing something he disliked on her behalf. She did not want to be responsible for Steve taking a job he would hate. Thus when he said he was thinking of doing it, she responded mildly, saying only, "Well, whatever you think."

This is an important point to reach in a major conflict, because when each partner is ready to yield ground, both partners are mollified. Each person gets a taste of what it would be like to have things his way; each person understands that the other wants him or her to be happy. Moreover, each partner feels *consulted*. Part of the reason for

Susan's anger had been her feeling that Steve was taking a unilateral action that would affect her life as much as it would his. As she saw it, Steve was not only deciding to turn down a job, he was also deciding that Susan should continue to work full-time. This, of course, was not how Steve saw it. Regardless of who was right, however, both needed to feel that they had had real input into how the decision finally came out. Here they were following a principle common to most happy couples:

• **When compromise is not possible, happy couples make sure that each partner at least has a <u>say</u> in how things will turn out.**

This was where the matter stood when Steve and Susan were invited to attend a barbecue given by one of the firm members. From the beginning, neither warmed to the tone of the event. It was made clear that their children would not be welcome even though the party was to be held on a Saturday afternoon; Susan felt this as an intrusion into her time with her family.

The gathering itself was pleasant enough, but Susan was put off by their host's relationship to his own children. He seemed completely removed from his young son and daughter, barely acknowledging their presence when they crossed his field of vision. Susan gathered from the conversation that he was rarely at home; apparently the firm's attorneys were expected not only to work long days but also to travel frequently on business. All the wives but one were full-time mothers.

Susan and Steve drove home sobered. While both had begun to think that Steve was going to take the job, and both had begun to fantasize about the financial benefits that would accrue, now the price this opportunity would exact in terms of family life became clear. A few days later, Steve said tentatively that he thought he should turn the job down, that if he were to take it he would "never see his children again."

Susan instantly and wholeheartedly agreed. "It was funny how I could go from being completely furious with him to being in complete agreement in just three weeks," said Susan. This drastic change of heart reveals how powerful, and important, the framing of an issue is to its ultimate resolution. So long as the new job was framed as a question of what would be good for Steve (reasonable hours, interesting work), Susan objected. But when the issue was reframed in terms of what would be good for their family, Susan came "on board."

This is the final lesson to be drawn from the way in which thriving couples resolve important issues. Instead of framing an issue in terms of separate wants and needs, they approach it in terms of what *they* want and need, both separately and as a couple. They reframe in terms of their dreams, then follow their dreams to the solution they demand. This approach offers the enormous advantage of drawing a couple together even in the midst of serious conflict, because instead of thinking "I," the couple is thinking, or at the very least trying to think "We." *We* value family; *we* want Steve to be there for his children; therefore *we* decide to take this road and not another.

With the "We" approach to conflict, each partner can and does emerge a winner; each gets at least something of what he or she wants. For the thriving couple this is frequently true no matter which way the decision ultimately goes. While Steve's first reaction was that he did not want the job, by the day of the party he had convinced himself that he did. In fact, had he taken the position, he would no doubt have focused upon the satisfactions offered by his new life, not the drawbacks. He would not have become a martyr to his wife's wishes, just as she did not become a martyr to his. For most of us there is no *one way* in life; it is not that one outcome will be heaven, another hell. Usually, when major disputes arise, both alternatives offer positives and negatives. The vital couple settles accounts by focusing upon the positive aspects of whatever decision they reach. Their operating principle is:

• **When an argument is resolved in terms of what is best for us, rather than what is best for me, both partners come out happy.**

Making Amends

Wisely, Steve and Susan did not allow themselves to reach the point—or even to come close, for that matter—of wounding each other's pride. But even though vital couples do not draw blood when they quarrel, they certainly do inflict minor scrapes and bruises from time to time. They can be petty, irritable, unfair; they can even be mean spirited. But when they are, *they know it*. This sensitivity was another of the more striking features of thriving couples, which once again flows from an abundance of the twin virtues of self-awareness and empathy. When a happy husband or wife said something mean or uncalled-for, he or she knew he or she was in the wrong. Their operating principle:

• **Happily married people believe in being able to admit, at least to <u>themselves</u>, that they could be wrong.**

It was quite amazing, this capacity to think of themselves as being in the wrong. Most of us dislike being wrong; most of us avoid any suggestion that we *could* be wrong. (And if you will notice, Steve and Susan, by not openly voicing any accusations, carefully constructed their dispute so as to avoid putting either of them in the position of having to be wrong.) But time and again, when I asked couples how they ended arguments, they would volunteer comments along the lines of, "Well, whoever's wrong eventually apologizes" (or "drops the subject," or "makes a joke," or "says something friendly"). They would offer this explanation as if it were the obvious response, requiring no further elaboration.

But of course for most of us it is never obvious when *we* are wrong, only when the person we are arguing with is wrong. "Do *both* of you always know who is wrong?" I would ask couples. The answer was yes.

Here again the answer could be yes because of the shared identity these couples had developed over the years. They now held so many values and beliefs in common that it could not help but be obvious to both who was (furthest) out of line. And they were so sure of each other's love that even in a pitched argument their defenses were down. They were capable of seeing themselves as wrong because being wrong held no threat. They would still be loved; their partner would still be there; life would go on as before whether they were wrong or not.

Couples were so sure of each other's love that they often viewed their tiffs with a sense of humor. One wife, married for seventeen years and now in her mid-thirties, humorously described her most recent marital battle. It had begun, innocuously enough, with a flat tire. Her car had the flat and, when her husband drove her to work late, she "bugged" him about it—to the point where he called her a "bad word" and then she hit him on the arm. Having regressed by this point to the level of two preschoolers, both went their separate ways. Things did not end there: that night after work her husband did not show up in his car to pick her up. So she called home, "just to nonchalantly ask the kids where he was," as she put it. He was in the garage, they told her, fixing the flat.

While the fact that her husband was working on her car even if he had not seen fit to pick her up might have mollified her, it did not. Both partners were now sticking stubbornly to their pride. He wasn't going to pick her up unless she asked him to, and she wasn't *about* to ask. Instead she called her sister. Even that wasn't the end of it: she and her sister picked up the kids to take them out for hamburgers, without asking her husband whether he wanted one, too!

Finally, after a spirited exchange concerning the hamburgers, the two made up. "I don't know," she said, when I asked how they had managed to extricate themselves from this seemingly self-perpetuating series of minor insults. "I guess all of a sudden it's just over. One minute it's 'You're so ignorant,' and the next we just start talking to each other as if it never happened. For me my anger just sort of evaporates, and I think it's the same for him."

The point here is not that happy couples (and after a rocky first five years this couple had been very happy indeed) are always operating out of a noble and mature regard for each other. Sometimes, obviously, happy couples can behave like two children squabbling in the backseat on the family vacation. It is not that happy couples never behave like squabbling children but rather that happy couples are well aware that they are behaving like squabbling children when they are. They know what they're doing when they're doing it, and they can laugh at themselves afterwards. And afterwards generally comes sooner rather than later.

Thus, fighting "well" is not purely a matter of technique. Some happy couples develop excellent techniques for conducting an argument; others do not. Good technique alone cannot work without the vital couple's love for each other, without the union of two souls into one. A marriage cannot stand as a house divided against itself, and the happy couple's shared identity is an invisible force working to draw both partners back to center.

And, just as importantly, the happy couple's love for each other allowed the "wounded party" to forgive and forget. In ending an argument it is just as important to accept an apology as to offer one. And vital couples told me that they accepted all apologies, in all forms. Many couples apologized outright, but many did not. More than a few errant spouses remained too prideful to confess to wrongdoing outright; instead, they apologized *implicitly* by becoming especially solicitous and attentive when the storm had passed. Their apology was spoken through gesture and tone, accepted by the heart.

Even with all the vital couple's capacity to end the fiercest of arguments happily for both, there remained some topics not open to negotiation. Sometimes, long-married spouses told me, they reached the breaking point. Something, someone, had to *change*. And as we see in the next chapter, in many happy marriages, someone did.

4

℃

Change

"**W**hatever bothers you about him today will bother you ten times over five years from now. People don't change."

Many a parent has given this advice to a daughter, or its obverse to a son, and rightly so from the parent's perspective. No mother or father wants to see his or her child take a risk in love, and choosing to marry a decidedly flawed human being is undeniably to take a risk. But how true is this notion, really? Do errant spouses never change?

Most couples told me that in fact they had changed a great deal throughout the course of their marriages; only a few felt themselves to be exactly the same people they had been when they set out in life. Moreover, all believed that they had changed for the better—and their mates agreed.

This is an important finding indeed because it offers hope to those couples who have reached an impasse, to couples who despair of anything important changing between them. A surprisingly large number of very happy couples had reached this point themselves at some juncture. A good quarter had thought of leaving their marriages more than once; a few had actually packed their bags and gone. And yet their marriages had not only survived, but flourished. The marriages endured because one or both partners, quite simply, *changed* whatever it was about himself or herself that was driving the other away. In marriage, change can and does happen.

Thus the question is not whether people change, but how much they change, and under what circumstances. What forms of personal change can we hope to see in our mates and in ourselves, and how do we bring about these changes?

Change Through Maturation

To begin, most people change naturally—regardless of the promptings of an impatient spouse—as they age. Within marriage maturational changes follow a predictable pattern, with couples moving from a frequently chaotic and confused period in their twenties into calmer years that begin somewhere in middle life. (Couples who married at age thirty or later had an easier time of it, at least in my group.) As we would expect, the most dramatic stories of marital conflict often came from a couple's early days together. Take the case of Marjorie and Henry Williams. Their problems with his gambling occurred almost exclusively during their twenties, coming to an end as Henry entered his thirties. Henry was twenty-six when they married, Marjorie twenty-four. By the time Henry was thirty he had two small daughters to support and a gambling problem that was draining away what little salary he could bring in. "I gambled a lot, and I lost a lot," Henry told me.

Everything changed when Henry reached his thirties. While undoubtedly Marjorie's love helped him to overcome his problem, much of the change in Henry appears to have been due to the process simply of growing up and settling down. "I really didn't get hold of myself until after the kids were one or two," Henry said. "I became a man at age thirty-one."

For Henry, as for many men and women married or not, age thirty was a watershed. Not only did Henry conquer his gambling, but he also made important strides in his work life as well. "I finally realized I'd better straighten myself out," Henry recalled, trying to explain the sweeping nature of the changes he found himself able to make at this stage of life. It was now 1941, and Henry was able to get work at the film studios as a laborer, a job that offered clear possibilities for advancement where his earlier job had not. Henry worked hard, moving up from laborer to plumber, then on to special effects and from there into construction where ultimately he became a foreman. All these advances were hard won. "I had no background in any of it," Henry told me, "but I learned because I watched everyone else." Particularly daunting was the necessity of being able to read engineer's plans, a skill for which he was not only entirely untrained but which was especially difficult for him to pick up because he was a slow learner in any case. "I learned how to read plans because I'd hire people smart enough to read the plans, and then I'd watch them," he said. Henry's advancement did not come easily; his was a difficult and highly stressful rise. By nature an anxious man given to restlessness and self-reproach, Henry found these years of taking on jobs for which he was not prepared harrowing. And yet he worked hard and succeeded in each new challenge—strong testimony to the highly motivated husband and father he had become.

Although some of his personal development was the inevitable outcome of maturation, Henry's growth was also nurtured by his family. It is a truism of human nature that people will try to live up to positive expectations, and Marjorie, for all her distress over the gambling, is and was an innately positive spouse. Also, it hurt Henry to see Marjorie suffering as she left her children to uncertain care each morning when she went out to work; he became fiercely determined to make it possible for her to stay home. Even today, so many years later, his memories of this period are intense: "I made damn sure that she could stay home with those kids," he told me, tension clouding his face. A scant five years after he had set his mind to this goal, he prevailed.

This brings us to our first principle concerning change:

• **A happy marriage can help both partners to outgrow the worst character flaws of youth.**

It is easy to see why the passage from the twenties to the thirties brought welcome changes to so many couples. The period from late adolescence through early adulthood is often fraught with difficulty. These are the years of lowest income and highest anxiety; a twenty-five-year-old parent of young children can feel besieged. The important lesson for a young couple going through these tumultuous times is that things do change. Universally older couples counseled patience; all of them had seen their relationships deepen and strengthen as they themselves matured.

Often couples who married young told me they had practically raised each other, especially when one or both partners came from dysfunctional families. Two such people, Diane and Josh Hayworth of Van Nuys, California, met when Josh was sixteen and Diane fifteen; they had been together for thirteen years when we met. Their path throughout the tempestuous years of their twenties can only be described as a saga: both have had to deal with family problems, drug problems, financial problems, and, in the midst of it all, the birth of two babies.

Josh's family was chaotic. Both parents were alcoholic, and they divorced when Josh was small. Josh's mother was out of control; Josh would come home some days to find her passed out on the bed, other days he was met with screams and hurled objects. For a time he was given real support by his stepfather (though his stepfather, too, was an alcoholic, albeit a functioning one), but when his mother divorced for a second time Josh was on his own. He bounced from foster homes to his sister's house to his mother's place and back.

Diane's family was considerably more stable, but her emotional life had been sadly complicated by the fact that she was adopted. Her parents had not told her about the adoption until she was twelve and, she says, they had not handled the revelation well. "I didn't feel wanted," she told me. In reaction she began taking drugs and hanging out with older kids who were already well on their way to ruin. At age fourteen, feeling she did not belong in her own family, she ran away from home. She left California and journeyed to Oregon where she rented a room, lied about her age, and found work. She stayed there for a year.

Her relationship with Josh developed in this context of overwhelming family crisis and chaos for both. Josh was the neighborhood "bad kid," riding motorcycles up and down the quiet streets, staying out late, behaving as provocatively as possible. He was going nowhere in life. Diane's parents were so appalled by his interest in their daughter that whenever he would cruise past her house, her mother would stand in the front yard and blast him with the garden hose.

Predictably, the course of their relationship mirrored the inner turmoil both were suffering—and their struggle to survive has been nothing short of heroic. Diane was sixteen years old and three months pregnant when they married. Wanting a healthy child, she immediately stopped smoking the angel dust she had been using, a first and crucial step toward happiness and a better life. Josh reacted constructively to the pregnancy as well. Though he had been working at a "get-nowhere" job as a photo developer, now his stepfather pulled strings to get him into the technicians' union at the film studios. Still teenagers, both were reaching out, together, for a stable and loving adult life.

For many years, this was to be an elusive goal. Couples do not overcome major childhood trauma overnight. Both feel, too, that they were damaged by the era in which they lived. The late 1970s, they told me, was a particularly destructive time to come of age. "We were a lost generation," Josh said. "By the time our day came there was no war to worry about, all we had to do was party and exist. We didn't grow our hair long to symbolize peace and love, we did it because that's what rock stars did." It was the beginning of the "heavy metal" period in popular music, and Diane and Josh were swept away in its turbulent currents. Though both were delighted with Nicole, their new baby girl ("We used to fight over who would get to feed her," Josh recalled), eighteen months later they separated. "I had become reckless and crazy," said Josh, "and Diane had, too."

They parted by mutual agreement, and for Josh the drug culture took over. He was now using large quantities of cocaine and taking Quaaludes—and looking forward to the day when he would be old enough to drink in a bar.

Still, his connection to his young wife was strong. They saw each other twice a week; no doubt as a sign of his continuing attachment to her, Josh freely supplied as much money for her support as he could. When the two met in the hall at the courthouse where they had gone to sign a formal separation agreement they said to each other, "Let's not do this." And they didn't.

The months wore on. At increasingly loose ends, Diane took her baby and moved north to Oregon where she set up house with a man she had been seeing. Even this did not significantly disrupt her bond to Josh. Though he wasn't enamored of the situation, he accepted it without rancor. "Life was life," Josh said, trying to explain his casual attitude toward his wife's love life. "I figured, that's the way it is."

They were drifting. Too many drugs, too many arguments; neither was in control of any aspect of his life. Finally they reunited in the same careless spirit: "One day I just decided to come back," said Diane. She moved in with Josh as soon as she reached town. They were now twenty years old.

Their second baby arrived a year later. The new baby brought more stress into their small family because she was the classic active child. Whereas Nicole had been an easy baby from birth, Stephanie was her father's child, climbing out of her crib, knocking things over, throwing tantrums at the slightest provocation. She was a handful.

Even with all the myriad sources of stress in their young lives, Diane and Josh managed to stay together through the next eight years. But while they had stabilized as a couple and a family, life was still not under their control; far from it, in fact. Without either of them quite realizing it, a new and potentially even more devastating problem had arisen: having reached legal drinking age, Josh rapidly developed into a serious alcoholic. He was drinking heavily; he could drink all day at work with no one being the wiser, and would often stay out until three or four A.M. at a bar with friends.

Neither Diane nor Josh saw his alcoholism for what it was, and neither was aware of the toll it was taking on their life together. Diane told me, "I was aware that he was drinking, but I didn't really see it as a problem. I did want him to stop, but not consciously." They were too young to be able to put their lives into any kind of perspective; too young to be able to stand outside themselves and see the "alcoholic parent" or the "problem drinker." They were living in the moment, without pause to reflect.

When we met, both were changed people. Josh was an active member of Alcoholics Anonymous; Diane was attending a community college and planning a career as an optician. Both had developed the habit of reflection; instead of acquiescing passively in whatever life brought their way, they gave every impression of knowing who they were and what they wanted. They were *on track*. And they were fully aware of the cultural dangers that they faced living in the midst of a heavily drug- and alcohol-dependent social world. In short, they conveyed an acute clarity, about themselves and the world, that is the sign of a productive adult life. They had changed from passivity in the face of overwhelming obstacles to activity; life no longer happened *to* them.

They made this leap together. A second arrest for driving under the influence of alcohol proved to be the precipitating crisis. "My first arrest was a slap on the hand," Josh said, "but by the second, the law had changed and I woke up in jail wearing paper shoes—the whole nine yards. There was a Mexican guy five inches from my face who had been totally beat up. It was like waking up to Freddy Krueger [from *A Nightmare on Elm Street*]. He said, 'I want your bed.' " Breakfast, Josh remembered, was a microwaved burrito.

Diane found a friend to bail him out, and in the car, driving home, he said simply, "This is it." And it was, for both of them. At home Diane took the bottle of Xanax her doctor had prescribed for anxiety and flushed the pills down the toilet. It was the end of their twenties.

After the age-thirty watershed, the other major period of personal change seemed to occur somewhere around age fifty. Here, for once, the commonplace notions held true: men told of mellowing, women told of becoming confident and assertive. (One wife, in fact, said that the reason she and her husband were doing the interview was that she had grown more adventurous, and answering an advertisement in the paper for long-married couples seemed like an adventure!) It was a happy time for wives and husbands both. The changes men made at this time of life were the most dramatic. Wife after wife told me that men who had long been fiercely workaholic, or who had had violent tempers, even men who had been chronically unfaithful, simply calmed down. Sometimes, as we will see, they calmed down in the face of an ultimatum from their mates, but often these changes evolved as much from a process of personal growth as from a response to an unhappy wife.

A. J. and Marta Long's trajectory neatly illustrates this evolution. The two met in high school in San Diego nearly fifty years ago. She was fourteen, he was seventeen. Their relationship developed slowly, punctuated by summers apart which Marta spent with relatives back East in Pennsylvania. She saw other boys during these sojourns, but her feelings for A. J. continued to grow. Finally, at age twenty-one and fresh out of college he said, "Let's get married."

Their first years of marriage were happy. A. J. was called into the service, and the two moved around the country with his transfers. Two of their three children were born while he was on active duty.

In Marta's view, their life together began to deteriorate in 1946 when they returned to San Diego so that A. J. could go into his father's business. This was the start of, as she calls it, a "horrendous period" between the two of them. A. J. became obsessed with his work, so driven to succeed that he would leave home at 8:00 A.M. and return at midnight. As he himself now says, "The business was my mistress."

By her own account, Marta seems to have kept up an almost continuous pressure upon her husband to pull back, to find time for her and their four children. She and A. J. would have regular "knockdown drag-outs," and once, in a state of crisis prompted by a sexual proposition from a man she had met at church, she left home and drove to Malibu in a state of chaos and despair. Finally, at 9 o'clock that night she drove home, where her family greeted her with blankets and warm tea. She was exhausted and drained.

Marta had made her point, but even so A. J. needed something more. The extra push arrived in the shape of his father's tragic business failure at age sixty-eight. "My father got old in the saddle," A. J. told me. "He tried to keep running the company after it was time for him to move on, and he ended up losing a million dollars." The loss put his father in the hospital with a heart attack while A. J. sold the business.

By this time A. J. had built his own thriving enterprise, an offshoot of his father's once prosperous company. At forty years old and the top of his game, he was profoundly shaken by his father's fall. Determined to avoid his father's fate, he decided to sell. "It owned me," he said of the business, "and I decided to give myself to myself." Of Marta's role in this change of heart he said, "We loved each other. I wanted to get to know my family better."

He realized $2 million on the sale, enough to leave them independently wealthy for the rest of their lives. Over the next twenty years A. J. continued to work for other people's companies as a consultant, limiting himself to reasonable hours that gave him ample time at home. He retired at sixty-one.

While few men told of changes this dramatic, A. J.'s story was similar in its outlines to those of many. At a certain point in their lives, fiercely driven men tended to pull back a bit—a happy change for both husband and wife.

As far as wives were concerned, their change from meek to strong, from timid to confident, was often a transformation that their husbands welcomed—and had helped to bring about. Howard Spencer, a sixty-year-old account executive living in the suburbs of Chicago, told me he had consciously tried to mold his wife, Joyce, into becoming a more aggressive person. He hoped to see this change in her character because he wanted to rely upon her for advice and counsel in his business. Over the years, whenever he had contemplated a potentially risky move, he had sought her advice, wanting her to say, "Do it!"— or "Don't do it," if he was making a mistake. Instead Joyce would mull the situation over for a time, then tell him mildly to do whatever he thought best.

Howard wanted more. He needed a full partner in the family decision making, not just a loving wife who offered him generalized support. He wanted her to share in the process of building their financial future.

Over the years Joyce gradually became the aggressive, fifty-fifty partner he wanted and needed her to be. Once the children were grown she began to sell real estate, becoming successful enough to begin investing in property herself. She became so sure of her instincts that once she bid on an investment property entirely on her own while her husband was out of town. It proved to be a wise decision.

One final note: Obviously, their story completely reverses the classic scenario of the oppressed wife demanding respect from the domineering husband. While I did speak with couples who had struggled over this issue, the husbands in my sample were far more likely to foster a wife's self-confidence than to suppress it—a fact that speaks volumes as to what kind of man ends up lucky in love.

The principle here:

• **Spouses are happiest, and most likely to change for the better, when their mates bolster their self-confidence.**

Change Through Union

Another force working for change in married men and women was the marital union itself. At the simplest level, when you live in close quarters with a person—almost any person—inevitably something of his habits and outlook will begin to "rub off." That person changes you, and you change him. When that person is your spouse, the deeper psychological processes of internalization are triggered. Over the years, as we have seen, married people "take each other in"; just as the child can summon his mother's voice even when Mother is away, so the happily married spouse comes to "hear" the voice of his absent spouse.

And, much as the child is guided by this inner voice, so a married person is shaped by the inner voice of his spouse. When this process is working at its best, each spouse absorbs the other's virtues. Joe and Karen Compton illustrated this process perfectly. When they started their family, they were diametrically opposed in their approach to child rearing. Karen was tolerant and nurturing, Joe a harsh disciplinarian. "When our first son was two years and ten months," Joe recalled, "he drew on the car and I whaled the hell out of him. I used to spank him with a belt—by today's standards I would be guilty of child abuse."

Karen did not overtly interfere with these scenes. At times she would say, "You were awfully hard on him"; typically she would grow distant. "The house would get *cool*," Joe said. But she did not ask Joe outright to change his ways. She did not nag.

Joe traced his overbearing approach to his own mother, who had been very cold. "She probably did not want kids," he said. "I could never kiss her without feeling 'She doesn't care for this.'" Having felt unloved and unwanted as a boy, he now reacted with a cold anger toward his own small son whenever he stepped out of bounds.

By the time we met, however, Joe had reversed his attitude entirely—a change he attributed to his relationship with Karen. "I watched how Karen dealt with the kids," he said, "and I saw that she also got what she wanted out of them, but through love, not punishment."

Joe's was the form of learning psychologists term "social imitation." But even more importantly, at the same time that he was changing through sheer imitation, his marriage to Karen was transforming him psychologically, making him into the kind of man who could and would adopt her loving techniques. "Karen taught me how to *receive* love," Joe told me, neatly summing up the startling changes that marriage to his wife has wrought in him.

Feeling loved for the first time in his life, Joe began to be able to give love to his wife and children. And he relaxed. Somewhere in his late thirties or early forties (Karen dated it earlier, Joe dated it later) he mellowed. Now, in middle age, he was on close terms with all three children.

Of course there is nothing to prevent a married couple from absorbing each other's failings as well as their virtues. This happens all too frequently; it is what takes place in the *folie à deux*. A couple can unite in darkness as well as in light. But in the happy marriage partners do not encourage each other to acquire their worst characteristics, only their best.

To illustrate, I spoke with many couples in which one member was frequently sad or anxious while the other was constitutionally cheerful. In theory, for such couples the lines of influence could run either way; the happy person could bring the sad person up, or the sad person could bring the happy person down. But within good marriages, couples characteristically opted for the former. Over and over again, a downcast person would tell me that he/she hated seeing his partner become depressed. Whenever the normally cheerful partner slid into a funk, the normally depressed partner would rally. Within happy marriages, a pessimist who had married an optimist wanted the optimist to remain that way.

The pessimist wanted the optimist to stay optimistic because the pessimist was seeking happiness. These were marriages in which both partners grew toward the light. While many a couples' counselor might argue that it is not a good thing to lock one partner into the role of the ever-cheery optimist, the reality of the healthy alliance is more complex. When a pessimist insists that his normally optimistic mate remain upbeat, he is trying to fight the forces of depression. The pessimist is signaling that he does not want his partner to be drawn into the vortex of his dark thoughts; he is asking that the two of them, as a couple, follow the optimist's lights, that their marriage be grounded in the positive rather than the negative.

The healthy marriage so fosters the good in spouses that even a partner's bad habits can be ameliorated through association with a beloved mate. When I asked Marjorie Williams how she coped with Henry's gambling during their early years, she told me that she had gone out and learned to play poker herself: "I joined him!" she exclaimed merrily. To this day she is an avid card player. "When I play poker," she said, "I can play all night." The difference, of course, is that Marjorie did not gamble away their earnings.

These were cases of a wife's closeness to her husband reshaping their problem, cutting it down from catastrophic dimensions into something more manageable. Marjorie and her husband formed poker clubs with other couples, and eventually Henry became an entirely recreational player rather than a gambler. His love for poker, minus the gambling, was assimilated into their shared identity.

Here again, many counselors might balk. Gambling is an absolute breach of faith, they would tell us, and a spouse should say no. But a flat no is seldom effective when we are dealing with adults; one does, indeed, catch more flies with honey than with vinegar. Marjorie's circumspect and positive approach worked well for them; by sharing in her husband's "interest" in cards she avoided labeling him an abject failure as a man and a human being. In picking up poker as a hobby Marjorie managed to express a simultaneous "no" *and* "yes." Yes to the game, no to the gambling.

This points to the way in which the shared identity of a marriage works to transform its partners. When a partner absorbs an interest or attitude from his mate, he *reinforces* and *validates* that interest or attitude. Over the years a well-married spouse, sustained by the active interest of his or her mate, becomes more of what is best in him/herself. A good marriage nurtures growth in each partner just as surely as good parents nurture growth in their children; in the happy marriage, partners blossom. The principle is:

- **Marriages work best when partners encourage each other to come into his/her own.**

At the same time, many of the most commonplace problems dividing men and women yield to the steady pressure of daily exposure to someone who is part of you yet different. One couple in their early forties told me that they had had difficulties for years over the issue of intimate conversation. It was the classic opposition: She wanted to talk about feelings; he did not. Now, both said, he was better at intimate exchange than she. Their path to this happy state of affairs had not been smooth. They had had their ups and downs; once they even separated for several months.

But eventually they learned. As the husband grew more intimate, at the same time the wife also grew a shade more distant, learning to let things drop. In time, watching the way in which her husband functioned in the world, she began to see the wisdom in not subjecting each passing sensation to scrutiny. While the men and women in my survey often began life stereotypically polarized by sex, in time they drew closer together. Husbands absorbed the values and interests of their wives; wives absorbed those of their husbands. Thus Marjorie learned to play poker, while Henry learned not to gamble, and both came to unite body and soul in a shared life.

Ultimatums

All of these couples' experiences offer cause for hope; all show that when it comes to a spouse's flaws, patience, fortified by a positive outlook, is a supreme virtue. People do change, and they can change for the better.

Nevertheless, there remain some differences that even all the subtle forces for change at work within a marriage cannot bridge. Not every wife can ease a husband's gambling problem out of her life by joining him in a weekly game of cards; not all problems can be solved by a big heart and an open mind. Sometimes, couples told me, someone had to take a stand. And someone had to change.

Connie Lang's long history with her domineering and distant husband offers a glimpse into a marriage no one, least of all Connie, thought could change. Handicapped by a desperately unhappy family background, Connie had made a troubled match of her own that most observers would have dismissed as irretrievably flawed. The child of financially distressed alcoholic parents—parents who abused her mentally, physically, and sexually—Connie said, "My parents were extremely indefinite people. The only ideas they conveyed to us were, Don't steal, and Don't have sex. They had no control over their own lives or even any knowledge of what a life was—they just popped babies. All seven of us were accidents. I was born eleven months after my brother and my mother never forgave me."

Connie's father was equally disturbed. Forced to retire from the military for emotional reasons at age twenty-eight, he showed no interest in his daughter until she became a teenager. Then he developed a sexual attraction to her. This set off a pattern in which he would "handle" her, as Connie put it, then grow angry, then apologize abjectly. Within days this sequence would be repeated. Connie and her brothers grew up desperate to escape from their parents' home as soon as possible.

By dint of sheer intelligence, all of them did. Connie was accepted on scholarship at a major university where she did well. But emotionally, she seems to have arrived upon the threshold of adult life a shell-shocked young woman. Chaotically seeking love and attachment, she collected proposals of marriage; by her own count she had had twelve to fifteen offers of marriage by age twenty-one—"mostly," she told me, "because I could shape myself into whatever image a man wanted." Eventually she became engaged, to a young and sweet graduate student whom she did not truly want to marry. When he was killed in a skiing accident she found herself feeling completely "turned off" to men and love.

It was at this point that she met Greg, a graduate student three and a half years her senior. Her early feelings toward Greg sound restrained in the extreme: from Connie's vantage point, Greg "was this not very interesting person, staid and harrumphy and gray haired at twenty-five." Connie recalled feeling safe; this was someone with whom she wouldn't fall in love, she told herself.

In some ways already an old man at twenty-five, Greg seemed to have offered Connie a kind of leadership, a clarity of vision and goals, that had never been present within her own family. "I was looking for a god," said Connie, "and he was as close as I could come. He seemed utterly sure of himself and in command, though in retrospect there were lots of signs that this wasn't true. But I avoided them."

Greg appeared to have been a rather rigid young man, certainly one not able to easily and fluidly fall in love with his future wife. His way of declaring himself to her was to observe dryly, "Rats, I've fallen in love."

"He had a terribly rational mind," Connie said. "He told me he was in love with me because logically he knew it was now time to say something." This first "I love you" was as far removed from the swept-away joys of the sunnier couples in my sample as one can get. To Connie, Greg seemed to have no emotional needs whatsoever, not even for sex.

Emotionally crippled in their separate ways, the two made a match. "I'm sure a lot of the reason he married me was that I was so malleable," said Connie. Having had a great deal of practice, Connie was willing and eager to shape herself into whatever kind of person

Greg wanted. "He was a liberal Democrat," she said, "so I became a liberal Democrat." Greg needed to be in control of all aspects of his life, including the people in it, and Connie was a willing subject.

This was a far from promising start and, predictably, their marriage moved from bad to worse. Within a few years Greg had established himself as a high-profile architect, achieving a level of success that only increased his arrogance. Now he demanded that the marriage revolve entirely around him and his career. Connie was expected to entertain his business associates weekly, and to submerge everything to Greg's continued success. The question of a family was only glancingly approached, Greg telling her that "she could have children if she wanted to." Emotionally fragile after her own childhood, Connie would have needed considerably more support and enthusiasm on her husband's part to have been able to risk motherhood. The subject was dropped.

Connie's unhappiness grew by the year. It was a constant struggle to be what her husband wanted her to be, and she found their domestic arrangement intolerable. When, six years into their marriage, Connie went to work, her husband's demands only increased. She was still doing all the housework as well as tending to a continually growing list of duties as hostess to Greg's business associates. Finally she saw a therapist: "I went into therapy and stayed fifteen years," she said, adding, only half in jest, "I would have committed suicide without my therapist."

With continued success Greg grew increasingly distant, emotionally "impermeable." "At the height of his career," said Connie, "he was a very forbidding, cold, and harsh person." His staff feared and avoided him; frequently someone would approach Connie and plead with her to intervene on his behalf with her husband. "They all saw how he treated me," Connie said. "They must have thought I was a real jerk."

When the fall finally came, it was devastating. Greg had made enemies at work and, when his firm hit a rough period, they were able to push him out. Suddenly, his career was in a shambles. Connie hadn't even known there was so much trouble at work; self-sufficient to the end, Greg had not confided in her.

Greg was deeply embittered. Wounded by his colleagues, he also felt betrayed by Connie, who, toward the end, had refused to "be the geisha." Terribly unhappy, he withdrew into himself, dropping out of the world of work and, as Connie remembered it, doing little else but play his flute for a year. Connie's work supported them.

Eventually he began to rebuild, though his career had never fully recovered from the initial blow. But personally, even in the face of nearly overwhelming evidence that his harsh authoritarianism had made him his own worst enemy, he remained the same. This surprised no one: "Nobody expected him ever to change," said Connie. "My therapist didn't, and I didn't."

And yet when I met Connie, her husband was an altered man. "The past three years have been very happy," Connie said. "I really do feel 'lucky in love.'"

Greg's dramatic change of heart came about when Connie finally laid down an ultimatum. He changed, said Connie, "when I got to the point where I didn't love him and I was ready to leave."

The confrontation came one day, after "he had been acting like a bastard for months. Even I could see it." Finally Connie said to her husband simply, with a clear sense of resolution, "I don't like this, and I may well leave."

Greg told her she was out of her mind, and left the room.

And then the miracle occurred. "Not half an hour later he came back and said in the sweetest way, 'I'd like to go to a museum,'" Connie told me. She was floored. Throughout all of the thirty-odd years of their marriage Greg had flatly refused to take time for the normal outings most couples enjoy; even with their high income they never had dinner out, never saw movies, never went to museums or plays. Greg had no interest in anything beyond his work. Now, he was suggesting an outing of his own accord.

They went, and Connie had a lovely time. Greg bought two kaleidoscopes for them in the museum shop, and they stopped for dinner at a local restaurant on the way home.

It was a personal transformation that had held fast for the last three years of their marriage. Even Greg's response to our interview signaled his change of heart: an intensely private person, he did not want to discuss his marriage with a journalist himself, but he was entirely willing for his wife to do so—and interested in hearing about it afterward. Just a few years before, her participation would have been out of the question.

Connie's was a case of an ultimatum that worked. Faced with a clearly defined choice between changing his ways or losing his wife, Greg chose to change.

I heard more than one such tale. While the laying down of an ultimatum can lead to disaster, ultimatums work more often than one might expect. And they work because people are more fluid than we have been led to believe. You *can* teach an old dog new tricks. It isn't easy; on a purely physiological level the neurological pathways in the brain of an adult are far more fixed than those of a child. Adults are rarely as impressionable as children. And yet if we think of flaws like workaholism and thoughtlessness as being—at some level—simply bad habits, the possibility of change makes more sense: all of us have seen people change bad habits even very late in life. If a sixty-year-old can stop smoking in the face of a cancer threat, it should not be surprising that a fifty-year-old can start taking his wife out to dinner in the face of divorce.

Of course, change must come from within; for an errant spouse to change dramatically, he or she must be strongly motivated to do so. And it is probably impossible to estimate beforehand how powerfully an ultimatum might motivate a spouse to change—if at all. Returning to the marriage of Marta and A. J., Marta chose not to issue an ultimatum concerning A. J.'s workaholism because, having witnessed the sad fate of his mother, she feared that A. J. would not concede. Marta had long identified with A. J.'s mother who, neglected by A. J.'s workaholic father, had eventually told her husband she was leaving. He did nothing to stop her. They divorced, and two years later he remarried, leaving A. J.'s mother an aging and embittered woman who was to live out the rest of her life alone. "It always frightened me that A. J.'s father let her go," Marta told me. "I knew I didn't want to end up like her." Wisely, she chose not to press the issue of A. J.'s work life to the limit.

When Ultimatums Work

Under what circumstances did ultimatums work? They worked when an overarching love was present, however strangled its expression. As difficult as Greg was to live with, he clearly loved and even prized his wife: when she wrote her first book he insisted she see its worth as he did. Painfully shy (so shy she would attend parties without her glasses to avoid being overwhelmed by the sight of so many people in one room), Connie might never have shown the manuscript to anyone beyond her husband; Greg pushed her to send it out, helped her compose a cover letter, and celebrated when a publisher offered her a contract. "He helped me with every aspect of the book," she recalled. "He has pushed me into having a fuller, more spacious life; in many ways he is very, very generous." As a man Greg was riddled with contradictions, at once a tyrant and a gentleman. When Connie's ultimatum came, the gentleman prevailed. Greg responded to his wife's sharp demands because he loved her, in however complicated a fashion. He loved her, and he did not want to lose her.

Interestingly, Connie and Greg's story proved to be typical: within my sample the successful ultimatums came from wives who had heretofore been retiring souls. (Unfortunately I did not interview a single man who had given his wife an ultimatum, and thus cannot offer any observations about the situation with the sexes reversed.) Connie had deferred to Greg for years; she had never directly challenged his authority over their life together. Thus when she finally did, her threat carried real power—certainly the power of sheer shock value, if nothing else.

This would not have been the case for Marta who had regularly, once every three months by her own reckoning, incited major conflagrations with A. J. A threat to pack up the children and leave leveled during one of these battles would probably not have been particularly effective. But when a self-effacing spouse suddenly put her foot down, her husband listened.

It is entirely possible that husbands listened under these circumstances because this was the first time their wives had truly spoken up. The underlying principle here:

- **Marriages thrive when couples set clear limits.**

Setting limits is just as crucial to nurturing a marriage as it is to nurturing a child. Spouses need to know what is acceptable, and what is not. All happy couples appear to do some form of limit setting; over and over again I heard people say, "If he had an affair with someone else, he knows I would kill him!" *That* is a limit: people do not draw boundaries much clearer than this.

Thus happy marriages are seldom based entirely upon trust in one's mate to do the right thing. Instead, happy spouses shored up their trust with clear limits. They trusted each other implicitly, yet let each other know what the results would be if the other failed to live up to that trust. In this they were pragmatic: it is a far sight easier to live up to a moral code when you know something very bad will happen to you if you don't!

Thus a wife who does not set limits is depriving her husband of crucial information (where she draws the line) and of crucial motivation (what will happen if he crosses it). When such a wife suddenly delivered an ultimatum she was in some ways doing her husband a favor: she was making her feelings known, at last. As the saying goes, you can't expect your spouse to read your mind. Those marriages in which spouses *were* reading each other's minds were also those in which both spouses had been clearly expressing their thoughts to each other all along. No spouse can be expected to divine the inner wishes of a partner who has been too timid to speak up.

Ultimatums worked, too, when they were positive demands that, if acceded to, would benefit both partners. Greg had everything to gain from moderating his tyrannical approach; when he lost his vaunted position to company politics he was made painfully aware of how few real friends he had. Greg probably could have used some sound advice from a loyal wife much earlier on in life; a more vocal spouse might have helped him see that he was on a collision course with his colleagues as well as with her. The principle is:

- **As with all marital arguments, formulating an ultimatum in terms of what is best for <u>both</u> partners is the wisest strategy.**

This was the case in another family in which differences between husband and wife ended in a successful ultimatum. Nearly fifteen years ago John and Rachel Kanter, a well-matched and for the most part happy couple with three teenage boys, came to a standoff over the issue of John's career. Highly ambitious, and with a tendency to be abrasive on the job, John's pattern was to move on just before he was asked to. Each move brought him a somewhat better position, but the disruption was terrible for Rachel. Closely attached to her family, she had suffered when the two of them first left their native Allentown to move to Cleveland; it had taken her several years to set up a new life with friends and neighbors there. Then, just when she had come to feel at home in Cleveland, John uprooted them all for a move to Minneapolis. While some wives might have found the change of scene an adventure (I spoke to at least one couple who loved to move and did so often), Rachel needed roots. Pulling up stakes and heading west was, for her, nothing short of traumatic.

Now, when the Minneapolis job did not work out—it lasted only a year—Rachel was furious. "I hadn't wanted to go to Minneapolis in the first place," she recalled, "but I was still the obedient housewife so I went." She had reached a new low.

Still, life improved when John took a job in sales. Here, for the first time, he flourished; the rough edges that had hampered him working in an office setting were good qualities for the outgoing and aggressive person he needed to be in order to sell his company's products. The household settled down, but even so it took Rachel a full five years to think of Minneapolis as her home.

It was at this point, just as Rachel had fully adjusted to her new world in Minneapolis, that John accepted a promotion from his company requiring yet another move. Devastated by the prospect of once more uprooting herself and her sons, Rachel finally took a stand. She had two sons in high school, one in junior high, and she loved her house. She refused to move. "I felt that you really have to go with your gut feeling," she told me. "This was not a good thing for us to do again. I didn't care about the extra money—if we needed extra money I could always work. I didn't want to take another five years to be depressed and adjust." Rachel didn't want to move again at this point in her life, and she wouldn't. "I told him," she recalled, " 'If you want to move, good-bye.' "

Taking this absolutist position was not an easy thing for Rachel to do. "I took a risk I had never taken in my entire life," she told me. But the risk paid off. Seeing how strongly his wife felt, John turned down the promotion, and he did so freely, without bearing her a grudge. Confronted for the first time in his life with a choice, he had no difficulty reaching a decision: his family came first.

But it is what was to come next that is so remarkable: within months John was offered the same promotion, without having to leave Minneapolis. And it was at this point that John's career finally took off. He has been highly successful ever since, with no more of the tumultuous job-switching that so marred his early work life. "It was a real turning point," said Rachel. "We both look at it as one of the best things that ever happened."

It is entirely possible that this moment of truth actively helped John at work. "When I was younger, all of my problems were job related," John told me. "I was a job-hopper. I left jobs because I wanted to better myself, but I also left jobs because I wasn't getting along with the people at work." John had been a restless and ambitious man, fiercely—perhaps too fiercely—driven to succeed. Rachel's ultimatum may have helped him put his ambition into much-needed perspective. Having come to see that success was not all, he may have been even more valuable as an employee, certainly an easier person to work with.

Whatever the cause of their subsequent good fortune, the lesson to be learned from John and Rachel's experience—and, indeed, from the experience of nearly all the couples with whom I spoke—is that in the good marriage partners change, and they change for the better. Whether they change through the natural processes of maturation, through mutual influence across the years, or through the head-on collision that is an ultimatum, the changes help. Both partners emerge from a long and healthy alliance enriched; at the end of their lives they are larger human beings than they would have been on their own.

Thus, while it is obviously not a good idea to go into a marriage hoping that our partners will change, the fact is that people do change; they cannot help but change. Life changes us: it is impossible, as the saying goes, to put one's foot in the same river twice. The good marriage helps people change for the better. This is a crucial function of the good marriage, because, as we will see in the next chapter, the arrival of a baby requires all the flexibility, creativity, and courage we can muster.

5

Children

For many couples, the Dream is the dream of family. In spite of all the changes we have witnessed since the first half of the century —the sexual revolution, the rise in the divorce rate, the mass entry of mothers into the marketplace—the desire to raise a family remains fundamental to most marriages. For many couples happiness and children go hand in hand. And certainly, census data show, couples with children are significantly less likely to divorce than are couples without.

Nevertheless, if children could bring great joy, they could and did bring pain in equal measure. This was the paradox of the dream of family: couples could break their hearts in the trying. Even couples for whom all had turned out well spoke feelingly of the stress young children could bring to a marriage. There have been various studies attesting to this fact over the years, a number of which have found that marital satisfaction declines during the years in which children are living at home, rising again after the children have left. While these studies are disputed by some, at least one has found that childless couples are happier than those with children. Certainly the two childless couples in my own survey were very happy.

Perhaps the proper way to interpret these results is to say that what makes a marriage happy is not so much the reality of children, but, rather, the *sharing of the dream* of children. When two people strongly want children, both are fully and wholeheartedly united in the same quest. They are of one mind. By this reasoning, a childless couple who shares an alternative dream would be just as happy as couples who do want children—perhaps more so since the childless couple does not suffer the worries that children can bring.

Thus the subject of children's relationship to happiness in marriage is a complicated one. Children brought their parents joy, sorrow, and all the many feelings in between. Bringing up children, couples told me, was like boarding a roller coaster; there were dizzying highs and plunging lows and always the swift rushing of time.

When the Dream Does Not Happen: Infertility and Adoption

When the time came to start their families, several of the couples in my survey met with serious difficulties. Interestingly, the subject of infertility underlined the importance of temperament in shaping a marriage: two individuals of the same age, social status, and background could respond to infertility in completely different ways. While we have all been schooled to believe that infertility is inevitably a traumatic and tragic event in the life of a couple, this simply does not hold true for all. Amazingly enough, I interviewed one couple, Martha and Hugh Juniper of Los Angeles, who said they had not been greatly affected by the dawning realization of their infertility. Recalling their four-and-a-half-year effort to have a baby in the 1950s, a time during which they fruitlessly saw three different doctors (none of whom could offer any answers), Martha told me that she found all this only "occasionally stressful." "We were both of the same mind," she said. "We didn't see having to adopt a child as any kind of denigration. We were always open to it."

Of course, her memories of this period may be muted by time. She and Hugh went on successfully to adopt a baby boy, after which they eventually had two children of their own. Their period of infertility came to an end. Even so, speaking with Martha it is clear that infertility simply was not the scarring experience for her and her husband that it is for so many. It was not scarring for the simple reason that Martha and Hugh were difficult to scar. Martha was by nature a happy person; like Marjorie Williams, she, too, was a constitutionally cheerful soul. Hugh was also conspicuously upbeat; theirs was a marriage of optimist to optimist. I should add, too, that both were highly self-confident, a trait that prevented them from construing infertility as a personal failure. Being happy people, neither was prone to catastrophic thinking. They did not say to themselves, as other couples in the same position did, "We will never have children." Both saw children coming into their lives in one way or another, through pregnancy or through adoption. That was enough for them.

In sharp contrast, for wives (wives were far more *obviously* affected by this subject) who were at all inclined to anxiety or depression the struggle with infertility pierced to the very core of their beings. Women who had married in the 1950s, a time when the bearing of children was the essential goal of all young wives, spoke of profound feelings of isolation, rage, envy. "I was devastated," Rachel Kanter told me, describing her three years of trying to conceive (which ended finally with the birth of the first of three boys). "I couldn't imagine a life without children." To a woman like Rachel, who was subject to bouts of anxiety and depression, the possibility of adoption held no comfort. To this day she remembered the experience vividly, as Martha Juniper did not.

Interestingly, every couple, including those who had found infertility to be genuinely traumatic, said that their inability to conceive had not hurt their marriage. For the happy couple the principle governing the experience of infertility was quite different from what we have been taught:

- **Infertility may hurt happily married spouses <u>individually</u>, but it does not hurt them <u>as a couple</u>.**

Couples flatly refuted the universal belief that infertility can destroy a marriage. Rachel Kanter told me that the experience of infertility had actually strengthened her marriage: "I became so depressed that I went to a psychiatrist for help," she recalled. "And John was extremely, extremely supportive. He was very unusual in this; there was such a stigma against it. I never told my parents, I never told anybody. I don't think I could have done it without John." It would be impossible to exaggerate the depth of her husband's support. Not only was it the 1950s, when a wife in psychotherapy would have been a highly embarrassing secret for any man, but it was at the very beginning of John's career. Although he and Rachel together were earning next to nothing, John unquestioningly put what little they had toward his wife's therapy bills. That was what she needed. When a wife finds herself this profoundly supported by her husband, the marriage can only grow stronger.

All the couples who had trouble conceiving eventually became parents; if they could not bear children themselves, they adopted. But the issue of infertility continued to haunt those of a more somber temperament. One woman, the adoptive mother of a baby girl now middle-aged, told me that she was contemplating writing a book she would call "Letters to the Mother of My Daughter." This was not a woman whose adoption had gone sour; her relationship with her now-grown adoptive daughter was excellent. It was not childlessness that haunted her but the sheer fact of failed biology. In her early seventies, she still cried every time she saw a baby being born on TV. "I simply can't get over the process—it's so overwhelmingly amazing," she told me. Of her feelings about her own infertility she said, "I don't think you ever solve it."

Thus couples filtered their experience of infertility through the lens of their own temperament and outlook. For some it was an ongoing source of trauma; for others it had been merely a temporary frustration. But for all, the marriages remained strong. When a happy couple found that they could not achieve their dream, they made adjustments; they opened the door to adoption.

Little Strangers

The reality of children, as opposed to the dream, could be a challenge indeed. More than one couple told me that they had found fitting a child into a close relationship difficult. Cuber and Harroff reported that in the 1960s it was commonplace to view obviously romantic marriages with suspicion: when parents were too much in love with each other, the feeling ran, they loved their children less.

In the 1990s I found that there is more than a grain of truth in this perception of the sometimes adversarial relationship between marriage and children. Children absolutely do come between parents—and parents who are "too close" can resent or neglect their children. A new baby in particular can so split apart two partners that Martha Juniper attributes her first pregnancy to her husband's jealousy of their adopted infant. "All I was thinking about was the baby, and Hugh suddenly got twice as sexual as he had been before"—giving them twice the chance of finally conceiving. A scant two months after the adoption, she was pregnant. "Looking back, I'm grateful for those four and a half years [of infertility]," she told me, "because we got to know each other so well." Having raised three children to adulthood, she fully appreciated how little time and energy children leave for a marriage.

Not every couple was able to make room for children. Nancy and Mark Walters, the couple who were so close that they once gave each other the same Christmas card, offered the bluntest account of this phenomenon: They agreed that the experience of having had children had been, in Mark's word, "traumatic"—traumatic because, once the children were born, they lost all privacy as a couple. Of course, living in a small two-bedroom duplex in the city of Chicago with Nancy's parents in the unit upstairs had greatly exaggerated the problem. The bedrooms were so closely situated that the only room in which Nancy and Mark felt comfortable making love was the living room, hardly a sanctuary for sexual abandon. Clearly Nancy and Mark felt crowded, both physically and emotionally, by their two sons. "In all honesty," Mark said, "having kids is the one thing I would never do again."

Why should children be experienced as so disruptive? To begin with, the time constraints that children impose upon a marriage are obvious; children take away from the hours and the attention their parents once devoted exclusively to each other. But the impact of children upon a marriage goes deeper than this; it goes to the very essence of the shared identity. Children enter a family as little strangers; even though a child is flesh of our flesh he possesses his own temperament, and he knows nothing of the family identity that we, his parents, have created before him. As every parent universally observed, children come into the world on their own terms: they are who they are, regardless of what our hopes and dreams for them might be. Parents and children can suffer their irreconcilable differences; when two parents who value books and education confront a child who is slow to read and unmotivated in school, they are confronting a challenge to the identity that binds them. Their family myth, their concept of who it is they are or want to be as a group, is called into question. The challenge with children is to assimilate these little outsiders into a new and enlarged family identity, an identity expansive enough to contain the *difference* children introduce.

Sooner or later, of course, most couples were able to adjust their sense of marital identity to accommodate the addition of a little "third party" into the system. Lianne and Brian Voight offered a vivid account of their ultimately successful passage from Married Couple to Family. They, too, like Nancy and Mark Walters, found the arrival of their first child very difficult. When their daughter, Jennifer, was born, Lianne and Brian, then in their mid-thirties, had been together for sixteen years, a long time in which to build an intensely intimate relationship with each other. As with so many happy couples, Lianne was (and is today) powerfully invested in Brian's career as an independent filmmaker; before they became parents she had spent years working on his films. She was accustomed to being intimately involved in every phase of production up to and including the trips to Cannes to market the finished product. Their marriage was intense, creative, glamorous.

All this ended with a jolt when their daughter arrived. Perhaps unavoidably, the new baby broke up her parents' work partnership. Brian was working on a new film for which he was producer, director, writer, and actor, which meant that he was out of the house for twelve-hour days. When he was home, he was too exhausted to talk to his wife. "I felt like an outsider," Lianne recalled. "I always told him my whole day and when he didn't tell me anything about his I felt totally alienated and locked out." As if the emotional and physical separation weren't stressful enough, Lianne was also coping with financial uncertainty: Brian had refinanced their house in order to maintain a controlling interest in his picture. She was overwhelmed.

She was also, in her word, grieving—mourning the loss of so important a part of her relationship with her husband. "My sister pulled me through it," she said. "Her husband worked for Brian so she was in a bit of the same boat. She understood." Torn apart by their now entirely separate existences, for the first time in their marriage Lianne and Brian argued constantly. Lianne was shot through with a consuming anger she could not bring under control. "The whole time I knew that I was being terribly demanding and really laying it on him," said Lianne, "but I couldn't stop. We went to bed mad a lot. We had two very tough years, and Brian would be the first to admit it."

But finally all the struggle and turmoil passed. The movie ended production, and Brian flew off to Cannes to sell it. The loans were repaid. "Suddenly," Lianne recalled, "there was no more movie." They went on two family vacations, and began to come together again. Belatedly, they began the transition from happy couple to happy family.

Even so, the memory of those first two years after the birth of their child remained painful enough for both of them that for some time afterward neither wanted a second child. Lianne, in particular, could enjoy no breathing space at all during those early years because her daughter was so intensely attached to her: "She was my little Velcro baby," Lianne told me.

The birth of a first daughter can be particularly difficult for a marriage because of a new daughter's intense attachment to her mother. Using census data, sociologists at the University of Pennsylvania discovered that parents of sons are much less likely to divorce than are the parents of daughters. While no one knows absolutely why this should be so, survey results show that children tend to feel closest to the same-sex parent. First-time parents of little girls tell stories of their daughters actively rejecting their fathers, insisting that their mothers put them to bed, or read them their stories, or give them their baths. Little boys can also prefer their mothers, but it is not at all uncommon to hear of little boys who actively prefer their fathers. The bond between mother and son simply seems to be less all-encompassing, less all-consuming than that between mother and daughter. A marriage may falter when the new father of a little girl feels excluded from a close and intensely felt mother-daughter bond—or, as in Lianne's case, when the mother feels overwhelmed by a complete and total responsibility for her small daughter's well-being.

Fortunately for Lianne and Brian's marriage, "Velcro babies" soon grow up to be delightful and independent children. At the time I first spoke with Lianne, Jennifer was beginning first grade and Lianne and Brian were expecting their second baby. Both were very happy, their small family thriving.

To reach this point, Lianne told me, she herself had to come to feel

more independent. "Especially since Jennifer I've felt very vulnerable," she said, capturing a common feeling among new parents, perhaps especially among new mothers. "Trapped and vulnerable. Even
when I was pregnant, my car broke down on the way to work one
day when I was just about to deliver and I became hysterical. I felt
helpless to do anything about the breakdown; I felt I would never get
the car off the road. After Jennifer I would feel dependent on Brian
and I would think, What if something happened to him? I would be
completely lost." Lianne could only move on to her second child by
regaining her strength. "People have to suffer to get ahead," Lianne
concluded. "It's probably all going to happen again with the next
baby, but I hope that this time I'll be able to see it as finite."

Two years after my interview with Lianne, her life had indeed
worked out as she hoped. She and Brian were the parents of a little
boy, who had taken his place in the family without causing the turmoil
his big sister created. They were all four very happy. As with many
couples, Lianne had found life with her second baby to be immeas-
urably easier. The appearance of a second baby is a far less trying
affair because where the first baby creates the family, the second baby
simply joins it, a welcome arrival to a party already in progress.

When a Child Does Not Fit

Although it is true that all children introduce a disruptive element
into their parents' marriages, it is also true that some children are so
different from their parents that the family must confront a fundamental and destructive incompatibility between parent and child. This
was the case for Irene and Jerry Kolb, a vital couple in their sixties
whose sole source of sorrow was Jerry's relationship with their eldest
son, Alan. Although Alan was now a grown man nearing his fortieth
birthday, father and son fought constantly—so much so that Jerry
had sought help from a therapist. For her part, Irene, who had long
been the mediator between father and son, was being ground down.
"It takes an enormous amount of energy," she said of her invariably
unsuccessful efforts to keep the peace.

Some of the battling was fueled by their worry over their son who,
in middle age, had yet to "find himself" professionally. Although
highly intelligent, he had not been able to finish the doctoral program

that he had entered some years ago; nor had he stayed with a romantic relationship for longer than a few months at a stretch. From his parents' perspective, his life remained in limbo, a source of ongoing friction between father and son.

For his part, Alan seemed to be in the grip of a consuming rage toward his father that had not mellowed with time. Even in middle age, Alan's anger was intensely focused upon his father; he seemed intent upon doing battle with Jerry—so much so that the family therapist whom Jerry consulted spent most of her time discussing ways for Jerry *not* to respond whenever his son "pushed his buttons." While Jerry was now trying to maintain calm in the face of his son's attacks, he clearly felt besieged.

No doubt many factors went into damaging the relationship between father and son. Because relations with their other two children, both of whom were doing very well in life, were happy, Irene suspected a birth-order effect, noting that there were three troubled first-borns in their sisters' and brothers' families. But apart from whatever stress Alan may have suffered by being the first child, an important part of the problem between himself and his father was the fact of Alan's homosexuality.

Alan was, quite simply, different from his father, different along a dimension that would challenge the sexual identity of many fathers. Leaving aside the issue of how homosexuality develops, the fact is that at some point the homosexual child of heterosexual parents is clearly following a different path in life. Alan was not present at my interview to give his side of the conflict; nevertheless, his parents' belief that Alan's chronic rage stemmed from having felt rejected by his father for his homosexuality was probably not far off the mark. While both Irene and Jerry had taken pains to accept their son's sexual preference—and while both now spoke of his gay life-style without a trace of open disapproval—the truth is that they would have been happier if he had been straight. Deep down, they wanted him to be like them, just as all parents wish their children to be like them in important ways. Like attracts like; the evidence for the appeal of sameness is overwhelming in the annals of "social-attraction theory." Cohesive groups form around a commonality of interests, values, behaviors. The presence of a gay son in the midst of a strong marriage founded upon heterosexual love can only be felt as a challenge to that marriage. A couple like the Kolbs cannot help feeling most validated when their children lead lives like their own: like father, like son. Jerry and Alan had never been able to savor the satisfactions of the kindred soul.

When Children Are in Trouble

The most distressing stories that couples shared were, of course, those of children in trouble. Marriages groaned under the weight of two partners struggling with a wayward child, each spouse suffering his own fierce sense of loss. A child in trouble invaded every crevice of a marriage: the parents suffered for the child, and they suffered for the lost dream of a strong and healthy family.

Bill and Eva Whitman told the saddest story of wrenching conflict between parents when confronting the harsh reality of a child out of control. After their son, Jody, the second of two children, began to experiment with drugs at the age of thirteen his mental condition deteriorated rapidly. In a horrifying downward spiral, his problems moved well beyond the petty delinquency and chronically inebriated state that can accompany adolescent addiction. He developed paranoid fantasies; he became convinced that unknown people were trying to kill him, and he began to tell his parents that he would have to kill these threatening strangers before they killed him. One night Bill awoke to find his son standing rigid in the living room, staring out the sliding glass door into the darkened yard beyond. There was something out there, he told his father. Bill and Eva were terrified not only for their son, but also for the very lives of those with whom he came in contact.

Trying to cope with their son's problems very nearly tore Eva and Bill apart. They disagreed violently over how to handle Jody, who, at age thirty-one, was only marginally functional as an adult. He was a good plumber, his dad said, but unreliable. Inevitably, when he missed enough work, he was let go.

When he was in trouble, he came home. Bill always took him in; he was too softhearted to turn his son away. These indulgences infuriated Eva, who believed that the only hope for their son was for them to take a tough stance. She felt that they should quit helping him, stop letting him come home whenever he encountered difficulties in the outside world. She wanted to force him to live like an adult.

It was an unresolvable issue. While Bill did not entirely disagree with Eva's position, the fact was that he simply could not live with it. Sporadically, Eva would issue an ultimatum, telling her husband to choose whom he wanted to live with, his son or his wife. "Bill shapes up whenever I blow up," she said, "but he goes back to his own shenanigans the minute I relax. I feel as if I have to constantly keep up my guard." Bill was painfully torn between wife and son; while he saw the sense in what his wife was saying, he also saw the need in his son's eyes. The only time Bill had ever refused his son was the period during which Jody harbored murderous fantasies. Horrified, his parents told him that if he did not get help for his problem he could never come home again.

Jody did get help, checking himself into an inpatient drug-treatment program. But even though his behavior and outlook improved—his parents no longer lived in fear that their son would become a murderer—his mind may never be completely right. While Bill and Eva did not say as much, they clearly suspected that a tendency to drug addiction is innate in Jody. (This is a possibility many researchers into the biochemistry of the brain now support. *The New York Times* quotes Dr. Kenneth Blum of the University of Texas, one of the scientists who recently shared in the discovery of a gene linked to alcoholism, as saying, "My guiding hypothesis is that there are specific neurotransmitter irregularities for each addiction." In other words, many neurologists now believe that people often take drugs in order to "self-medicate" for biological abnormalities of their brain chemistry.) Jody was a troubled child from birth. "He always had a negative attitude, from the outset," said Eva. "He didn't want to get dressed in the morning, he didn't want to get undressed at night, he didn't want to get in the tub, he didn't want to get out of the tub." It was entirely possible that Jody's drug use was a desperate and destructive form of self-medication.

Philosophically divided on how to deal with the problem, Bill and Eva were nevertheless united in a love and concern for their son bordering on the heroic. I was able to see this for myself when Jody stopped by near the end of the interview. The warmth flowing between parents and son was palpable. He offered to mow his parents' lawn and made friendly conversation with me—this despite the fact that he clearly felt nervous seeing me sitting unexpectedly at his parents' kitchen table. It seemed an effort for him to chat with me, and he was making the effort. He was trying.

I came away feeling that these were two people who had done the very best they could with what they had. Their son came into the world a brittle little boy, and although he had grown up to be a brittle man he was also possessed of a sweetness, a loving nature as well as a fearful and paranoid one. He was alive, he was law-abiding apart from his sporadic drug use, and he was not violent. He was able to spend stretches of time holding down a job and living on his own. This might be the best he could do and, if so, he owed much of this to his parents' steady love.

Under these circumstances, Bill and Eva's marriage can never be the seamless union of that of other couples; their son was and will always be between them. Barring a miracle, there will not be a happy ending: "This will be with us until we die," said Eva. "You have to really adjust your mind to these things. I enjoy my son when he's doing well, and I tune him out when he's not. If he's on drugs, he's not welcome."

For some couples with children in trouble, there *was* a happy ending. Jill and Richard Frank of Los Angeles told me that their entire marriage had been turned around in response to their daughter's drug problem. Until that point, they had never been really happy together. In fact, they were radically disconnected, Jill desperately yearning for more contact with her husband, Richard just as strongly resisting.

They married when Richard was still in school studying electrical engineering. Committed to a highly demanding course load, he was the classic workaholic, leaving his studies to come to bed only at midnight or one—at which point he would find, to his dismay, that his wife wanted to *talk*. "I thought that was totally unreasonable," Richard said wryly. They quickly evolved into the equally classic angry-wife–unresponsive-husband alliance: she would throw temper tantrums, and he would be reasonable ("reasonable to the point where you could puke," Richard told me). "I was a very unfeeling person," Richard observed. "I was brought up in a home where feelings were not allowed, and I used to think I was a good person, being so even tempered."

Not surprisingly, their daughter's drug problems wreaked havoc on a marriage that was none too sound to begin with. Ever the reasonable party, Richard at first denied that there was a problem, while his wife grew increasingly frantic. Worse, when he did finally acknowledge the problem, he blamed Jill. Things became so bad that Richard referred to this period as "World War III": "There was no respect between us, no love, no communication. Just blaming and denial."

When I met them their lives and marriage had changed radically, thanks largely to their involvement in their daughter's recovery program. All three entered the program as a family, their daughter becoming an in-patient for a time. "With her removed and safe," Richard said, "we could relax and take a look at ourselves. The program insisted on it."

This period of self-examination helped both to understand what it was that had gone wrong between them. Richard in particular began to see the reasonable nature that he had so prized in a new light; confronting the distant way in which he had initially reacted to his daughter's problems, he now saw himself as an ambitious and hard-working man who had effected a near-total divorce from his feelings. Detached from his own emotions, he had not been interested in those of the family around him, and he had not been there for his daughter when she needed him. "I wasn't even there for myself," he told me.

He finally began genuinely to connect with himself and his family when he and Jill entered a training program that would teach them to counsel other parents coping with their children's drug problems. Talking to these parents, Richard was forced to open up; the subject, after all, was their children's drug use.

Jill, too, began to come to grips with herself. As a mother she had always been a shouter; she had yelled at the kids so much, all three told their parents that if the marriage ended they would go with their father. Family relations had deteriorated to the point where both Jill and Richard were "ready to walk." The only thing stopping them was the sad fact that neither wanted to take the children.

Jill's change of heart came during a lecture by the family therapist John Bradshaw: "My light bulb went on," she said. Suddenly, blindingly, she saw that her tempestuous relationship with her own mother was poisoning her relationship with her children. This perception overtook her with the force of truth revealed, and she decided to change. "At age forty-four," she said, "I divorced my parents." Belatedly she began to teach herself the twin virtues of patience and tolerance.

Their marriage was far better than it had been at any point in the past. The two had begun to "date" again, to arrange small treats to surprise each other, to take weekends away together. Not surprisingly, their relations with their children, all of whom were in their twenties now, were excellent. The oldest daughter had remained drug free since her treatment; she was now married herself. "We have an open family where everyone comes over and visits," Richard said, "and it's an absolute miracle."

Richard and Jill's was a case that showed how a child's troubles can act as a catalyst for the parents, forcing them to rethink their relationship. Without the crisis provoked by their daughter's drug use, both would doubtless have gone on as before, Richard work obsessed and removed, Jill beside herself with frustration and rage. They were able to use a family crisis to reshape their marriage into a relationship that today nurtures and sustains both of them.

Their story reveals a heartening principle concerning children in trouble:

• **If a child in trouble is a blow to any marriage, it is also equally an opportunity for wife and husband to build new love and respect for each other.**

The fact that Richard and Jill could do this while Eva and Bill could not should be taken as no reflection upon the Whitmans. The truth is that Richard and Jill were enormously lucky in that their daughter's drug problem proved to be treatable, her mind unaffected by the drug use. Unlike Eva and Bill, who must continue to cope with their son's problems for the rest of their lives, Richard and Jill can relax. Not all problems can be solved by loving parents, or by drug clinics and psychiatrists, and Bill and Eva have done their best.

Richard and Jill can also congratulate themselves for having handled a crisis effectively—a pleasure forever denied to Bill and Eva, whose problems are ongoing. While the Whitmans were and are coping heroically, in all likelihood they will never be able to feel that they have prevailed, because it is realistic to expect that their son's crisis will never fully pass. One of the fundamental bonds that happy children forge with their parents is a sense of mutual pride, of a job well done. In short, when all goes well, raising children is a highly validating experience; it is one of life's successes. For Richard and Jill this sense of validation is even stronger in some ways, because their child came so close to the brink. Because they saw their daughter through her problems, they are now drawn together in triumph, having conquered their family problems together. As a result, they both feel a profound sense of happiness and pride.

As their happy experience shows, a child's problems *can* create a renewed sense of appreciation between a couple. Thirty-eight-year-old Hannah Winslow told me that she deeply appreciated her husband Keith's support during their recent discovery that their seven-year-old daughter, Molly, was dyslexic. A psychologist herself, Hannah felt terribly guilty for "not having seen it sooner." She had been intensively tutoring the little girl every day after school with no improvement to show for it; mother and daughter were growing daily more frustrated and upset with each other. Molly had long had other problems as well. She had great difficulty adapting to change; she could not be taken on family vacations because of the difference in routine that a vacation creates. Hannah now felt that she had ignored all these trouble signs, to her daughter's detriment. She could have sought help sooner, she told herself.

Finally, just a few short weeks before I met her, she had realized that something was seriously wrong. Having just learned of her daughter's diagnosis, she was living in a state of near panic. Although in the popular media "dyslexia" is routinely described as a relatively minor reading problem involving the reversal of letters on the page, in fact it can mean far more than this. Problems in the brain's functioning are rarely simple, and they are almost always mysterious. Not all people with learning disabilities are able to achieve independent lives as adults—one of a parent's worst fears—and this was the fear Hannah was trying to hold at bay. Having one's child diagnosed as learning disabled immediately makes the future very uncertain indeed; it is a highly traumatic passage in a family's life. "I start thinking, what if she never learns to read?" Hannah said. "She won't be able to go to college, she won't be able to have a job . . . I get terrified. It costs eighteen thousand dollars a year to send your child to private school for special education, and I don't see how we can get the money together."

Keith was the only person holding her together during this traumatic period. "He gets me back into the normal operating range," she said with a grateful smile. With her husband's help she was managing to avoid panic, to focus on the here and now without projecting disaster scenarios into the distant future. When I talked to her, she was in remarkably good spirits, thanks largely to him. She was very worried, it was clear, but she was holding on. She was indeed living within the normal operating range—an achievement as important to maintaining her young daughter's confidence as to her own.

Listening to her story brought home to me how crucial a strong marriage is to meeting the needs of young and vulnerable children. It is difficult to imagine how a single mother could cope with revelations like that of Molly's learning disability; in the face of severe stress and worry, it takes two to remain anywhere near the normal operating range.

More Problems with Children: The Blended Family

Not surprisingly, second marriages brought with them all these same problems, only several degrees more intense. If children by nature come into a marriage as little strangers, the children of someone else's marriage can seem to an overwhelmed stepparent like members of an alien species. What is more, stepchildren are not only different, they can be hostile as well. Married couples living in blended families probably told me the most dramatic stories of sheer, unmitigated, day-in-day-out *stress* caused by children. Not tragedy, not life-threatening drug problems, but constant conflict, turmoil, tumult. Seeing how these marriages survived offers insights for us all.

Marilyn and Max Harper, ages fifty-four and sixty-two, had been married for twenty-two years when we spoke. They met at Parents Without Partners when she had been divorced for six years and he had been widowed for one. He was forty years old; she was thirty-two. For Marilyn, Max was "very, very special. I had been out there in the jungle for six years, and I had heard every line there was. I told Max, 'You're so different.' "

Max *was* different. "I had no axe to grind," he said, describing his approach to dating again at forty, "because my first marriage was good." In short, Max was not a member of the walking wounded.

He was an uncomplicated man who had been happily married for thirteen years when he lost his wife to cancer, and who hoped to be happily married once again. Their relationship blossomed.

The hard part was their children. "I knew I had to marry someone with kids," said Marilyn, "so he would be able to deal with my kids." When they married, Marilyn had two boys, ages seven and ten; Max had three boys, ages seven, ten, and thirteen. The mix proved volatile. With their wedding vows behind them Max and Marilyn embarked upon a ten-year period of, in Marilyn's words, "absolute mayhem."

Much of the trouble stemmed from their profoundly clashing disciplinary styles. "I was an only child," said Marilyn, revealing the source of her own child-rearing philosophy. "The sun set and rose on my head and I could do no wrong. I raised my own kids the same way; instead of saying no I was always explaining everything." In sharp contrast, Max was of the affectionate disciplinarian school of fatherhood. His style was to issue simple commands; he expected nothing more than simple obedience in return. Uncomplicated in his relations with women, he had long had an uncomplicated relationship with his children as well. The problem was, Marilyn's children would have none of it. Unaccustomed to any paternal limit-setting whatsoever, they saw Max not as a respected head of the household but as a tyrant to be defied at every turn.

Not surprisingly, given the sharply diverging philosophies of child rearing that both parents brought with them to the new family, both sets of children took an immediate dislike to their new stepparent. Max's children hated Marilyn; Marilyn's children hated Max. This is the stubborn truth of children; unlike a new husband or wife, a new stepchild does not necessarily feel compelled to put his best foot forward. With blended families, the new couple does not enjoy a period of private time in which to work out the kinks in their relationship. Instead they are forced to face the small differences that all couples must smooth over in the presence of children who may be trying their best to divide and conquer.

It is no exaggeration to say that with their marriage Marilyn and Max embarked upon life in a war zone. There was constant, unceasing conflict; the children fought all the time with one another and with their parents. There was no letup, ever. Dinnertime in particular was horrendous: there was always a conflagration. The marriage buckled.

Finally, after five years, Max said to his wife, "Let's just call it quits.

We'll walk away as friends." He recalled his frame of mind at the time as simply "resigned." He was not angry with Marilyn, whom he continued to love very much; he just could not see any way for the family to struggle on.

Marilyn rallied him to the cause with a pep talk. "I told him, 'You know they'll grow up and leave, and we're great together,' " she said. Unconvinced, Max nevertheless stayed on and was rewarded for his resolve by the dawn of an even bloodier era as each and every one of their five children swung full force into a highly tempestuous adolescence. Needless to say, battles with a sixteen-year-old can be considerably more taxing than battles with a seven-year-old, and this was the phase the family had now entered. Marilyn and Max both vividly recalled one major confrontation over her son's hair length. When Max told him either to get his hair cut or leave, the boy left. It was Marilyn who pulled the family through this crisis. She sheared off the ends of her son's long mane ("I gave him a one-inch designer haircut," she told me, joking) and told Max to "keep his mouth shut." Max did, and the compromise held. Her son returned home, and the family lived on to fight another day.

How did their marriage survive? Primarily, both said, by means of sheer retreat. Marilyn and Max took weekend trips alone together as often as possible; they even went so far as to build a second-story master suite, a sanctuary situated literally above the fray. To some degree their bond must have been akin to that of soldiers at war; outnumbered by their five battling offspring, they hunkered down in their new bedroom, a team of "us" against "them." They refused to allow the children inside this private space: by mutual agreement they avoided even discussing the children during their time alone.

Needless to say, Marilyn and Max were one couple who stood on its head the usual notion of a sad and lonely passage to the empty nest. When their last child left home at age twenty-two, Marilyn and Max were overjoyed. Both vividly recalled the night their son went out the front door for the last time: "We leaped and danced and shouted," said Marilyn. "I had had to be a lady around the boys for so long that I ran all through the house shouting curse words." Life without children proved to be as happy as they had hoped it would be, illustrating once again the 1950s belief that happy coupledom and happy familyhood do not necessarily go hand in hand. Marilyn had been right: she and Max, miserable as a family, were wonderful as a pair. And still are.

Might there have been a better way of handling the challenge of bringing together five boys of the same age, all on the cusp of adolescence? Possibly. Family therapy might have helped; more open communication between Marilyn and Max might have done some good, too. Nevertheless, communication can accomplish only so much; young boys who have lost a mother do not want open communication, they want their mother restored to them. Judging by the outcome, Marilyn and Max did not do so badly. All five children were doing well in adult life; three were now close both with their natural parent and with their stepparent. (In fact, our interview was set up by Marilyn's eldest son's girlfriend, who told me that I must talk to Marilyn and Max because they were one of the happiest couples she knew. Obviously there was a rich current of affection running between the son and his mother and stepfather; I could hear it in his girlfriend's voice.) The hallway in their duplex was lined with photos of the children, and of mementos from one son's successful career as a rock-and-roll musician in Los Angeles. Both Marilyn and Max were lively and flamboyant people; clearly they were dealing with a lively and flamboyant group of children. It is entirely possible that the kind of child who is going to grow up to star in a heavy-metal band is also going to be a handful in childhood—no matter how much good communication and family counseling he is exposed to.

In short, there may be real limits to the amount of peace and harmony that some blended families can achieve. Even the most calm and optimistic of spouses could be defeated by a child who was desperately opposed to a parent's second marriage. Louisa Holman and her husband, Rob Mattox, told me that their marriage had so upset Louisa's son that the two had finally taken the extreme step of establishing separate households during the boy's high school years. The mother went with her son; the stepfather remained behind, living alone in spite of his marriage. This was a case of the child being completely derailed by his mother's divorce and subsequent remarriage. Children, of course, may suffer from the geographical dislocations involved in remarriage much more acutely than do their parents, and that had been true for him. With his mother's move into his new stepfather's house, the boy had lost his entire social circle. Overnight he went from a suburban public school filled with childhood friends to a highly competitive private boys' school filled with the sons of the wealthy. His grades plummeted, and he began to flirt with drugs.

It is impossible to know what exactly was happening to Louisa's son. Louisa's first husband, the father of her son, had been a seriously depressed alcoholic. As is now well established, a tendency to depression runs in families; it is thus quite possible that Louisa's son simply was more prone than other boys his age to being thrown off track by major changes in his life. (In fact, Louisa's daughter by her first marriage—who had already left home when Louisa remarried—was even today seriously depressed.) Furthermore, because her son had lived for so many years with a profoundly unhappy father, his close circle of friends may well have functioned as a major source of inner stability for him. Nor did he respond well to Rob's firmly paternal style of discipline. The mix between stepfather and stepson was bad; entering adolescence, Louisa's son was simply not at a stage where he could accept a strong new father figure in his life.

But whatever the problem was—and probably all of these factors contributed—the reality that confronted Louisa and Rob was that her son was rapidly deteriorating. Desperate to save him, Louisa, with Rob's full cooperation and support, finally pulled him out of the new school and returned him to the suburban home she had shared with her first husband. Rob stayed behind, further reducing the tension of his unwelcome presence in his stepson's life, and the two settled into a two-household partnership; husband and wife were not to share the same home for four years. Their sacrifice is a measure of how far parents will go to protect their children: "I really feel that we saved him," Louisa told me, her voice filling with pride. Reunited with his old friends and teachers, her son thrived. At twenty-eight, he was happily married and expecting a child of his own, his career as a graphic designer well under way. And he was now on very good terms with both his mother and his stepfather. He understood what both of them did for him.

Their marriage was a profoundly happy one—one of the happiest love matches I encountered. And yet for them her child was so incompatible with their existence as a couple that they had to choose temporarily between the boy and a life together. They chose the child, and they had been richly rewarded. Their bond, like Richard and Jill's, was strengthened by the knowledge that they brought a child through a troubled adolescence into a strong and healthy adulthood. And Louisa would always carry with her the knowledge of Rob's selfless generosity.

Life Without Children

Minus the complications created by children in trouble, childless couples could lead very harmonious lives indeed. Only three of my couples had chosen to go through life without children, and two of them were also two of the closest, and happiest, whom I interviewed. (One of them was James and Ellen Wagner, the couple who were so intimate that they frequently read each other's thoughts.)

But children or no, the dynamic animating a happy couple remains the same: all couples without exception were happiest when they forged a shared marital identity and committed themselves to a transcendent marital goal. When that goal was not children, it was something else. One of the childless wives, then aged thirty-seven, told me quite explicitly that she and her husband were thinking of buying a house to fix up together as a substitute for having a baby. The other couple were highly involved creatively; they worked together on financial projects; they had designed and built a house together; they had even made short films together.

Thus the irony of children is that while the basic impulse to *create* is fundamental to the happy couple, children—the most common form married people's creativity takes—are a particularly demanding form of creation. Unlike a house or a movie, children are not a creation that parents can ultimately control; they possess their own realities, and they go their own ways. In bringing children into the world, couples had to relinquish a certain sense of control over their fates; they gave hostages to fortune. All couples had to make peace with this truth.

What Children Give to Parents

But for all the heartache a child can bring, in the best of all possible worlds children are a blessing, a source of tremendous strength and happiness. Among strong couples the need to care for a child brings out the best in husband and wife; they grow in stature and character as their children do.

The principle:

- **As marriage enriches the self, so do children enrich the marriage.**

Lucas and Debra Lyon-Jones, now ages thirty-five and thirty-three, told the most vivid tale of a relationship strengthened by children. Both hailed from a hardscrabble background of near poverty and sometime family violence. By dint of sheer will, they had forged a strong and vital family life; they had created a house and home of which Lucas said, "I will fight furiously to maintain this family." Theirs was a marriage in which they had always taken care of someone vulnerable: before having children they had already assumed primary responsibility for Debra's young sister, for Lucas's ailing and impoverished mother, and finally, just when these responsibilities had begun to lift, for a small boy whose sixteen-year-old mother was too young to care for him but unwilling to give him up for adoption. Lucas and Debra took on these responsibilities in their twenties, at a time when other young men and women have their hands full just trying to date and begin their work lives.

As they saw it, it was precisely these responsibilities that had made their marriage strong. This is an important point, and one that is underestimated by many. A traditional couples' counselor might well disapprove; he or she might object that Debra and Lucas had used their weaker dependents to make themselves feel strong by comparison. But even if this analysis were true, and it certainly could be, it ignores the positive aspects of "role-playing." People grow into the roles they take on—be those roles good or bad—and in taking on the admittedly idealized role of fearless caretakers, Lucas and Debra had given themselves something to live up to. Assuming the role of responsible son, sister, and foster parent may have been their way of compensating for the extreme vulnerability both of them felt in the world. If so, however, it was a form of compensation that worked.

Becoming a parent spurs many couples on to new heights in work and love, because children pose a challenge to which both partners must rise. Speaking of this phenomenon, one wife told me bluntly, "I believe children bring money." What she meant by this was that the responsibility of providing for children frequently spurs people on to greater heights in their careers, necessity being the mother of invention. The data showing that married men are more successful financially than single men supports her insight.

Nevertheless, for Debra and Lucas, living up to the demands of parenthood did not come without extreme struggle. By the time the children came Lucas was in law school, a step he was able to take only at Debra's urging, and only because of Debra's unswerving belief in him. Debra was working full-time as an accountant to support them both. It was exhausting even to listen to their account of this period. At one point they were $8,000 in debt with Debra's job hanging by a thread. Her employers were cruel; each day at work they would taunt her, telling her this might be her last day. She hated her job desperately, yet needed to hold on to it just as desperately. Each night Lucas would come home and say, "I don't know what we'll do if you lose your job." And each night Debra would come home and sob. "I had a nervous breakdown," she told me. Their first child was born on a Sunday, and Debra returned to work on Monday. They were living that close to the edge.

All of this they coped with entirely on the strength of their own emotional resources; neither could draw upon the solid middle-class backup of stable parents ready to lend a helping hand. Unlike the "yuppies" who are now Lucas's colleagues at his law firm, they could not turn to their parents for loans or tuition, or even for emergency child care. They had, and have, only themselves to count on. "Neither of us grew up in the house with the white picket fence," said Lucas. Lucas's father, though a hard worker, was an alcoholic; now deceased, the best of his life was over by the time Lucas was born to him at age fifty-two. His mother, Lucas said, was a cruel woman given to playing frightening practical jokes on her children, such as the time she told all of them that they were moving—and then proceeded only to move the furniture around the living room. She, too, abused alcohol as well as prescription drugs.

Debra's childhood was even more chaotic. "My father was probably a genius," she said. "He would have brilliant ideas and get great jobs and then not go to work." Headed by a brilliant but dysfunctional man, the family was always perched on the brink of disaster. And Debra's mother could not make up for the deficiencies of her husband. "I really had no mother," said Debra, "because when I was fifteen months old she gave birth to a blue baby who died." The family never recovered from this blow, and the parents ultimately divorced. By age thirteen and a half Debra had been thrown out of her mother's house by her mother's boyfriend; she took her younger sister, Marcia, with her. Already, just into her teens, Debra had taken on the adult role of mother.

Having witnessed a constant stream of disappointment and tragedy in both families, Lucas and Debra shared a profound sense of the precariousness of life. To the outsider it seemed something of a miracle that their marriage had survived. But both agreed that it had not disintegrated in part precisely because of the enormous burdens they had shouldered together. "The fact that I had so much responsibility for my mother and Debra had so much responsibility for her sister held us together," said Lucas. "We couldn't do it alone, we needed each other emotionally and financially. She was a buffer between me and my mother, and I was a buffer between her and her sister."

Their shared commitment to family had already seen them through one marital crisis, a crisis not entirely resolved when I met them. This trauma had involved a breach of faith having to do with Debra's sister, Marcia, who, said Debra, "is a real agitator." Two years earlier Marcia had developed a crush on Lucas, and, for "one brief moment," Lucas had responded. On the night of Debra's thirtieth birthday, Lucas and Marcia kissed.

Things went no further than that, and Lucas promptly withdrew from the flirtation. This might have been the end of it but, two years later, on Debra's thirty-second birthday, he confessed. He told Debra about the kiss. His reasons for revealing this momentary transgression a full two years later were complex. In part he was afraid that Marcia might be on the verge of telling her sister about it herself, but more than this he wanted and needed to clear his conscience. He had felt intolerably guilty; "I was really a rat," he said. Though he had managed to live with the secret for two long years, when Debra came home the night of her thirty-second birthday and emotionally confessed her undying love for him, he was undone. Full of love for her husband, Debra told him that night that she might be willing to have the fourth child he wanted; she had never felt so close to him, she said, as when she had been carrying his babies. Listening to his wife's trusting expression of love and faith, Lucas could no longer carry on the deception.

But his confession, motivated by a desire for love and union, proved devastating to the marriage because while the secret no longer stood between them, the kiss now did. Debra reacted only mildly that night, but by the next morning she was furious. She called her sister, who volunteered to let Debra read the journal she had been keeping at the time, apparently as a means of supporting Lucas's account. But the journal only made matters worse since it was from her sister's diary that Debra discovered the kiss had taken place on her thirtieth birthday—a wounding detail Lucas had wisely chosen to omit. All her good memories of that night, which she had treasured as a particularly tender one shared with her husband, were abruptly wiped away.

The result was explosive. Debra was furious, and their family life descended into chaos. Whenever Lucas came home from work, Debra went out to a bar. There she grew close to one of her sister's boyfriends, flirting with him while keeping the involvement platonic. She thought constantly of divorce; ever the take-charge family planner, she worked out on paper every financial detail of a possible separation. She even went apartment hunting to find a place for Lucas.

And yet six months later they were still together, and were finding their way back to the trust and connection they felt before. Their children held them together. "I look at these three children," said Debra, "and I say I'm just not going to chuck this all. I don't like failure."

The broad parental streak in their love for each other also held them back. Two days after the Sunday when Debra finally told Lucas she wanted a divorce, she fell suddenly ill; she was sick enough to be rushed to the hospital, where she was initially misdiagnosed as having spinal meningitis. Lucas dropped everything to take her to the hospital; he stayed with her during the CAT scan and did not go in to work the next day. His attention to her illness had the important effect of shifting them out of the sexual realm and into the nurturing realm, where there had been no betrayal of trust. "It really brought into focus how reliant we are on each other," Debra said. Moved by his devotion, Debra dropped her request for a divorce and they began the process of rebuilding trust.

There is a happy postscript to their story. Two years later, as I was finishing the revisions on this manuscript, I received a letter from Debra. She and Lucas were still together and happy. And they had had their fourth child.

Although in a complex way, for many couples children serve as a stabilizing influence. Most obviously, of course, children give a couple a powerful reason beyond themselves for protecting and nurturing the marriage. In finding a way through bad times devoted parents understand that they are doing more than preserving a relationship; they are sustaining a family, an intact home for their children. But more than this, there is a quality to the very nature of parental love that is more stable and less volatile than romantic love. Nurturant love is always a long-term proposition; we do not speak of "crushes" or "infatuations" when we are trying to describe the love that ties parent to child. The same thing holds true between adults. People might fall in love with each other across a crowded room in one electrifying moment, but they do not fall in "nurturance" with each other in this way. The nurturing bond takes time to develop; by the same token, it takes a great deal of time and trauma to undo.

What this means for the couple in conflict is that simply making contact with the nurturant, parental side of their feelings for each other can help resolve a divorce crisis. A marriage based entirely upon an essentially parental love between partners might not be our ideal, but certainly a broad streak of parental love should be present in even the most lusty of attachments. For Lucas and Debra, it was the strongly developed parental side of their relationship that saw them through Marcia's sexual challenge to their marriage.

For most couples, the creation of a child together was the ultimate expression of their love. Whatever that child's fate, once two lovers had become family, they were forever joined in pride or grief, joy or pain, happiness or sorrow. And those who knew themselves to be truly *lucky* in love—lucky in the most random and happenstance sense of the word—had been blessed with children who were lucky in life. Because when children were not lucky, when children suffered, parents suffered, too.

And, when a child died, wives and husbands reeled. In the next chapter we hear from couples who had confronted, and survived, great loss.

Tragedy

> . . . for better, for worse,
> for richer, for poorer,
> in sickness and in health,
> to love and to cherish,
> until we are parted by death.
> —*The Book of Common Prayer*

The abiding strength of the good marriage revealed itself most starkly in a couple's capacity to survive the most profound of losses and grief. Here, too, the lives of children inflicted the greatest wounds to the soul. Many couples had lived through the death or terrible injury of a child. They were marked forever by these experiences, but their love survived intact. It was their love that pulled them through.

Life is not fair: I met with couples who had suffered not one tragic loss of a child, but two. How these people remained standing, I could barely fathom. And yet there they were, sitting together before me, living their lives. Their courage in the face of devastation was inspirational. Couples whose past had been saturated with loss stood by each other; they worshiped in church and went to work; they pursued their hobbies. They carried on in the face of lasting sorrow.

Harvey and Marian Spicher of suburban Chicago, married for thirty-three years and the parents of four sons, had experienced such a double loss. How they dealt with each blow tells us much about what a marriage must be in order to support its partners. They were a young couple struggling to get by on Harvey's income from a mom-and-pop grocery store when their infant son succumbed to crib death in 1964. The pain of this tragedy, with each partner reacting in different ways, badly strained the tie between them. Marian took the death much harder than did her husband, who says that he coped with it "pretty fair." But Marian felt acutely guilty. "I thought maybe I didn't take care of him right," she told me.

It was a conviction she could not shake. She began to fight with her husband; she did not want to be close to him. Withdrawing from home and family, she began to frequent bars with her unmarried girlfriends. These women exerted an extremely negative influence on Marian's marriage. She would complain about her husband to her friends, and the friends would side loyally with her, urging her not to "take any crap" from Harvey.

At the time, Marian was only dimly aware that her behavior was in any way connected to the death of her baby. Though she understood that "I felt like the baby hurt me a lot and I didn't want to be hurt anymore," this perception did not help her put her actions into any kind of real or useful perspective. She was acting directly out of her pain, bypassing the rational filtering processes of consciousness. That she *was* in fact inventing reasons to withdraw from her husband is clear. Near the end of this dark period Marian found herself wanting to bring together the two opposed camps she had created. Now, for the first time, she introduced Harvey to her circle of friends at the bar. All the women took an instant liking to him, and he to them; they remain friends to this day. It was Marian who had artificially engineered the hostility between the two "sides" out of her need to separate from the father of her lost baby. In choosing now to foster affection between her husband and her friends she was symbolically returning home.

If Marian was only vaguely aware of her motivations during this time, her husband was completely in the dark. All Harvey could see was a wife who withdrew from him and defied him at every turn. He made no connection between the crib death and his wife's five long years of rebellion following the loss.

By the time we spoke, he did see the connection; he saw it clearly. It was part of the healing that had gone on between the two that both now *shared* a vision of what happened to them thirty years ago. Again, we can invoke the shared identity of the strong marriage: Harvey and Marian fully shared one unified interpretation of what was to be the very worst period of their thirty-three-year-long marriage. Sharing that perception allowed them to put those years behind them, prevented them from reliving those terrible times via arguments over what they meant, over who was at fault, over who did what to whom. The past was settled.

Thus the most essential piece of wisdom to emerge from couples who had weathered tragedy was this:

- **Just as the strong couple must share a vision of life, they must also share an understanding of loss.**

Marian and Harvey's shared vision of life and loss, forged through the death of their infant son, allowed them to stand together when, years later, a second tragedy struck their family. In 1980 their son Ken, twenty-one years old, was hit by a car while riding his motorcycle. The accident left him in a coma that was to last five and a half months—a period during which Harvey's innate optimism kept the family afloat. "I love getting up in the morning," Harvey said, describing the quality that allowed him to maintain his hopeful vigil, "I always think things can be better. I never worry." So optimistic was he concerning the prognosis for his son that the doctors felt he did not understand the seriousness of Ken's condition. Marian, too, was sometimes puzzled—albeit heartened—by her husband's unreasoning optimism. As Marian said, "Harve would sit by Ken's bedside and say, 'Look what he's doing!' and I'd think, 'He's not doing anything.' "

But Harvey's faith held, and, against all odds, his son emerged from the coma, badly brain damaged but alive. He could recognize his parents; he was conscious. Harvey and Marian had been coping ever since, and it had been ten years when we spoke. Both were united in Harvey's view of their son's life; both focused entirely upon his halting progress forward. Every penny they could borrow or earn went into his care, and they took full responsibility for his physical needs. Their small living room was filled with the steel apparatus essential to the rehabilitation of the desperately injured. It was a constant physical reminder of their son's terrible loss.

And of their own loss. "He was a beautiful person," Marian said, dry eyed and composed. "He was only twenty-one and he was a giving person. He always helped people. He bailed out an ex-friend of mine one time, and he tried to help out the son of a friend of ours who was on drugs."

"He still is a beautiful person," Harvey said, correcting her gently.

They had been through so much. To protect their son at night, they would put him in his bed and then move a sofa up against it so that he could not fall out. One night, as he was turning in, Harvey heard a sound. Marian heard it, too, but thought it was only Ken settling himself in. But Harvey had a presentiment of danger. He went to his son's room to check, and found Ken gone. A panicked search through the house quickly led them to their son, who had unaccountably climbed up over the sofa and gone out into the freezing Chicago night beyond. Wearing only his thin pajamas, he was sitting on the steps outside the back door. If Harvey had not found him, he would have been dead by morning.

It was likely, they believed, that he had gotten up in search of food. The damage to his brain had left him ravenously, insatiably hungry. He had difficulty settling himself for sleep as well. During our interview Harvey excused himself to put his grown son to bed; some minutes later I heard a low, guttural growling coming from the rear of the small house. That was Ken, his parents told me, working his way toward sleep. Frequently, he talks to himself.

To the outsider, it was an unthinkable burden of pain for two parents to bear. And yet bear it they did. "It's brought us closer together," said Harvey, "because we both have the same idea of what we want for his care." They were both following Harvey's lead in this; they were focusing upon therapy, upon treatment, upon the small but very real gains their son had made over the past decade and continued to make. They accepted the fact that he was irreparably damaged, and yet they rejoiced in each small step forward. They were remarkably strong in their faith, and in their marriage—which, at this point, amounted to the same thing.

For the rest of us, what is so heartening about their story is that Harvey and Marian had managed to reach this point in the midst of a marriage that was far from perfect: these were not two people whose union came easily. They had fought frequently over the years, sometimes fiercely. The issues dividing them were the ordinary stuff of daily life that could cause any couple to jump the tracks. In their early years they argued about money. Having been accustomed to earning and managing her own income, Marian found the financial dependency of marriage intolerable. "I hated having no money of my own," she said. "It was a very bad thing for me."

Unfortunately, her options were severely limited. Though she longed to take a part-time job no child care was available, making paid work out of the question. Soon she and her husband locked horns over her use of the family credit cards. Harvey had been brought up not to spend money he did not have; Marian now felt as if the only money she *did* have was the credit line on their MasterCard. And she chafed at the fact that in other families it was the wives who handled the family finances. (She was entirely accurate in this perception; I found that many traditional families shared finances by assigning breadwinning to the husband and the managing and handling of funds to the wife. In this way, both partners could be financial equals in spite of the fact that only one partner was contributing income.)

But Harvey kept full control of their finances, a situation in which Marian acquiesced because she had been brought up to believe that the man handles the money. "I didn't handle the money," Marian said, a note of lingering resentment creeping into her voice. "She *couldn't* handle the money," Harvey objected at once. It was and no doubt always will be an issue between them, a flash point that finally exploded when Harvey closed down every credit account they had, including the one Marian held in her name alone—an action she continued to resent. "You had no right to do that," she told him in the strongest of tones, mid-stride through our interview.

Nevertheless, they had worked out some degree of accommodation on this issue. "For the first five years I was a flake with the credit cards," Marian said, fully confirming Harvey's complaints. And, she added, "Things got much better when Harvey turned over the electric bills for me to pay. Then I saw how careful we needed to be." As in any strong marriage, both made concessions; both began to see the issue from the other's point of view. Harvey came to understand that, "flake" or no, Marian had to have some real involvement in the family finances; Marian came to see that she needed to acquire Harvey's unflinching sense of financial responsibility.

All of which is to say that Harvey and Marian are no perfect couple. Neither life nor marriage had been easy for them; they had struggled with the world (when I spoke to them, Harvey's small grocery shop was on the verge of going under) and with each other. And yet their marriage, the very fact of their marriage, strengthened each profoundly. United they stood: they coped with the terrible devastation of their strong and handsome son's accident by drawing strength and sustenance from each other, and from their remaining sons. Committed for life, they endured. They even looked to the future with a cautious hope, focusing each day not upon Ken's disabilities, but upon the small steps forward he continued to take.

Temperament, Once Again

As always, the remarkable diversity in temperament, in people's innate abilities to cope, struck me with enormous force. Needless to say, the sunny souls among us are blessed when tragedy strikes. Hugh and Martha Juniper, the couple who revealed that they had not been seriously affected by several years of infertility, told me in all sincerity, "We've had very lucky lives." Listening to them describing the activities of an obviously affluent retirement, sitting in their lovely town house decorated by Martha with an inviting clutter of country colors and furniture, including a coffee table she had built herself, hearing about the accomplishments of their grown children, I could only agree. These people, I thought, have been lucky.

So it was with a shock that, in the midst of hurried note taking, I realized suddenly that they were now telling me of the accidental death of their second daughter only a few short years before. At first, I could scarcely register this revelation. Here before me were two happy, lively, relaxed people occupied with their many friends and hobbies, people whom I saw as extraordinarily blessed by life's bounty. And suddenly they were telling me that they had suffered one of the most terrible fates that can befall any parent.

How did they do it? I asked. How did they live on after her death? How had they managed to so obviously *thrive?*

Martha and Hugh themselves could give me little in the way of an answer: they were not people who would jump at the opportunity to tell other parents how to conquer grief. Nevertheless, this very incapacity to describe their innermost workings offers us an important clue. By temperament, both had an ability *not to think about* a subject they wished not to think about. "We're not brooders," they told me, and they were right.

This is not to say that they had not mourned their daughter's death, had not deeply experienced the loss. Written upon their kind faces were the traces of suffering, of irremediable loss. But their focus was entirely upon the positive. "After Debbie died," Martha told me, "people from the neighborhood we had never even spoken to stopped to tell us how sorry they were, how lovely they had always thought Debbie was. Everyone brought us food." Both were warmed by the heartfelt—and unexpected—support they were given; both came through the experience feeling better loved and appreciated than they had before.

Debbie's death was a turning point in their lives, and afterward they made several changes. Soon after the accident, Martha advised Hugh to retire, and he did. "Life is short," Martha told me, "and in most careers you don't get any thrills after sixty." They now began to visit the cottage in Colorado that Martha's parents had left her, dubbing it their "Versailles West." They had a full circle of friends in Colorado, and they enjoyed their time in the small house immensely. When their son asked whether they might be retreating, running away from the city whose freeways had claimed their daughter's life, they answered him no. They were embracing life. Still, it was a complex embrace; it *was* a retreat in precisely the same sense that a "fresh start" is a retreat. They were able to withdraw, to withdraw *partially*, from a scene of great pain without causing further hurt either to themselves or to their living children for whom Los Angeles was home. Theirs was a graceful mix of acceptance and flight.

Or perhaps the proper way of understanding their capacity to withdraw is to see it as a form of *deflection*. This pattern showed up throughout their marriage: they staged the most heated of arguments, but these arguments were never, unlike the quarrels of many couples, sparked by some transgression one or the other has committed. It was Hugh and Martha, in fact, who told me that they routinely argued about the correct definitions of words. Very likely, when a wife and husband can happily resolve a battle over word definitions, they have also managed to symbolically express and resolve some more personal tension—with the great advantage that no one's feelings have been hurt. With the move to Colorado they may have deflected some small portion of their grief simply by leaving the scene.

In any event, it was a sign of how successful they had been at creating a good and loving life that they would have a son who could ask them this question. And some of their success in marriage came down to temperament. They were happy people, by nature (Martha more so than Hugh); they were naturally gifted with an ability to see the glass as half full.

But more than this, Martha and Hugh told me that they were at peace with themselves. Their capacity to shed guilt, to accept and forgive themselves, is crucial to the survival of a family tragedy. It would be devastating to confront the death of a child whom one felt one had in any way failed. Martha and Hugh, blessed with an acceptance of themselves and their failings, felt no need to assign blame. This quality saw them through their children's adolescence as well, a period fraught with the standard woes of that time of life. At nineteen their son had grown his hair long and had acquired a van and a girlfriend with whom he was sexually active. Hugh was, in Martha's phrase (Hugh nodding agreement), "being very hard on him." "It was a hard time," both said, "but not for our marriage. We didn't blame ourselves or each other." It was this fundamental self-respect that saw them through their daughter's death.

The principle that Hugh and Martha illustrate:

• **Couples cope best with tragedy when they are at peace with themselves.**

Acceptance

Hugh and Martha appeared to have benefited from a temperamental advantage in weathering enormous loss; nevertheless even the more emotionally delicate of couples found the strength to cope. I think here of Jeanie and Leonard Hollings. Their marriage had been marred by Leonard's virtual breakdown at work; overwhelmed by the fierce and deadly politics at the advertising agency where he worked, he had left home one morning, pretending to be on his way to the office, and had simply driven off into the desert, ending his journey on a lonely mountaintop. He stopped only long enough to call in sick, telling his boss "not to tell Jeanie."

His boss, of course, called Jeanie at once, who felt, by turns, betrayed, furious, and terrified. She knew this was the end; Leonard had enemies at work, and his unreasoning flight into the desert would give them reason enough to force him out. She was right, more right than she knew at the time; he was never to have a full-time position in the advertising business again.

What is remarkable about their lives is that in the midst of all this professional trauma they had stood staunchly together as they coped with their young daughter's chronic illness. Their firstborn had been a tiny hydrocephalic baby girl who required life-threatening surgery when just thirty days old. There was only a fifty-fifty chance that she would survive. Even if she did come through the surgery, her chances of surviving childhood were unknown.

For all his fragility in the realm of office politics, Leonard was very strong in helping Jeanie to survive this period. "The night before the surgery," she recalled, "I was putting my hair up in pin curls the way I always did. And suddenly I said, Why am I doing this?" The minutiae of personal grooming seemed to her utterly meaningless in the face of the harsh truth that by this time the next evening their beloved infant might be dead.

Leonard was there to show her why putting her hair up in pin curls that night, as she did every night, was the right thing to do. He taught her what his superior officers in the Marines had taught him: that in the face of terrible danger, the way to avoid panic is to maintain routine. "They never explicitly told us *why* routine was so important," he told me. "It was just that you *don't break step.*" Jeanie finished setting her hair and never forgot this lesson; it was, she said, an "epiphany."

The next day their baby survived the surgery. Now they were faced with the challenge of living daily with an uncertain future. Would their child be mentally retarded? Would she live to see adulthood? No doctor could tell them.

Again, they coped. "We had two ways we could go," Jeanie said. "We could scrutinize her for signs of mental retardation, or we could treat her as normal and just see how it went." They chose the second course, one Jeanie sees as "accepting." "We didn't deny the problem, or resist it," she told me. "We saw it as being like having a child with diabetes. We thought, This is what God has dealt us and we're going to play it as best we can."

Nine "joyous years" followed. Their daughter proved to be a bright little girl, and they lived their time with her fully in the present, without thinking of sad things that the future might bring. Once it became clear that she was going to be mentally normal, of course there *were* times when they were "awash with relief," but it is clear that they would have coped beautifully with mental retardation if that was to be their daughter's fate.

Their daughter lived to be nine years old. On her last night Jeanie rode with her in the ambulance to the hospital. Once there, a young doctor asked Jeanie if she "needed anything." She refused. "Sedatives are not a way to live," she told me. "You don't run away; you face a situation and deal with it." Watching his wife absorb the news of their child's death, Leonard must surely have been sustained by the sight. "What I've always found most admirable in Jeanie," he said, "is her strength in the face of adversity." It was a strength upon which he could draw.

They handled their child's death well. "We handled that better than other things," Jeanie said, "because that was final, decisive. It couldn't be changed." The death produced no quarrels or distance between the two of them; there were tears and grief but no angry words or withdrawal—important testimony to the strength of their bond. The sheer, unrelenting *stress* (far too mild a term) of a death in the family can create tension between even the happiest of spouses, as we will see later on. Today, nearly twenty years later, they considered themselves "recovered." "We can talk about it now and not feel sadness," Jeanie told me, though Leonard added, "I still miss her an awful lot."

They, too, sounded the theme I heard first from the Junipers. "We don't need to punish ourselves," Leonard said. For the Hollingses, as for the Junipers, this was an important principle:

• **Self-forgiveness is an essential element in coming to terms with family tragedy.**

The Refusal to Blame

The capacity to forgive oneself was essential, too, when a parent tragically did bear some responsibility for the loss of a child—perhaps even more essential. Though it is wrong to draw comparisons among people's private tragedies, to try to rank pain on some abstract scale of ascending anguish, for me, the very saddest story was that of Mary and Lou Hawkins. Thirty-some years ago, Mary, sick with a head cold and home alone with a two-year-old and a new baby, put her older son, Tommy, in his crib for a nap. He awoke two hours later in convulsions.

She rushed him to the hospital, and the family began its anguished vigil. Tommy, they discovered, a child who "never put anything into his mouth," had slipped into his parents' bedroom and swallowed an entire bottle of antihistamines. The brain damage was irreversible. Tommy was left with a mental age of two; he would never learn to speak. There was a period, early on, when Mary and Lou held out a desperate hope that he might somehow improve: they were encouraged in this by the fact that when he had awakened in the hospital he had spoken a few words. Their doctor found this promising.

But those words were to be his last. Caring for him after the accident became an unceasing nightmare because his difficulties went well beyond simple mental retardation. The trauma to the brain left him enormously hyperactive; he had to be watched and restrained every second that he was awake. At home he was so destructive they were forced to nail their furniture to the wall. Their ordeal would never end; recently Tommy had escaped from the county home where he lived and was lost in metropolitan Chicago for several days, a grown man incapable of speaking or identifying himself to the authorities his parents hoped desperately would find him. Now in their sixties, they worry what will happen to him when they die.

Mary and Lou suffered indescribable guilt. The responsibility for their son's terrible accident, they knew, was ultimately their own. This was an ironic case of a double failure, the kind of double failure a couple can have when both parents are present in the home. Together Mary and Lou had made a strict rule that their bedroom door was to be locked at all times; it was only because of this rule that Mary had left her cold medicine within reach of a little one. But someone, very likely Lou on his way out to work, had left the door unlocked. Mary went about her day assuming the door was safely locked; Lou went off to work assuming all harmful substances were out of reach. Neither double-checked, because each trusted the other to remember the rules. The terrible irony is that Tommy's accident might never have occurred if either Mary or Lou had been a single parent—if only one person had been in a position of ultimate responsibility, not two.

Neither has ever fully recovered from the loss. Given Tommy's condition, Mary said simply, "It would have been better if he had died." "He would have been the tennis player and the runner," his father said. "He was Lou's son," Mary told me. "He was an easy baby. We took him everywhere. After the accident I don't think Lou smiled for several years."

Although this tragedy will be with them for the rest of their lives—"You never recover," said Mary—they have coped. Tommy's accident, they said, made them need each other more. Both were well aware that this might not have been the case; they were once friends with a couple whose marriage had been destroyed by the birth of a mentally retarded child. Lou said that he believed the loss of a child affected the mother more, and that because of this, once Tommy was lost to them, he could never, ever have left Mary alone with that pain. He did not abandon his wife in any way either emotionally or in terms of the sheer physical work involved in caring for a brain-damaged child. "He pitched in and did whatever housework was necessary," said Mary. Horrifyingly, their suffering did not end with Tommy's accident; some twenty years later they were to lose their second son in a freak bus accident. Only two of their four boys were now alive and well. "I don't think a day ever goes by that we don't think about all of the kids," said Lou.

Like the Junipers, they had found the capacity to go on only by searching out some way to forgive themselves. Together, the two reached out to the world for help. Mary saw several therapists (one of whom destructively "churned up" some terrible feelings toward her mother) and, when these efforts at healing proved unsuccessful, Lou finally found an answer in the form of a popular book on love and marriage. Never a man to express his feelings openly, he nevertheless purchased the book and brought it home to his wife. She was so moved by what it had to say that the two of them took a seminar given by the author. His thesis was simple, Mary said: "It was, Don't waste your time blaming anyone—not your parents, not your spouse, not yourself—just accept the situation and get on with it."

They took this wisdom deeply to heart, and they lived by it. Neither blamed the other for Tommy's accident. But the tone of their comments revealed more than a simple lack of blame; it was, rather, that each actively *refused* to blame the other. They knew that blame, after the fact, could only destroy. They would never recover, but they would live; they would love their two remaining sons, and see friends, and faithfully offer their volunteer services to their church. This was the best they could do with what life had brought them. Some small measure of self-forgiveness made that life possible.

When Tragedy Comes Between Wife and Husband

Sometimes tragedy did wound even a very happy marriage, for a time. Joanne and Scott Allman learned this sad fact in 1985, when their infant son was stillborn. Simply at the physical level, it was a horrendous experience. Joanne's medical treatment was terribly deficient; it took the nurse a full hour to attach the fetal monitor. The minister of her church arrived in the delivery room well before Joanne's doctor did, and she nearly bled to death.

Joanne, already the mother of one child, was profoundly traumatized by this loss. Though her church and pastor offered the one source of strength and comfort upon which she could draw, she found herself angrily questioning her faith. "I was literally hanging on to religion by a shoestring," she told me. "I would think, Oh, God, are You there? And if You are there, why did You let this happen?" It was a question she could not answer, a doubting that seared her soul whenever people, meaning well, would tell her that the stillbirth had been "God's will." The possibility that the death of an innocent child could be God's will nearly severed her from her faith for good.

Perhaps unavoidably, her faith in her husband had also been shaken. Tim had been born on March 28; on April 1 Scott began his new job as a communications specialist with a major corporation. He was overwhelmed by pressure at work and, in private, a doctor had diagnosed him as having cancer, a misdiagnosis as it ultimately turned out. He kept this news from Joanne, hoping to avoid adding to her grief. But the effect of his withholding such momentous information was to make her feel shut out of his life and thoughts altogether. "I felt I was suffering alone," she told me.

To make matters worse, Scott's way of coping with his infant son's death was to withdraw: if his wife was sobbing on their bed, literally prostrate with grief, he was stoically cleaning up the dinner plates, doing what needed to be done around the house. Joanne read his self-control as a lack of feeling—or worse. "He would be sad," she recalled, "and I would think he was angry." They grew distant.

Finally, three months after the stillbirth, Scott broke down and wept. Joanne needed to see this, and afterwards they were able to talk. Gradually, things improved between them: "That was when I really learned to *ask* him what he's feeling," Joanne said,—an insight that their marriage continues to benefit from to this day.

Still, Joanne's recovery was to be a long and tortuous road back. She grieved for four years. Like many other people who have successfully recovered from tragedy, she turned outward, looking outside herself and her marriage for help, trusting that help would be there. And it was. She found what she needed in a close friend who had lost two husbands to cancer. "She gave me tremendous support and advice," Joanne said. "I could tell her what I was thinking and have her say, 'That's normal.' She would tell me, 'Don't have the "shoulds"—do what you *need* to do.' " This last was crucial advice, because as time wore on and her grief did not abate Joanne found herself being continually urged to go back to work, to keep busy, to get on with her life. It was a constant litany from friends and family whose concern, while heartfelt, was only making matters worse.

She found help, too, from her minister. She would ask him, "How can I trust God again? How can I tell my son to trust God?"—questions of the most profound pain to the deeply religious person she had always been. For Joanne, such questions were tantamount to asking, "How can I go on?" Her faith, her fundamental sense that life can simply be *lived* from day to day, had been shattered. She could take nothing for granted, not even God's love, and to take nothing for granted is not to live at all. A "normal" life, the very sense that one is leading a normal life, depends upon being able to take things for granted: to take for granted that the sun will rise tomorrow and that we will, too, that our mates will be there, our jobs will be there, our children will be there. These are the simple elements of life that must seem solid and fixed in order for people to feel that all is well with God and the world.

Joanne had lost this sense; she had lost her faith. It was her minister who helped her find the way back. In her own words, Joanne had never had to work through the question of why, if God exists, so much pain and suffering is our lot in life. But her minister had given this paradox a great deal of thought. Talking Joanne through her crisis, he gently convinced her that while God does have the power to control events he does not always do so, that accidents—real accidents, not tragedies born of "God's will"—happen. He told her, too, that Satan and sin exist, that these are the twin sources of war and disease. And the Lord, he told her, could create good things from bad.

Joanne's minister was shepherding her through a crucial process of healing, a healing that every couple, every person who has faced tragedy, must undergo. He was helping her find her way to a more complex view of the world, toward a view that allowed for tragedy and yet still held out hope and belief in the value of life. He was telling her, in effect, that a baby can die, or a nine-year-old can die, or a two-year-old can drink cold medicine and awaken in convulsions, and there is still a *point*, a reason for living despite a senseless tragedy that makes life seem without value. This insight was particularly crucial to Joanne, whose mind did not easily accept contradiction. She is a woman of strong opinion, for whom black is black and white is white. After her baby's death, life was, for her, entirely black. "My minister would tell me you can have two fists, and both can be right," she told me. She struggled to absorb this lesson.

Their minister proved to be correct: good can be created from bad. Their baby's death ultimately brought Scott and Joanne closer; theirs was a very strong marriage when we spoke. "Before Tim's birth, we had never really had to share our feelings," Joanne said, "and we had never had to discuss religion." Eleven years into her marriage, Joanne so loved and respected her husband that she could not name even a minor flaw in his character. "I can't think of a time he's ever let me down," she said. "There's nothing about him that I accept, but don't like." She liked and admired every facet of her husband's character; their marriage, steeled by tragedy, had grown far beyond mutual acceptance to mutual devotion and esteem.

In confronting tragedy, happy couples followed this principle:

• **The strong couple finds a way to create good from bad, life from death.**

Joy Out of Sorrow

The capacity to create good from bad was most movingly obvious in the lives of Judy and Harry Jacobs, a suburban New York couple who lost a son to AIDS at age thirty-three. He had been a young man of extraordinary promise; a product designer, at thirty he had already had his work published in the magazine *GQ*. He was making his way in the world of New York fashion and design.

All this had come at a cost to his relationship with his parents, middle-class American Jews living out unglamorous lives centering on their synagogue and a set of old friends in the far suburbs. "Sam was a snob," his mother told me, without a trace of resentment, or guilt at speaking ill of the dead. "What he was, he was." As Sam moved into the world of high fashion, he grew ashamed of his parents, of his roots in the unsophisticated land of suburban America. A gap widened between parents and son.

Sam's illness brought the family back together. Judy and Harry had long known their son was gay; he had told them soon after graduating from college. "We were surprised," said his mother, remembering that time. "It hit us hard. But he's our son, and we treated him like a son. He knew that and appreciated it."

Thus it was not the diagnosis, with its revelation of a son's secret homosexuality, that brought parents and child together. It was the illness itself. His parents rallied behind him. Harry, long retired, moved in with Sam in order to nurse him; Judy, forced by her job to remain at home, drove into the city once a week. Thus began their final days together, days that erased the estrangement between the Manhattan life of the son and the Long Island life of the parents.

Everyone was supportive. Sam's friends stood by him, and the owner of the restaurant below Sam's apartment brought up dinner for Sam and his father every night. As time went by, Harry and Judy became part of Sam's small circle of friends: "They became our kids," Judy said. Before Sam got sick, Judy had known none of his friends; they had never been introduced. Now she was intimately involved in their lives. "I got completely immersed in the fashion world," said this middle-class suburban mother. "I know *all* the politics of who's hiring and who's firing." Some years after their son's death, this closeness remained. "We're very involved with our surrogate kids," Judy said with a mixture of pride and humor, "especially with who the girls are dating, and whether they're going to get married or not." In short, they now performed for their "new" children the standard functions middle-class, suburban parents perform for their real children: they worried about whether they would be happy.

Thus they had managed to make something happy and good out of a terrible loss; they had embraced life in the midst of death. Their friends openly admired their resolve and strength. Recently the Jacobses had given an enormous party for Harry's seventy-fifth birthday; everyone came to celebrate a long and good life.

As to how their loss has affected their marriage, both said that it had brought them closer together. They went through Sam's death together, and they mourned it together. Together, they set their hearts upon recovering. They, too, like all couples who had faced family tragedy, spontaneously brought up, without prompting, the issue of blame. These were, after all, people who had raised their children in the 1950s, a period when mothers were thought to be the source of all the problems their children might encounter in life: the "castrating mother" was a notion invented not by Sigmund Freud, but by the American ego psychologists who interpreted his work for parents and analysts this side of the Atlantic. The 1950s was the time, lest we forget, when the book *A Generation of Vipers*, Philip Wylie's damning account of American motherhood, became a best-seller.

A couple of Harry and Judy's generation, two people well schooled in the doctrine of parental omnipotence, could easily be swallowed alive by guilt. Whose fault is it that a son grows up to be gay; whose fault that a son has died of AIDS? Harry and Judy did not shy away from these questions; together they had confronted, and resolved, the issues. "No matter what you say," Judy offered, "it is a terrible blow finding out that your son is gay. You ask yourself, 'Why is my child gay? Did we do this to him?' " Judy went over this conundrum in her mind time and again, though she could not say how long it took her to come to the answer at which she ultimately arrived. "I finally decided that, no, being gay comes from within."

Perhaps, given the limitations of what science knows about genetics and inheritance, there can be no right answers to such questions now, as the twentieth century draws to a close. But within the emotional realm Judy's was the true answer. Very likely Sam would have said so himself; certainly he gave no indication that he saw his homosexuality as a deformation of character, or as the result of being raised by a Freudian monster. As a designer who traveled in the frequently homosexual circles of fashion and design, he was entirely comfortable in his world. As far as Sam was concerned, certainly, and his parents as well, his gayness "came from within."

Thus parents and son alike came to the same belief; they lived their lives without blame. Being able to feel sure in their hearts that they had been good parents, *knowing* they had been utterly devoted during their son's year-and-a-half-long illness, they could accept his death as an act of fate. Fate can be cruel and, knowing this, they could live on peacefully after they had laid their son's body to rest. It is entirely possible that Sam, too, met his death with a peace of mind he could not have had had his parents been riddled by guilt and shame. He knew himself as himself, not as the damaged product of his parents' failures. He did not die a victim of rejecting parents. He died instead a son whose parents were deeply proud of all he had accomplished in the few years given to him on this earth.

Saving a Life

If a strong marriage could pull two people through great loss, for Anne Klonski a strong marriage was literally the only thing keeping her alive. Anne emigrated to America from the British Isles with her widowed mother shortly after World War II. By the time she reached adolescence, her young head was filled with dreams of marriage to a wealthy American who would look like Elvis Presley. Instead she met Adam at North Hollywood High. He was not the man she had envisioned for herself; like her he was an émigré, from Poland, but unlike her he had not been "Westernized." His clothes, his manner —all were so foreign. Yet, from the first, their relationship seemed inevitable. Both had lost family members to the Holocaust; both recognized and understood something crucial and profound in the other's history. "It seemed as if we were destined to be together," she told me.

And so it was Adam, a solid and loving immigrant very different from the hard-driving young American men making their fortunes in postwar California, whom she married. Unlike Anne, Adam was not ambitious. Worse yet, Anne soon discovered that her new husband was a classic "couch potato": "When he's watching TV a bomb could explode," said Anne in a tone of long-standing exasperation, "and he wouldn't notice. He could watch twenty-four hours a day; he is totally addicted."

The marriage was off to a troubled start. "I dreamed of having the perfect American home with a swimming pool," she said. "I thought a husband and wife should work together to *build* something." But Adam was possessed of no such driving ambition; he wanted only to go to work and come home to relax. This difference in temperament caused them a great deal of strife during their early years together: Anne trying to change her husband, Adam stubbornly absorbed in his television viewing. A hard worker at his small factory job, he withdrew into silent resistance at home.

Gradually Anne came to accept the idea that she would have to be the one to make things happen. She was filled with plans. Having originally wanted to be an actress, she now set her sights on doing commercials; she began, too, to take her children to theatrical interviews; she planned to found a nursery school. With the postwar population boom under way, she had found a piece of property they could purchase and renovate for resale. It would have been an excellent investment: the asking price for the house she found in West Los Angeles, today some of the highest-priced real estate in the world, was at that time a mere twenty thousand dollars. Her energy was boundless, and her dreams, some of them at least, might well have been realized.

Then, when she was twenty-eight, her life came to a halt. The victim of a terrible accident that she will not talk about even today, she awoke in the hospital, a quadriplegic for life. At that time, the younger of her two boys was only nine months old.

At first, the children stayed with Anne's mother; Adam simply could not manage them. His grief was too great. He would visit Anne faithfully in the hospital, then go home and immerse himself for hours on end in the happy images of a televised world.

Then slowly, heroically, he began to pull himself together. "I remember telling him in the hospital," Anne said, "that he would have to be mother and father both and he said, 'I can handle it.' "

Handle it he did. "The first years we were married," she told me, "Adam was a boy. He didn't grow up until after my accident." Now he metamorphosed into a profoundly responsible adult: breadwinner, father, mother, doctor, nurse, husband. Eighteen years after the accident, he still called his wife from work two or three times a day to check on her. He was her connection to life.

That life had not been a happy one, although it had been a triumph of the spirit for both. The children were grown and were appealing, healthy young adults. Both were attending college, something neither of their parents did. Their childhood had been unbearably painful for Anne, who could not even wipe her baby's runny nose. "I felt like an outsider," she said, describing herself as a young mother unable to do anything at all for her children, having to watch as her husband fed, bathed, and raised them.

Adam had stayed by his wife, though her utter dependence upon him had been a terrible thing for her to bear. She feared, always, that in spite of all his evident devotion to her, one day he would walk out. They quarreled frequently, and each argument struck a primal fear of abandonment in her heart. All of their quarrels now flowed from her terrible handicap; invariably they revolved around the routine household tasks that only one of them was capable of performing. Their running argument concerned when and how things would get done: Anne would see something lying on the floor that could cause an accident and would insist that Adam pick it up, now rather than later. Adam's preference was invariably to opt for later. He had worked hard all day; he wanted to sit in his chair and relax in front of the television set. And there was Anne, helpless in her wheelchair, nagging.

Their marriage was so strong that they had managed to work around even such daily reminders of the wreckage her accident left behind. For his part, Adam had come simply to accede to his wife's wishes that things be picked up around the house, and he had told his two sons that "it's easier just to do it than to argue about it." For her part, Anne, each day, carefully organized in her mind exactly *what* needed to be done *before* her husband settled in for the evening. She took care to phrase these requests tactfully: "Dear, before you get involved [in your television programs] could you just . . ."

For all her fears, she understood that Adam is devoted to her. He had traveled throughout the world with her, searching for cures; together they had tried everything. She had tried healers, hypnotists, spiritualists. Adam was ever hopeful. Recently when she found an article on electrical implants for the spines of the paralyzed he told her they must write away for more information at once.

The Klonskis' marriage was whole; theirs was a highly sexual involvement from the very beginning, and remained so after the accident. "Adam is a very sexually active man," Anne said, smiling. "He could make love twenty times a day. And I've never had a headache."

Although she could not feel any sensation physically, she desired her husband emotionally. Sometimes she would wake him in the middle of the night and ask whether he was too tired. "Not for that" was his invariable response. He is a romantic man; the day of our interview, Anne told me later, he came home from work bearing a pot of red tulips for his wife.

This marriage, even under the constant stress of Anne's handicap, was strong and vital. More than this, it was lifesaving. "I used to think about suicide a lot more," Anne said. "But I don't think about it very much anymore because I'm afraid he would do it, too. He always tells me that if I go, he's going to go, too." Certain that he meant it, Anne had resisted the temptation to end her life. This was a marriage that had held its partners' very lives intact.

People cope, and their marriages help them to cope. If time heals all wounds, blessed are those for whom that healing will be shaped by a strong marriage. Couples shored each other up; together husbands and wives made the essential decision to move forward. Beloved by their mates, married people found what they needed from within, and from each other. They rose to life's fiercest challenges, and were changed forever in the process.

But if they were able to turn to each other, they just as importantly were able to turn outward as well. Early on in the course of my interviews I began to understand how fundamentally trusting happily married people are; I saw, too, that their trust was a function not only of their marriages but also of their basic personalities and outlooks. Happily married people trust each other, and they tend to trust the outside world as well. I was struck by how firmly most couples— perhaps especially couples who had survived a family tragedy— believed that help was to be had for the asking. All revealed a fundamental faith in life, or in God, or in, simply, other people, friends, family, or therapists; all believed that if they were so bowed by troubles they could not stand on their own, there was someone or something outside their homes that would help. This quality endowed their marriages with the blessings of the self-fulfilled prophecy; seeking help, they found it.

Almost every happy couple with whom I spoke, whether they had ever encountered serious problems or not, told me the same thing:

• **When they need help, happy couples instinctively assume help is available, and they keep looking until they find it.**

Often, the fates met them halfway. Mary and Lou Hawkins, parents of one younger son and an older child so brain damaged that they were forced to nail furniture to the walls, agonized over the decision of whether to have a third child. They wanted a normal sibling for their second son, who, practically from birth, had been completely absorbed in the need to care for his damaged brother: "Ta-ta c'ying," he would say in his little baby voice. "Ta-ta need Joey." They wanted a normal child for Joey, and they wanted, for themselves, to "dilute the grief."

The prospect of a third child should have been, was—in fact—impossible. There was no money for household help, and Tommy's needs already required more than full-time care from his mother and tiny brother. But finally they decided just to do it; something would happen, they told themselves, to make things all right.

Something did. Mary was eight months pregnant when, with no warning, Lou was called by a company in Chicago. They wanted to hire him, and they would raise his current salary by 50 percent. It was the money they so desperately needed to support a terribly handicapped child. Mary gave birth to her third son and, eventually, to a fourth. "We always wanted four sons," Mary said. Fate intervened to ease their way.

Fate, and the bond they had forged together. The marriage that survives tragedy, the happy marriage, is the marriage in which two people unite in sorrow as well as in joy. In the best of marriages, partners did not feel they were suffering "alone." Or, if they did feel that way, they ultimately came to understand that their pain was shared. For better, for worse; for richer, for poorer; in sickness and in health; happily married people lived life together.

7

C

Sex:
Cinderella and
Her Prince

Sex and romance proved to be far more important to the good marriage than even many long- and happily married couples understood. Like most of us, they had absorbed the conventional wisdom concerning the place of sex in marriage: sex, we are told, is not what the good marriage is "about." The good marriage, so it is said, rests upon the cherished qualities of friendship, respect, commitment: qualities that endure when passion wanes. Indeed, many couples said just this when asked what role sexuality played in their relationships. Friendship is more important than sex, they told me.

Nonetheless, scratch the surface calm of these marriages and frequently a strong and vibrant sexuality, a clear sexual *chemistry*, soon revealed itself. Certainly many, perhaps most, of these happy marriages began with a strong sexual attraction even if it had calmed over the years:

"It was pure lust," said one wife of twenty years.

"He had a very sexy voice," another said, describing her first impression of the man she would marry.

"I thought he was too good-looking to go out with me, but he did have a pretty large nose so maybe there was a chance."

"Were we in love? It was more like being in heat."

The men were even more frankly sexual:

"She met all the criteria," one said slyly, casting his wife a sidelong look that stopped just short of a leer. "Good-looking, long legs, blond hair—you know how that goes."

Contrary to the popular belief concerning love and marriage, this initial vibrant sexual attraction does not fade away into the dimly recollected prehistory of a marriage, but rather forms a sexual base supporting the complex marital and familial relationship that sprouts up around it. A large number of happy marriages, perhaps the majority, are founded on a deeply sexual love. Sexual connection permeates—frequently almost unnoticed—the friendship and working partnership that develop as time wears on.

We can think here of Larry Weissberg's shining vision of his wife, Jane, as "America's most beautiful woman." Certainly, to see one's wife as America's most beautiful woman is to see her sexually; it is to see her as *woman* first and always. Larry and Jane's love for each other was fundamentally sexual, whatever the frequency and intensity of their sexual encounters. Even if the two were not spending lost weekends in bed, they'd shared an enduring sexual chemistry, a chemistry that had been a strong force binding them together through the years.

Thus the first and most basic principle governing sex and marriage is this:

• **Most happy marriages are held together by a powerful and enduring sexual bond—even when partners do not fully realize it.**

In the Beginning

My first hint of the vastly underrated importance of sexuality to marriage came from happily married couples' descriptions of their courtships. Whatever their current level of sexual involvement, the majority of couples (though by no means all) could look back upon very lusty early days indeed. Many told me forthrightly that they had experienced love at first sight—and love at first sight is invariably about sex, not about companionship. People do not "fall" into "friendship" at first sight; they fall into the turbulent currents of desire.

Such, we recall, was Sarah Cohen's experience. Sarah had only to set eyes upon her future husband in order to know that he was *the one*. Obviously, to know that you are going to marry a man with whom you have not yet spoken (and whom you have mistaken for a lowly undergraduate!) is to judge his suitability almost entirely upon sexual grounds: Sarah knew she was going to marry Norman because she knew she was going to like being in bed with him—though this was not how she put it to herself at the time. In fact, she did like going to bed with him very much; Sarah and Norman were one of the couples whose sex life had remained liveliest over the years—a fact Norman attributed to a physiological match between the two of them. As a physician, Norman believed that sexual "chemistry" involved a special connection between two people that was based in biology as much as psychology.

Such tales were common. A couple destined to love each other would meet, and one or the other would say to himself, "This is the *one!*"

On rarer occasions both partners experienced this happy flash of recognition. When Maggie and Chuck Green, ages nineteen and twenty-seven, met on a blind date, both knew at once. They first set eyes upon each other on a Saturday night, and on Monday Chuck told a friend that he had found the woman he was going to marry. Maggie felt the same way, writing a letter home to her family telling them that Chuck was the "right kind." After that, Maggie said, "It was definitely a whirlwind courtship. There was no question in either of our minds." They met in July and were engaged by the end of October, married in December. Twenty-three years and two children later, their intuition had proved true. They were in love still.

Thus happy endings do happen in real life. These stories, suffused with the glow of wishes come true, were a delight to hear. Perhaps my favorite came from Debra Lyon-Jones. Ever the forthright and gruff young woman, Debra, in the midst of her second date with Lucas, declared herself before a group of his friends. Rising from her seat she fixed her eye upon him and, characteristically blunt, spoke her mind: "I just have one thing to tell you," she said. "I'm madly and passionately in love with you." Then she turned on her heel and sped out of the room, mortified by her outburst.

"I was left with a mouthful of Cheez Doodles," Lucas said.

Paul and Natascha Stein's tale of love at first sight is the stuff of which movies are made: only teenagers—she fourteen, he nineteen—when they met in Germany during World War II, they braved severe repercussions at the hands of Hitler's secret police, the SS, in order to join their fates. As the son of a Jewish mother and a Christian father, Paul was legally proscribed from becoming involved with Natascha, a Dutch national living with her parents in Germany. But they were too young to understand how dangerous the adult world of war around them was, and too powerfully drawn to each other to pay heed to the warnings of their elders.

The details of their first meeting were classically comic in spite of the danger to both. Paul, at nineteen renowned in his circle as quite the authority on women, was walking down the street with a friend who wanted to meet a girl. How should he go about it? the friend asked Paul. "It's easy," Paul answered, pointing to a girl both could see standing in a building nearby, framed by a second-story window. "You see that blond girl? I'll introduce you." It was Natascha.

Full of bluster, Paul rang the bell insistently until Natascha finally came downstairs to find out who this persistent boy was. Seeing her at the door, Paul was smitten. All thought of instructing his friend in the manly art of impressing girls evaporated as Paul now claimed Natascha for his own. On their first night together he declared himself: "You are my dream girl," he told the astonished Natascha, "and I will marry you." It was as much boast as statement of intent; "I don't know if I meant it or not," Paul says today.

"I didn't take him seriously," Natascha said, laughing, but she was smitten nevertheless. They were young and in love.

These were the boldest tales, and not surprisingly they took place in the lives of the boldest tellers. As one would expect, the more forceful the personality, the more vivid the courtship. Quieter personalities came together in quieter ways, as was the case with Brenda and Gary Mazursky. In their fifties now, they had passed twenty-five years in the classic "laid-back" mode of Southern California life prior to the roaring '80s: "I just kind of meander through life," Gary told me, trying to describe his essential nature. "I don't have strong feelings." As to whether his marriage is happy, he observed, "Most of the time I don't think about it. Our life seems very natural." Brenda, equally calm in the face of life's twists and turns, added that, to her, their marriage "seems like a strange, happy accident." Neither was an aggressive sort; both liked to explore, to learn, to try new experiences (such as volunteering for an interview with a total stranger) without feeling any great drive to stamp these experiences with the imprint of their own personalities. Both were quiet, observant, and witty people.

When they met, Brenda said, it was not a case of impassioned love at first sight, although, as Gary told his wife of nearly thirty years, "I think I liked you right away." The fact that his earliest feelings for her left no abiding impression upon either of them was characteristic. These two were simply not the swept-away *sort*; they were temperamentally pitched in a lower key. It was a difference of which both were well aware. "We had a strange romance for today," said Brenda. "We never went together, and we always dated other people, too"— a state of affairs entirely unproblematic for either. Love progressed in its own time. They saw each other steadily, Gary bringing a little present along to begin each evening. These offerings were mildly humorous, typically low-key; Gary recalled once presenting his future wife with a toy dinosaur.

Brenda was content. "A friend of mine told me," she remembered, " 'He's in love with you, but he's shy. It will be another year before he asks you to marry him.' " The friend proved to be exactly right. When Gary proposed ten months later, Brenda accepted, and their introduction to married life turned out to be as smooth and uneventful as the serene courtship that had gone before.

Brenda and Gary were best friends. They shared all of their interests and decisions; each was the other's first and favorite person in the world. How sexually involved they were was another question—a topic about which they, like many couples, remained reserved. Because both were calm by nature, they seemed, on the surface, to belong more to the companionate branch of marriage than to the vital couples of Cuber and Harroff's survey. To the outsider, at least, they looked to be more friends than lovers.

Nonetheless, an enduring chemistry clearly existed between the two. Explaining what held them together, Brenda said, "I think he's funny, and he thinks I'm pretty, and that's very powerful." Brenda *was* pretty; at fifty she had smooth skin, a trim figure, and an arresting streak of slate gray hair down one side of her dark pageboy. She was married to a man who had thought her pretty for nearly a quarter of a century, and *that* is sexual attraction however temperate their sex life may have been in reality. For her part, Brenda so highly prized humor that she believed it "will keep the world around," an attitude that endowed her husband with powerful attributes indeed. He was powerful, she was pretty: such are the classic poles of heterosexual romance. Theirs was not a simple friendship; it was not the kind of caring platonic relationship we create with cherished friends of the same sex. Instead, theirs was a friendship suffused with sexual attraction, a friendship whose very terms were defined by sexual difference. However mild-mannered they might (or might not) have been between the covers, their way of *seeing* each other, their way of loving, was fundamentally sexual.

The concept of an enduring sexual chemistry, of a fundamental sexual bond, proved to be very real indeed, real and alive among even the most low-key of couples. Intriguingly this could remain true even when a couple had all but shut down sexually. One wife, lacking any conscious sexual feelings for her husband during the two-year period following the birth of their first child, told me that throughout this time she had had almost nightly erotic sexual dreams—all featuring her husband. She had discovered for herself the reality of a sexual *bond* that transcends the actual day-to-day facts of any given couple's physical existence—a sexual bond that holds firm even when eroticism has vanished for the time being. A basic principle emerged from this wife's testimony, as from the experiences of so many others:

- **Happily married couples are more than friends. They are <u>mates</u>.**

The Bond

Some couples, of course, were well aware of the importance of sex and sexuality to their relationships. These couples offered a sensible explanation for other people's tendency to downplay marital sexuality:

Married couples, they said, simply took sex for granted. "If we weren't having sex," one wife said to me, "that would be a crisis. But since we are, we don't think about it." In other words, the reason sex seems less significant than friendship to the happy marriage is that in the happy marriage a couple's sex life is usually going well. Because married people spend only a small portion of their time together making love, as compared with the many hours they spend functioning as companions, sex seems only a minor aspect of their relationship. But in fact the sexual connection is fundamental to their friendship. As Margaret Hyde told me, "I feel that when the sex is gone the relationship is gone. And there have been periods for us when it was gone." Having weathered her husband's heroin addiction and a bankruptcy, she was in a position to know.

Thus the relationship of sex to marriage is the opposite of what people often believe it to be. While many of us think of sex and sexuality as an active danger to a long-term relationship, as the overpowering lure into infidelity and divorce, reality is far more complicated than this. While our sexual natures can lead us astray, within the happy marriage those very same drives and impulses also act as a major force operating *for stability*.

Sexuality holds couples together over the years because, in the happy marriage, the psychological phenomenon we know as romantic idealization does not end with courtship. In happy marriages idealization simply is not a passing phase; it is not the honeymoon period that mature mates are thought to grow out of. It is, rather, an abiding and fundamental aspect of a couple's bond. And because of this ongoing process of idealization, couples do not register the changes taking place in each other's bodies all that keenly. That first, radiant impression of each other lives on undimmed by time; sixty-year-old men spoke of their aging wives as if they were still seeing them for the first time, home from school for Christmas. My favorite anecdote along these lines came from a wife who said that during her first pregnancy her husband once told her in all seriousness that he found an actress they were watching on television unattractive because her stomach was "too flat." Such is the power of idealization; beauty truly does lie in the eye of the beholder.

On the other hand, while happy couples continued to idealize each other throughout life, their love was not blind. At the same time that they spoke of each other in glowing terms they were also quite realistic in their perceptions of each other. I was consistently struck by how remarkably accurate their perceptions were, particularly in those cases where I was not immediately convinced by one spouse's characterization of the other. I particularly recall one husband who seemed, to me, stiff, formal, and forbidding. When his wife, trying to explain a particular passage in their marriage, said to me, "Well, you know, Howard is a total sweetheart," I was utterly nonplussed. I certainly did not feel myself to be seated in the presence of a sweetheart. What could she possibly mean?

And so I was impressed when, at the end of our interview, Howard seemed suddenly to come to life. He began to ask me about my work, to talk about his own work, to speak animatedly about his volunteer activities at the church—and he was indeed, just as his wife had said, an *absolute sweetheart*. The colloquialism fit him perfectly; it was an entirely realistic perception. Other people saw him in the same way; when I interviewed another long-married woman friend of theirs, she remarked to me as we began, "Isn't Howard the sweetest man?"

It is significant that not once did I come away with a drastically different impression of a mate than the one held by his or her spouse. Happily married couples see each other as the world sees them. But, at the same time, happy couples also varnish the image: they see each other not only as they *are*, but as they want and hope to be, as they are daily *trying* to be. The fundamental principle governing the happy marriage is this:

- **Happily married couples see each other's <u>best</u> selves.**

This "rosy realism," I found, was characteristic of the thriving marriage. Psychologists speak of the capacity to "mirror," to reflect back an image of the other. When we like people, we like them in part because we see ourselves, our *best* selves, in their eyes. We talk to them and their responses indicate that they are *getting it*, that they are seeing us as we see ourselves. They believe us; they believe *in* us. Such mirroring is essential to identity.

This is what happy couples do for each other. They reflect back a real but flattering image of their mates. If Jane Weissberg was not America's most beautiful woman, realistically speaking, she was nevertheless a sexy and attractive woman—and her husband mirrored this truth back to her. Jane saw herself as dynamic, ambitious, highly intelligent; Larry reflected this image back; and she was confirmed in her sense of herself. It is here that "realism" and "idealization" meet. Realistically Jane *was* dynamic, ambitious, highly intelligent, and yet, as she herself was well aware, others could find her difficult. As a high-level administrator in a private college, she waged numerous battles in defense of her projects. Clearly, she was a prickly character. "Larry is a nicer person than I am," she said. "If I get mad at you, I'll call you a son of a bitch." Her husband understood that other people did not always share his admiration for his wife. "I think she's terrific," he said, adding diplomatically that "Other people may think she's terrific but maybe get irritated with her, too." He knew she could rub people the wrong way, but she does not rub *him* the wrong way; he admired her, pure and simple. (Interestingly, Larry reported that he *could* find these same qualities irritating in Jane's mother, whom he also admired. He was entirely cognizant of what it was about mother and daughter that got under the skin of other people.) Thus Larry reflected back to his wife her best self, the best possible interpretation of her behavior, and in doing so he was realist and idealist at once.

This long-term process of idealization was the alchemy that allowed passion to endure. When couples were truly lucky in love, they were able to sustain romantic perceptions of each other for an entire lifetime. It is not so difficult to see why sexual attraction within the happy marriage can last: there is very little reason for it *not* to. When two people who are strongly attracted to each other turn out also to be good for each other, the sexual bond is daily reinforced by each partner's flattering vision of the other. Being married to a spouse who sees you as you want to be seen is a highly effective aphrodisiac. And the sexual attachment lasts.

Chemistry

What precisely makes a good sexual match between two people remains a mystery—but it is a safe assumption that biology plays a major role. Judging by the testimony of happily married couples, sexual chemistry is a very real and vital factor in a couple's attraction. Jack Lund offered one of the more striking descriptions of his own primal attraction to his mate. At age forty-five he still vividly recalled his first contact with his wife of twenty-three years, Lisa. They were in junior high school, practicing for their graduation ceremony. Because Jack belonged to the popular crowd and Lisa did not, the two had never really spoken. But on this day, finding himself positioned directly behind Lisa on the risers, he tickled the back of her neck. The effect was immediate, and sharp. He felt himself shot through with a charge he can only describe as electric. Lisa, too, felt the current.

Nothing more passed between the two until some years into high school, but there it was, a chemistry. It is there yet today: "I still get turned on when I see my wife take off her clothes," Jack said. While the two had gone through more- and less-sexual periods together, that ineffable chemistry, that indefinable basis for attraction, always remained. More importantly, their enduring sexual connection had seen them through what Lisa called their "divorce times"—two periods during which their marriage very nearly came to an end.

Their first crisis came to a head when they had been married for only a year and a half. Still in their early twenties, neither had given much thought to what they wanted their marriage to be, and Jack quickly settled into his own father's regimen: going to work by day, coming home by night to put his feet up and read the newspaper. The problem with this for Lisa was that she, too, was working full-time at her own job. While Jack read the paper she was expected to begin her second shift at home, fixing dinner, cleaning the house, doing the laundry. She found this arrangement infuriating, but she had to reach the point of packing her things to leave in order finally to "wake him up."

Their second crisis arrived at the ten-year mark. For years they had had difficulties over the classic issue of feelings: Jack, an optimist by nature, never expressed his; Lisa, pessimistic and introspective, characteristically examined hers in detail. "He thought I was self-indulgent," Lisa told me, "and I thought he was out of touch." "I was sick of her dilly-dally shit," Jack added humorously. Adding to the tensions was the fact that neither was on track professionally. Having gone to art school in England, Jack had returned to America in a somewhat aimless frame of mind, spending a few years on the margins of the film industry, then a few years doing carpentry. He was drifting. Lisa, too, had yet to "find herself" in the world of work. They lived in a small house in Venice, California, both still part of the hippie beach culture of the day, and they argued constantly.

Things grew so bad that finally Jack left. But he could not stay away. "There is some primordial thing that draws us back together," he said, which he believed was highly sexual. Both acknowledged that they were sexually bonded, mated. In spite of how thoroughly at odds they were by then, his frame of mind was: "I'm not going to let this end."

Lisa insisted on therapy for both of them—something he had always resisted—as a condition for getting back together. Now Jack agreed. Happily, the therapy worked: "It made the second half of our marriage twice as good as the first," Jack told me. Their sessions with a couples' counselor radically changed their communication patterns. It was Lisa and Jack, in fact, who told me that he was now much better at discussing feelings than she. But for all the growth they experienced in the course of therapy, it was the *frisson* Jack felt in eighth grade when he touched the back of her neck that ultimately held them together. Their basic and enduring sexual chemistry gave them the motivation to *try*—the motivation to work out their problems even after a decade of conflict.

When I met them they were the happily married parents of an eight-year-old boy. Both had found their way professionally as well, although they would always be children of the 1960s at heart. Lisa was now a therapist herself, and Jack was a successful television director. Even so, he said he would still prefer to be a "beach bum" if he could collect a salary just for hanging out! These were not the fast-track "young professionals" of an American Express commercial; they were a long-term couple who, together, had come a long way. For Jack and Lisa the sense of being sexually mated had helped them stay together long enough to learn how to be happily mated emotionally as well.

The Neurochemistry of Desire

Given the staying power of the sexual bond, why do affairs occur so frequently? The answer lies, in part, in the biochemistry of the brain. In one of the best books on the subject, *The Chemistry of Love*, Michael R. Liebowitz, M.D., explains that the experience of newly falling in love is directly analogous to the experience of ingesting powerful mood-altering drugs such as cocaine or amphetamines. The "thrill" of a new love wears off for precisely the same reason that the thrill of a stimulant drug wears off: the brain develops chemical tolerance. Just as the same amount of cocaine cannot continue to produce the same high, the same amount of exposure to one's husband or wife will eventually yield lower levels of excitement. The fever pitch of desire that characterizes a new relationship, those weeks and months during which just brushing each other's hand over the dinner table can provoke an almost intolerable arousal, inevitably calms. As Dr. Liebowitz writes, "Novelty means something new, something which is not familiar, something to which one's brain has not become tolerant. . . . I don't think it is an accident that the great romances of literature, such as Romeo and Juliet, or Cathy and Heathcliff, occur between people who, for one reason or another, don't have a chance to stay together. Thus their brain pleasure centers have not had time to get used to, and therefore less excited by, having the other person around."

Seeing erotic love as a chemical reaction also explains why vacations can work the magic that they do. It is a fundamental physiological reality that the brain responds to *changes* in levels of chemicals more than to absolute quantities. Vacations supply the necessary change in brain chemistry that pumps up our responsive system, allowing us to take second honeymoons. In a long-term relationship passion ebbs and flows, with periods of relative inactivity allowing the brain to regain its sensitivity to a lifelong partner. A charged period can then follow. In other words, as biological beings we may require changing levels of sexual involvement over the years in order to recapture the highs; we may need periods of sexual disengagement to spark periods of intense sexual involvement. The fact that we require a romantic weekend away from home in order to respond to a spouse whereas we need only one charged look across a darkened room in order to respond to a stranger does not mean (necessarily) that we are any the less sexually involved with our mates. It means instead that we have been *very* involved with our mates, so much so that our brains have developed tolerance. What we are responding to in the stranger across the room is the sheer chemical jolt of novelty.

Thus for most of us a thirty-year marriage would feel entirely different from a six-week love affair, but it is not correct to conclude from this that marriage is about friendship while love affairs are about sex. Marriage and love affairs both are founded upon a basic and powerful sexual attraction, the essential tendency of which is to persist. The fact that in the day-to-day married sex may be less fevered than it was at the beginning of a couple's courtship is no indication that the fundamental attraction has waned. It is, rather, an indication that that attraction has been fully *satisfied* by daily contact.

The biochemical perspective also helps to clear up one further misconception that we as a culture harbor concerning the relationship of friendship to sexuality. What few of us understand is that friendship, like sex, is *also* a "chemical" state. Dr. Liebowitz offers evidence that the friendship aspect of marriage is akin to the powerful effect of narcotic drugs such as heroin, opium, and morphine. Experiments with animals reveal that puppies and other young animals who have taken a narcotic drug cry far less when removed from their mothers than do puppies who have not been medicated. The drugged puppies are calmer because narcotics suppress the activity of the locus ceruleus, an area of the brain involved in anxiety. Dr. Liebowitz speculates that a stable marriage may also suppress the locus ceruleus, resulting in much the same psychological effects as a narcotic drug.

Biochemically speaking, Dr. Liebowitz links passion to stimulant drugs, long-term friendship and security to narcotics. *Both* states are biochemically based; *both* states involve what we think of as "chemistry." This is why it is incorrect to laud friendship as a calm and rational mental state while condemning erotic love as irrationally physical, emotional, biological. There is no escaping biology, and we are ill-advised to try.

Thus we cannot solve the problem of infidelity and divorce by urging unmarried people to select their mates rationally rather than romantically. The principle guiding one and all is this:

- **Happy long-term relationships are based in a fundamental chemical <u>match</u>.**

This match may, of course, list more toward the "narcotic" side of the equation or more toward the "stimulant" side, depending upon the individual makeup of the partners involved. Thus there are couples who are best satisfied with a deep friendship and little else, while others lead lives filled with passion and drama. However, these two groups fall at extremes of the spectrum. Most of us are responsive to both forms of stimulation, and thus do best to marry a person who can give us both—excitement *and* calm. It simply will not do to urge a normally sexed human being to forget about sex if he or she wishes to create a stable marriage.

When you consider the lives of the real people who truly have created happy marriages, you find that in the beginning passion often holds sway. Research shows that sexual attraction figures importantly in the choice of mate. In one landmark study, college students were randomly matched on blind dates, then asked whether they would like to see their assigned partner again. Psychologist Elaine Walster and her colleagues had thought that personality and intelligence would decide the matter. But they did not. For men and women both the blind date's physical attractiveness was the most important consideration. First and foremost students wanted to date people they found sexually attractive.

The importance of sheer physical attraction is revealed by another set of studies described by Jessie Bernard in her classic work of 1978, *The Future of Marriage*. Bernard reports that in fact men marry the same girl they date: even during the repressive heyday of the 1950s, married women were in fact leading far less "virtuous" lives than their unmarried sisters. Bernard's survey of the literature shows that married women of that period and earlier had engaged in far more "unconventional heterosexual activities" than had the never-married, and that *unmarried* women showed less "antisocial behavior" and were more "scrupulous about family obligations" than were the married ones. In other words, the stereotype of the worthy spinster aunt dedicated to family and community service proved to be true. It was the altogether less righteous girls who were actually getting married and having children. Apparently, the "bad girl" held (and still holds) a very strong appeal for the eligible bachelor.

Thus stable marriages are based upon a rich and complex chemistry encompassing passion and security both. For most marriages the security element will *seem* the more dominant from day to day, but the sexual attachment is still there, waiting for the necessary spark to ignite the flame once more.

Passion and Pain

Of course, there do exist those marriages in which passion dominates for many years. But because of the way we are wired, typically a couple must undergo a great deal of tumult in order to lead a daily life shot through with longing and desire. Biochemically speaking, such couples require tumult in order to produce the changes in neurochemical levels necessary to the creation of intensely passionate emotion. When a couple swings wildly between rage and reconciliation, their brain chemistry swings, too. Emotions run high; desire burns bright.

Holly Lawson's marriage was a classic case of marital passion sustained through pain. Married to a chronically unfaithful and hard-driving businessman, Holly spent many years locked inside a passionate cycle of terrible fights followed by torrid lovemaking. The payoff for their inability to "settle down" into a calm and supportive dailiness was a terrific sex life. Throughout those years Holly lived in a state of constant emotional danger, placing frantic 3 A.M. calls to her philandering husband on his frequent business trips out of town, getting no answer, fearing the worst, confronting him when he returned. Denial, battle, and passionate lovemaking would inevitably follow, after which she would convince herself that he would not do it again. On Monday she would be sobbing in her attorney's office, on Tuesday she would be momentarily calm. It was the stuff of high drama.

All of us have witnessed marriages of this kind, and most of us have experienced the (initial) thrill of a bad relationship. This is yet another reason many of us are so suspicious of sexuality. Obviously, a relationship such as Holly's would create a difficult environment in which to raise a family. Not surprisingly, Holly's own children, now grown, had a very strained relationship with their father—this in spite of the fact that Holly had done everything in her power to protect them from their parents' tumult. "I kept the kids out of it," she said. "There were no explosions in front of them."

Now, after twenty-four years of pain, Holly and her husband were finally happy, their marriage no longer wracked by repeated infidelities and ensuing battles. They had achieved this state largely through the sobering pause of a six-month separation followed by a highly effective period of couples' counseling. The combination proved powerful. Finally understanding, at the point of divorce, that they truly wanted to be with each other, they changed. Holly's husband at long last abandoned his affairs, and Holly began to see that he had his own complaints concerning their marriage. If she felt constantly betrayed, he felt just as constantly criticized. Seeing his side of things for the first time, she learned to be more gentle. The two had declared a truce.

The fact that their marriage had survived years of infidelity, pitched battles, and a lengthy separation speaks to the staying power of sexual attraction. Whatever the degree of pain Holly and her husband were able to inflict upon each other over the years, they *fit*. Undeniably, there was a way in which those years of fierce warring suited both: "We are both very passionate people," said Holly. "That is one of the main reasons we have stayed together." The deeply sexual match between the two kept the marriage alive in the face of the powerful forces working daily to tear them apart.

The Longest Honeymoon

How long can the "thrill" remain, unaided by the artificial stimulants of anger and fear? I spoke with only one couple, married for thirteen years and the parents of two girls, who were as passionately sexual as any two eighteen-year-olds—and, amazingly, who were not tormenting each other as a means of achieving this state! "I have a problem," Heather told me humorously. "I can't say no." While I was absorbing this revelation—unique to say the least among the long-married women with whom I spoke—she went on to add, "We're almost at the point where we can come just looking at each other." I had every reason to believe her: simply sitting with the two of them, one could see how sexually connected they were. Throughout the two-hour interview she and Patrick did not once lose physical contact. They sat on a small sofa together, Patrick slouched and resting his head naturally on Heather's shoulder. They were the most physically involved couple I encountered.

They owed their luck on this score, Heather thought, to a lovely quirk of her own chemistry. "I've always felt sexual," she told me. "I masturbated when I was very little, and I remember lying in the sun as a girl and feeling turned on." In short, she saw her sexuality as a fundamental aspect of her makeup; she was naturally able to form a sexual bond to her husband that time and familiarity could not wear down. Even the bearing of children had had no dampening effect.

Whatever the source of their remarkable longevity as impassioned lovers (and I suspect that Heather's explanation was correct), their intensely sexual connection was a major source of stability for their marriage—perhaps *the* major source. They had seen very hard times: difficult childhoods, money problems, Heather's alcoholism and clinical depression. Only thirty-two when I met them, they had already faced more adversity than some couples confront in a lifetime. Theirs were the kinds of problems that could destroy another couple's sex life. Having conquered her alcoholism, Heather, even then, was battling a depression so severe that she frequently could not climb out of bed in the morning. (Here, too, her story defied expectation in that one of the classic symptoms of depression is a loss of sexual desire. Her level of sexual interest in her husband had been completely unaffected by a depression that was incapacitating in every other respect.) Both freely acknowledged that their sexual attachment had helped to hold them together in the face of the many, many forces working to wrench them apart. For them, desire served as a source of strength.

Although I met several other couples who continued to lead quite lusty lives after many years together, these two were probably unique in the sheer intensity and frequency of their sexual involvement. For almost everyone else, the passion of the early months and years inevitably faded somewhat in intensity. Among the wives the record for sustaining the "thrill of romance" was Barbara Weinstein's seven-year-long honeymoon with her husband, Ron. When this period came to an end she was distraught. "For seven years, every time I heard his car in the driveway my heart went thump," she remembered. "Then one day he came in the door and my heart didn't thump and I thought my marriage was over."

It was a personal crisis for her. She had been married at twenty-three and had lived out her twenties in the blissful state of a dream come true. She was doing what she had been groomed—and in fact wanted very much—to do; she had made a happy marriage with a loving man who was a protector and provider. "Our marriage was almost an unreal relationship during our twenties," she told me, trying to capture that time in words. "Ron was my knight in shining armor. I had been socialized to get married. I didn't have to do that well in college because someone would come along and take care of me. So after we married I was perfectly happy to give up teaching to raise little kids." Small wonder her heart raced at night when her hero returned home.

Now, at age thirty, she was losing her young woman's capacity for starry-eyed bliss. And, as the romantic imagery began to fade, Barbara suffered. But for Barbara the passing of their heightened honeymoon phase was a necessary part of coming into her own. "Before we met I had been a strong-willed person," she said. "I kind of lost myself once I met Ron. I was not my own person, I was His Wife, and my whole ego was tied up in being His Wife."

The transition to her thirties brought her up short. Now she began to reclaim her own identity, to think of returning to school for a graduate degree. Her husband gladly encouraged her in these pursuits; the dawning of his wife's thirties was not a crisis for him. It was only a crisis for her, for the very basis of her sexuality.

It was a crisis sexually because the classic female theme of being small and weak in relation to a lover who is strong and powerful is an important component of many women's fantasy life—however much we may wish it were not. This fantasy can be light or dark; it can take the form of the protector husband or the black knight. There are better and worse ways to be swept off one's feet. Barbara's sunny version of the fantasy was constructive in many ways, allowing her to feel supported in love and in motherhood, and sexually alive. But at age thirty, no longer a girl, she could not sustain this childlike identity. She had to move on; the dictates of maturity demanded no less. For Barbara it was a loss of innocence, an innocence that had made her married life considerably more romantic than most.

Although at the time Barbara was shaken by this transition, she emerged on the other side happily—if less dreamily—married. She continued "to adore my husband," and he her. Only now, some years into her forties, she idealized him from the vantage point of an adult, not a child.

Men and Women: The Current

Barbara's dilemma was far from unique, and in many ways she was lucky to have sustained a benign fantasy of protected wife-and-mother for as long as she did—lucky, too, in having married a man flawless enough to sustain this image; in most marriages reality dawns a great deal sooner! The very real and continued excitement she felt as the cherished child-wife reveals something important about the sexual dynamic of the happy marriage:

- **Vive la différence!**

No matter how firmly we believe in equality between the sexes, when it comes to love and marriage we reject sexual difference at our peril. Invariably, people told me that they were aroused by the classic outlines of romantic love: couples were at their sexiest when men were Men and women were Women in the most basic, primal sense. Happily married wives blissfully recounted their initial perceptions of their husbands:

"I instantly felt secure. He was in control, he knew what to do."

"He's a powerful man, and I was very attracted to that."

"My father was weak, but he was always in control."

"He protected me."

All were sentiments of yin to yang, frail to strong, feminine to masculine—and they provided the basis of thriving marriages.

Other women fell in love along the maternal axis of attraction. "His mother was married quite a few times, and he was sent to private school when his folks divorced," Holly Lawson told me. "After the divorce he lived with his dad and a wicked stepmother for quite a while before going back to his mother. Then when he was eleven his mom moved into an adults-only building and he had to go back to his dad. He blocked everything; he wouldn't admit to this day that he wasn't loved. When we married I thought I would nurture him and take care of him. Take all the pain away." Margaret Hyde's profoundly maternal response to her own husband's abusive stepmother ("Welcome home, my arms are open to you") was another example. Interestingly, these marriages were far more problematic than were alliances in which the man had been seen, from the outset, as strong and protective. Choosing a mate *because* of his or her emotional problems appears to be a dangerous proposition.

But regardless of whether a woman's fantasies ran to Cinderella or to Mother Earth, falling in love with the man she would marry was bound up in her sense of herself as *female*. Perhaps she saw herself as a sensitive young woman in need of masculine protection; perhaps she saw herself as the healing mother who would atone for the bad mothers and fathers of her husband's past; perhaps she saw herself as a vibrantly sexy life's mate; perhaps she saw herself as the un-swervingly loyal wife who would ensure her husband's future in medical school.

Whatever form her vision of the future took, falling in love with the man she would marry was a fundamentally sexual undertaking: sexual in the sense of physical passion, and sexual in the sense of the male and female *archetypes* written into our cultural and emotional heritage. Much has been written about the destructive power of sexual stereotypes, and when a stereotype limits a man's or woman's life it is indeed destructive. But that was not the case in these couples' lives: there is a difference between a stereotype and an archetype. When I say that the founding fantasy of a young wife's marriage was bound up in her female identity, I mean simply that as they fell in love with their future husbands, wives were fully in touch with their feminine selves. This did not mean that because of their marriages they were suddenly cut off from everything in their character that was remotely ambitious, aggressive, or tough. It simply meant that as they embarked upon their married lives they were fulfilling an important part of their identities *as women*.

Husbands were less forthcoming as to whatever their romantic fantasies may have been; at least on the surface of things, they appeared to be far less given to romantic fantasy in the first place. For the most part, they remembered simply being *smitten*. They met the woman they were to marry, they thought she looked terrific, and soon they were in hot pursuit.

This was not always the case, of course; it was not uncommon for the woman to be smitten first—as when Elaine Stassen held out hope that she might yet stand a chance with the handsome Jason because of his too-large nose. (He remembered thinking she was "nice and attractive"; just as she feared, it did not immediately cross his mind to ask her out.) But regardless of which partner took the initiative, men almost invariably remembered having been motivated by sheer sexual desire unmediated by glowing romantic fantasy. Of course, it is possible that husbands preferred not to reveal the more romantic aspects of their youthful courtships; nevertheless, what seems more likely is that these husbands were simply considerably less romantic in approach than were their wives-to-be. There seemed to be far less mental *content*—images, romantic fantasies, projections into the future—in their attractions to the women with whom they would spend their lives than in their wives' attractions to them.

Cinderella Redux

Thus the majority of happy marriages had been inaugurated in a strong and elemental sense of Man and Woman, yin and yang. The sexual opposition between husband and wife was frequently very strong even when a couple acted as best friends in every other respect. Companionship simply did not blot out the primal sexual connection; there was a tremendous amount of juicy male/female current flowing back and forth between husband and wife.

This will doubtless come as bad news to some. For a number of years women have staked their fortunes upon *not* falling prey to the Cinderella fantasies of our childhood, *not* giving in to the romantic visions that lured our mothers to their restricted fates. A romantic fantasy life in which one waits for one's prince to come hardly seems likely to promote the sexual equality so necessary to women's successful competition in a male world. And so we reject the romance, thinking the better to attain the career.

But how sound is this argument, in reality?

Not surprisingly, critics of marriage have offered evidence that men do in fact profit from marriage more than do women. It is a general truth of psychological life that people rise to expectations, and when a woman enters marriage expecting great things of her husband he may well be inspired to new heights. Thus married men, as we all must know by now, earn more money and live longer than do their unmarried brothers. Behind every great man, it seems, there does indeed stand a woman.

By the same token, married women, in the aggregate, do not appear to fare nearly so well. Various studies over the years have found married women to be, as Jessie Bernard showed, "passive, phobic, and depressed." Bernard attributed these findings to the fact that women married "up": women marry men whom they perceive to be older, wiser, and wealthier than themselves, men they can look up to. The danger in this, said Bernard, was that signing on for a lifetime of looking up to one's husband tended to lower a wife's standing in her own eyes and in the eyes of the world. Marriage enlarged a man, she argued, giving him a mate who saw him as grander than he was. But it diminished a wife. Wives, in Bernard's memorable phrase, "dwindled" into marriage. And although Bernard published her book in the 1970s, to a large degree her thesis still holds. Women continue to prefer men who are slightly "ahead" of them: the famous "man shortage" of the 1980s was based entirely upon the fact that women prefer to marry men three years older than they. And to this day it is undeniably uncomfortable for most women to marry men who are less educated or less successful than they. In spite of all the changes wrought by the women's movement, women and men still do not as a rule wish to create marriages in which the wife is clearly in the lead.

While Bernard confined her discussion of marriage to the purely socioeconomic factors of age and income, she could just as easily have been speaking of sex. When a woman falls passionately in love with a man whom she sees as a strong protector, when she feels herself to be "swept away" in his embrace, she is yielding herself to the sexual version of marrying up; she is surrendering her sexual being to what she perceives as a more powerful masculine force. This feeling of erotic surrender is precisely the element of heterosexual romance that has fueled much of the feminist movement's suspicion of love and marriage; it is this "inequality" of heterosexual romance that has given birth to such sentiments as the famous line, "A woman without a man is like a fish without a bicycle." During the heyday of 1970s feminism, heterosexual women were routinely told that they would do better to live life without married love; sisterhood and hard work were the new keys proffered to happiness and the good life.

The message took hold: In her book *100 Predictions for the Baby Boom,* Cheryl Russell reports that in the mid-1970s only 32 percent of the baby-boom generation, then ages fourteen to twenty-five, thought that marriage was a "great thing," while 13 percent said that people should "seriously consider" remaining unmarried for life. (By the mid-1980s, nine out of ten members of the baby-boom generation said that marriage is the "best" life-style of all.) In the 1970s, young people often took a dim view of love and marriage.

But, in fact, the reality of the happy marriage does not conform to the negative images of the 1970s. Explore the way in which romance actually functions within a good marriage and you find that women as well as men thrive upon romance, however illogical this may seem. People thrive upon sex and sexuality; they thrive upon fantasy when it makes them feel cherished and admired, when it makes them feel good about themselves.

Among the couples I interviewed, it was not only husbands who were doing well in life, wives were succeeding, too. In terms of worldly success, I met several wives who had in fact far outstripped their husbands in achievement—continuing all the while to see themselves sexually as the princess in relation to her prince. I remember in particular a wife in her sixties who, having started from nothing, had built an import business so successful that she and her husband were now living in a large and splendid home in Beverly Hills. This personal triumph was entirely her doing; she had been pushed into the labor force when, many years before, her husband had suffered the traumatic loss of his job as a university coach. His career at an end, she had gone to work and succeeded brilliantly.

And yet, in spite of the fact that she had almost single-handedly built the family empire, she continued to "look up" to her husband emotionally; she had never lost her image of him as the handsome young coach of so many years ago. For me, her continued idealization of her husband was especially affecting in light of his now-frail condition. He was not well enough to speak with me when I arrived; his wife told me he was taking a medication that caused him to sleep for long periods during the day. That she could continue to see him as a vital male presence even in his weakened state was a tribute to their love.

And, of course, her continued idealization of her husband was altogether good for her—and had been throughout their marriage. In essence, she had derived from her marriage what men are said to gain from theirs: a steady source of reinforcement, validation, simple appreciation. It cannot have hurt that her husband saw her—quite accurately—as a swimsuit beauty; their family album was filled with photos of her posing seductively beside him on the beaches of both coasts. While I did not interview her husband, his body language in the family photographs spoke volumes; his sexual attraction to his wife was palpable. Certainly *she* felt it, and continued to feel it to this day. In the fading black-and-white of thirty-year-old prints he was tall, strong, and handsome; she was a classic fifties pinup. Her strongly sexual identity had clearly served her well as she made her way through the man's world of entrepreneurial business. Certainly she suffered none of the estrangement from her feminine self that businesswomen sometimes feel: no matter how aggressively she might have been parlaying her business sense into the family fortune, she remained Woman at home, beloved wife and mother, uncontested queen of the boardwalk. Being entirely assured of herself as a woman, she was psychologically free to act as aggressively as she liked in business. She may have been the least ambivalent woman I have ever met; she was completely and thoroughly focused and committed to home, family, *and* career (not to mention her active sideline as a highly successful investor in stocks and bonds). Beloved by a husband who saw her as sexy and desirable for life, she could throw herself full tilt into every arena that drew her. And she had.

While this couple offered one of the most vivid examples of the way in which classic heterosexual romance promotes the interests of wives and husbands both, their story was common enough. Two-career couples in their twenties and thirties organized their marital identities around the emotionally satisfying sexual poles of masculine and feminine; happy couples did not become "unisex." Even when couples had the same professions, the same incomes, the same aspirations and education, they still, within their marriage, experienced their attraction to each other as one of Man to Woman.

The majority of the wives of an older generation had, of course, led more conventional family lives; in most households husbands were the dominant breadwinners. But traditional wives were not diminished by this imbalance in earnings; most felt that they were leading significant lives.

These wives were able to experience themselves as their husband's full partners in life because the founding romantic fantasy of their marriage did *not* involve great differences in perceived status between mates. Though Jessie Bernard was correct when she observed that "dwindling" into a wife is bad for a woman's morale, the truth is that entrance into the state of wifehood does not *intrinsically* diminish a woman. Among the romantic couples of my sample no one was being asked to dwindle; both partners had been enlarged by their marriage. In the quotidian detail of life, wives were fully equal partners:

• **For happily married couples, it is strictly in the realm of fantasy and sexuality that men were "superior."**

I remember being struck, time and again, by the apparent contradiction between the seemingly "sexist"—or at least highly traditional—way in which a couple had first been drawn to each other, and the way in which they actually conducted their daily lives. In the day-to-day course of events they were equals. This seeming paradox was most striking in the realm of family finances. Maggie Green was one of the few women who had in fact struggled fiercely (and successfully) to establish her own identity within a marriage to a strong man; it was she who had told me, "He's a powerful man and I was very attracted to that." Part of her husband's "power" derived from the fact that he was enormously driven—and successful—in the business world. But in spite of the fact that in the eyes of the world he was a successful man and she merely the wife of a successful man, within their marriage this distinction did not hold. "He always refers to it as 'our money' and 'our business,' " Maggie said. She wielded as much control over the finances as she wished, overseeing the household accounts while her husband made their investments. It was a division of labor she preferred. In short, Maggie may have begun life attracted to her husband's aura of "power," but that response belonged to the realm of sex and fantasy, not to the realm of the everyday. She and her husband were equal in the running of the family.

A *good* marriage is good for both partners. The problem with surveys revealing married women to be less well-off than the unmarried is that such polls make no distinction among marriages good, bad, or indifferent. It may be the case that a bad marriage is worse for a woman than it is for a man; it may be that an indifferent marriage can be all right for a husband but bad for a wife. But a good marriage is good for both.

The Changing Marriage

Even in those cases in which a marriage did begin with an unequal distribution of power and authority, the passing of time often corrected the balance. The truth is that while a happy couple might *begin* life intoxicated by visions of Cinderella and her prince, few couples actually continue in this vein for long. Marriages progress through predictable stages of growth just as do individuals, and as wife and husband mature, so, too, does the relationship between them. This is the factor many critics of marriage miss: a marriage may begin on one footing, but it moves on to another. If a young woman enters married life seeing herself as the child-wife, eventually—unavoidably for most—she becomes a woman; she may begin married life looking up to a husband who gazes benevolently "down" upon her, but this state of affairs is not likely to last. Life evens out.

For the couples with whom I spoke, life evened out because, quite simply, the wives naturally outgrew the ingenue role. Perhaps most dramatically, the coming of children pushed them into the profoundly adult role of mother and protector to the young. And, at the same time, the aging process dramatically altered the way in which others perceived these women. By the time a woman was in her thirties, people were no longer responding to her as the "sweet young thing" of her early years. For those women who had worked outside the home, colleagues reinforced a wife's identity as adult, responsible, *older*. Finally, as the years passed, wives developed an ever greater mental complexity; they grew older and wiser. It became less and less possible to live their lives within the confines of the role we term the "blushing bride"—even if they had wanted to. All of these factors combined to change the way in which even the most classically romantic and "girlish" of brides experienced herself.

Men changed, too, over the years. Universally husbands and wives conformed to the commonplace observation that with age men mellow while women attain new purpose and resolve. By the age of fifty even the most obsessive of male careerists was beginning to calm down a bit, and his wife reaped the benefit. The presence of these husbands at our interview often attested to this shift in the balance of power: more than one sixtyish wife told me that sometime after forty she had decided to become more adventurous, and had made up her mind that her husband would become more adventurous right along with her. "I saw your ad for couples to interview in the paper," one sweet-faced midwestern wife of a retired oil company executive told me, "and I thought it might be interesting. So I told Dave we were going to do it!"

Thus within marriage most women (and men) "grow up"—whether

they wish to or not. Moving into the quintessentially adult years of her thirties was not a happy passage for Barbara Weinstein; nor, because her husband *could* provide his family a safe and comfortable life, was it one that circumstances absolutely demanded of her. Her husband was earning a substantial living; her two children were trouble-free little girls. It was a charmed life. "I lived in a bubble for twenty years," she told me. And yet, even so, she *grew up*. There came a point at which she simply could not sustain her Cinderella identity.

And there came a point at which her husband would need all of her gathering strength to sustain him through a life-threatening illness. When we met, Barbara and her husband, having endured three hospitalizations for his cancer, were living daily with the possibility that it would recur. They did not expect him to be sick again, but, as Barbara said, "in the middle of the night you think about it." Barbara was bracing herself to face what might come. She would not falter.

"I realized this bubble had burst," she said, staunchly holding back tears. "We had a bubble around our house and family. Everything was perfect and we've been typecast as you're-so-perfectly-married, and I hate it because it's so scary. And so this illness has been freeing in a way. We go and we do and we take this experience and we make something positive of it. He's always worked all the time, but now we have three vacations plotted out for the next three months. And we've never been like that." Their newfound commitment to enjoying each day was the silver lining of a very dark cloud. Barbara paused, looked down at her hands, then met my eye again. "I'd probably give it all back to have the bubble again," she said simply.

Her story made me feel that it is wrong to question the nature of a person's happiness, wrong to reject a romantic love as sexist or unenlightened. Happiness is so fleeting a state that we must embrace and celebrate it while we can. Barbara is right about her bubble: she may have been young and naive while its fine membrane shone around her family, but it was a good place to be.

In the end, what we are talking about is no less and no more than the passing of the honeymoon phase. After a time the knight in shining armor ceases to appear so princely as he pulls into the drive after work; after a time he comes to seem simply a man, a husband.

Sometimes, of course, a wife's "coming of age" *was* difficult for her marriage; some husbands did, indeed, view their wives' emergence as a threat. But, as with Barbara Weinstein, not infrequently a woman's personal growth was more problematic for her than for her husband. The real difficulty for women who had made happy marriages was not that romance was crushing their sense of independence and resolve; the real problem was far more likely to be that their sense of independence and resolve was crushing romance! Practically speaking, keeping passion alive was a far more pressing concern to all than was the development and preservation of a strong ego. In the happy marriage strong egos in both partners naturally develop. Egos are the easy part; it is sex and sexuality that present the challenge.

Women and Men: Levels of Desire

Not surprisingly, keeping passion alive proved to be a greater challenge for wives than for husbands. Here women and men attested to another classic difference between the sexes: In most happy marriages husbands wanted sex more frequently and more ardently than did their wives.

This jibes squarely with the findings of Patterson and Kim in their book, *The Day America Told the Truth,* who report that overall men are more sexually frustrated than are women. Two out of three men, as compared to only half of the women, said they wished they could spend more time making love; 30 percent of men described themselves as sexually "insatiable" as compared with only 19 percent of women. Respondents generally agreed that men were more sexual: 46 percent believed that men enjoyed sex more than women, as opposed to only 20 percent who thought women enjoyed it more. Also, only 24 percent believed that men "can live without sex" as opposed to the 44 percent who thought women could do so. There is a general cultural perception that men are the more sexual sex—which was borne out by the husbands and wives with whom I spoke.

This is not to say that in all marriages it is the husband who experiences sexual frustration. Obviously many marriages exist in which the wife longs for more lovemaking with a husband who is not interested. However, in the *happy* marriage, certainly among the happy couples with whom I spoke, it is typically the husband who is doing more of the sexual pursuit. I do not believe it can be merely coincidence that not a single happy wife told me her husband was less interested in sex than she (though one did say that her husband was not very satisfactory in bed, which is a different issue). Nor did one happy husband complain that his wife was too lusty. The truth of the matter seems to be that while all people have problems, often the happy person or couple confronts a different *set* of problems than does the unhappy. In the happy couple the most common sexual problem tends to be too little sex for the husband; in the unhappy couple the sexual problem may be too little sex for the wife. Obviously the best of all possible worlds would be a marriage in which wife and husband actively and equally desire each other. But failing that (and I spoke with only a few couples who were matched in levels of desire), the "best" sexual problem for a married couple to have, it seems, is for the husband to be actively interested in making love to a wife who is sometimes distracted by the demands of daily life.

Wives gave various reasons for this troublesome difference in levels of appetite. One wife, married for forty years, said she thought breast-feeding an infant, by virtue of being an intense physical relationship in and of itself, tamped down desire for many women. Certainly it had for her. The presence of children in the home, she volunteered, had been profoundly distracting. In short, during this woman's child-rearing years sex was the least of her interests, a fact that had been extremely distressful to her husband as he reached forty and fell into a protracted and painful mid-life crisis. Just as he needed more sexual affirmation from his wife, she was offering him less.

The real obstacle for wives seemed to be the fact that for women sex and sexuality begin and end in the mind. Women simply could not, as a rule, approach lovemaking in the elemental, utterly physical way their husbands could. For all the stories of middle-aged men leaving their wives and homes for young secretaries, the men in my sample, as a group, could sustain sexual interest in their wives over the years far more easily than could their wives in them. (Interestingly, Patterson and Kim found that only 39 percent of men had fantasized about having sex with a "much younger person." Forty percent may be a fairly high figure, but it leaves a full 60 percent of men who had not had such fantasies. No doubt many of the 60 percent were happily married.) While men were less forthcoming on the subject of romance than were women, they gave every indication of being significantly less dependent upon romantic imagery in order to remain attracted than were their wives. The passing of the honeymoon phase had no effect upon their sexual appetites; desire for them was not dependent upon the magic of the moment.

By the same token, when it came to sex, the men I spoke to were far less distractible as well. They could "turn off" their brains whereas women could not. For a man, the fact that the baby lay sleeping in the next room was not a barrier to lovemaking: for him it was a simple truth that the baby was *there*, while he and his wife were *here*. This was not a function of a man's being any less involved a parent as is so often claimed; it was instead part and parcel of a man's being more purely physical in need and sentiment.

In this respect, the one highly passionate wife's sexuality was more classically male than female. Like many (perhaps most) men, she enjoyed a basic and unfluctuating level of sheer physical desire independent of mental content. She was not caught up in romantic fantasies concerning her husband; she had not maintained desire by preserving an image of him as a dark Heathcliffian hero. Far from it, in fact. She simply liked sex, and the better she and her husband grew to be at lovemaking, the more she liked it! He in return had grown more and more sexually involved with her. Theirs was a highly intriguing alliance, raising as it did the possibility that monogamy and lasting passion might be a great deal more attainable in marriage if women's sexuality were more like men's!

In any event, when it came to sexuality this couple was especially blessed. For wives and husbands both, the difference in sexual makeup was frequently a source of frustration. Husbands felt rejected or, at best, sexually malnourished; wives felt guilty or pressured or both. The only way out of this dilemma was simple understanding: couples agreed not to take each other's differing levels of desire personally. Husbands told themselves, correctly, that most wives were no lustier than their own, and wives told themselves that they did not always have to be "in the mood" in order to make love with their husbands. Two wives told me that they had finally come to the realization that making love with their husbands took so little time, and was so important, that they now felt it was a good thing to do—regardless of inclination. Much compromise was in evidence, with husbands settling for less sex than they ideally would want, wives agreeing to more.

Happily, over time some of these differences diminished. Said Maggie Green, "When we were first married my husband could have had sex every single night of our marriage"—far more contact than she desired since, although she liked sex and was very much in love with her husband, she had difficulty reaching an orgasm under any circumstances. Things grew worse when feminism swept the land in the 1970s and her husband now began routinely to inquire as to whether she had or had not had an orgasm. Now she felt pressured not only to have far more sex than she wanted, but to enjoy it more, too. Though she was eventually able to dissuade her husband from enshrining her satisfaction as his reigning standard of evaluation, the stubborn problem of their vastly differing levels of desire remained for years—remained, in fact, until her highly dynamic husband reached his fiftieth birthday and finally began to slow down a bit. "Now it's weekend sex," she told me happily. "And it's great."

Still, while married people often made each other feel happy and beloved in bed, they could, and did, disappoint as well. With desire does come peril, as we are so often warned; with desire comes the possibility of rejection, of infidelity, of sexual failure. In the next chapter we see how strong couples survived these passages in life.

8

ℰ

Sexual Problems

Apart from the stubborn problem of husbands who wanted more sex with wives who wanted less, happy couples encountered remarkably few sexual problems. Only one wife told me, in confidence, that her husband had never been a good lover. He had been a virgin when they married while she had not, and their sex life had been unsatisfying from the start. Out of loyalty to him, a good and caring man whom she loved and respected, she said no more on this subject. In her sixties now, she belonged to a generation of men and women who married for life, and her disappointment as a young bride had not moved her to think of leaving her husband. She simply accepted as her fate the fact that sexual love would not be part of her marriage.

How many other men and women may have shared her feelings is difficult to say, because most couples met with me together. Clearly, telling a stranger where one's partner falls short in bed is an entirely different matter from telling a stranger where one's partner falls short in, say, disciplining the children—an issue many couples were happy to discuss at length. Still, I did meet alone with a number of wives (no husbands, though), and all these wives professed to be very happy with their sex lives.

The one couple who did reveal the existence of serious sexual problems was entirely forthright and unruffled about the matter. Hugh and Martha Juniper, they of the cheerful and resilient temperaments, told me that nearly thirty years into their marriage Hugh, then fifty-seven, had suddenly developed problems with impotence. "It was a difficult period for both of us," Martha told me.

Hugh saw doctors. When the problem was discovered to be physical in origin, he was offered the option of an implant. Martha told him, honestly, not to undergo the surgery for her sake. While they had always been, in her words, very "physically involved," she now told her husband that she could live without sex if that was what lay ahead.

Hugh chose to have the surgery, which proved to be a modest success.

The Junipers' trusting and open approach to a problem that could have been devastating was characteristic of all happy couples. As we have seen, happy couples almost universally believed that, in times of trouble, the outside world could help. They did not create the insular, closed-off system one can find in the "dysfunctional" family. When a healthy couple encountered serious difficulties—difficulties they could not manage on their own—they looked to the world at large. And they found the help they needed.

Supporting this faith was an essential openness. Hugh and Martha, again, were typical. They spoke of their problem to each other, to doctors, eventually to their children. Their daughter told them that the only bad thing about the whole issue as far as she was concerned was the fact that her father had felt too embarrassed to mention it earlier. Such openness serves as a useful defense. In speaking of a problem a couple can define it, with public assent, as everyday. By discussing their situation with trusted confidants, Hugh and Martha made it seem normal—as in fact it was. Nevertheless, this is precisely *not* how most people deal with the problem of impotence. Hugh's and Martha's open natures allowed them to *connect*, to see themselves and their lives as part of the human experience and their situation as neither shameful, humiliating, nor even, finally, all that embarrassing.

Infidelity

One of the most fundamental tenets of the long-married happy couple was the importance of fidelity:

> • **Almost universally, happy couples strongly believe in, and stead-fastly practice, monogamy.**

This was such a powerful article of faith among them that most couples actually had little to say on the subject. For many, being faithful to one's spouse was not what made a marriage happy, it was what made a marriage possible in the first place. It was a basic, a priori requirement, like taking the vows and signing the certificate of marriage. Marital fidelity was the "of course" of marriage; happiness came from the good qualities a couple built for themselves upon the foundation of fidelity.

Most couples, when I inquired into their thoughts on the subject of marital fidelity, uttered a strong "Yes!" or "Always!" or "Of course!" and then fell silent, obviously expecting me to move on to the next, and presumably more interesting, question. The many surveys finding widespread infidelity among husbands and wives clearly did not apply to this group. The notion of an open marriage held neither logic nor appeal for these couples. As one husband told me, "When a guy sleeps with someone else, he's divorced within a year."

Only five couples said that either of them had ever been involved with anyone outside the marriage. Of these, interestingly enough, two had in fact *not* been wounded by the experience, contrary to what most happy couples predicted. Nancy and Mark Walters, the couple with the baby-snake collection and the duplex-too-small-for-four, went through a period, ten years into their marriage, during which they began to date other people. The trouble had begun when Nancy returned to work and Mark, in Nancy's view, did little to take up the slack at home. "Nothing was getting done around the house," Nancy remembered, "and I harbored resentment. Mark kept saying he didn't know how to use the washing machine."

As Nancy's resentment grew, the two withdrew into separate lives. "Mark was running seventy to eighty miles a week," Nancy told me, "and he had no energy to do anything else. He ignored me." In the meantime Nancy had taken up running, too, choosing as her running partner a man she knew from work. This relationship inevitably developed in the direction such relationships so often do. "He had a bad marriage because his wife couldn't make friends, or understand his running," said Nancy, who had put herself in the ironic position of sympathizing with another husband whose constant running was alienating his own wife. Meanwhile, he was a ready critic of Mark, taking Nancy's side in every complaint she made against her husband. "At some point this became a physical attraction," Nancy said. "He was playing head games with me, reinforcing my bad image of Mark."

Needless to say, Nancy's growing affection for her colleague did nothing to quell the rising storm at home, and eventually she and Mark reached what both see as a "critical period" in their marriage. On the brink of separation they agreed that both were now free to see other people.

This they did, to seriocomic effect. "If Mark went out with someone I would wait up," Nancy recalled, "and then I'd ask him about it when he got home." Mark dated two women during this time, and Nancy continued her involvement with her running companion. Neither of them actually had sex with another person, though both had tacitly agreed that this step was soon to come. "We would sit down and say, 'You can have the lamp if I can have the desk,' " Mark told me. Their marriage had become a strange alliance indeed: now they were two close, if irritable, friends talking about their love lives as they calmly divided the spoils of wedlock between them.

It was Nancy who finally registered the absurdity of this arrangement. "One morning I woke up and said, 'This is crazy.' We were still best friends throughout the whole thing, so I realized, 'Something is wrong—we obviously aren't as pissed off as we think we are.' " Her revelation sparked a long talk with Mark during which both of them decided "to just let things go and see how it was and just discuss things as they came up." Nancy in particular had learned an important lesson: "I'll never brood again," she reported. "It poisons a relationship."

They decided to stop seeing other people and begin again, their days of extramarital dating leaving both completely unscarred. Neither was in any way wounded by the fact that both had felt attractions to others—quite the reverse, in fact: having had a taste of freedom, both were now less inclined to pursue it. "Now we know what it would be like with these other people," they told me. "Of course you think about affairs, but the novelty would wear off and the rest of your life would be screwed up," Nancy observed. She "couldn't stand" the colleague to whom she was once so attracted, a development that taught her the fundamental truth contained in the saying that the grass is always greener on the other side.

For his part, Mark weathered his wife's attachment to another man with supreme confidence. "I kept telling her," he recalled with a grin, " 'Make up your mind, because if I need to go out and find someone else I will.' I learned there's a lot of single women out there. It took me a week to find a date, and I wasn't even looking." But beyond this, he was convinced that however angry Nancy was feeling at the time, ultimately she would not leave. "I had confidence in our relationship," he said. "I really believed she loved me, and would wake up." Besides, he reasoned, if nature ran its course his wife's attraction to her running partner would soon turn sour.

This prediction proved correct. "[My running partner] was the typical macho guy," Nancy reported. Even worse, he was a dog owner and his dogs did not like cats—of which, you may recall, Nancy then owned approximately ten. When he was inflexible on this point Nancy said to him in her characteristically blunt fashion, "I guess we won't be living together then, will we?" This was a turning point for her: "I realized not all guys are like my husband," Nancy said—an understatement, to put it mildly. A man who can happily accommodate himself to sharing a tiny living space with ten cats, numerous snakes, entire families of mice, hutches filled with Depression glass, and a large collection of stuffed bears does not come along every day.

"It was a very useful and productive time," Nancy told me, speaking for both of them, "even though it was very unpleasant and stressful. I changed because of this period. I accept Mark the way he is more." Before she had always chafed at Mark's "laid-back" nature, which, depending upon the context, she could experience as passivity, laziness, or lack of concern. (Even as we spoke the two were involved in an ongoing, if controlled, dispute over the bathroom light fixture. It was broken, and, Mark told me, "My tendency is to just let it be"—an attitude that was clearly provoking his wife.) "I was always expecting Mark to be a certain way," Nancy said, "and I thought I *wanted* him to be a certain way. I thought I wanted him to be a stronger figure, to take care of me. And then I realized people like that are like that *all the time!* They're too busy with their own egos."

Nancy began to appreciate the virtues of her husband's "vice"; she began to see that a man who has trouble getting around to minor repairs around the house may also be a man who can readily adapt to his wife's ever-changing enthusiasms for household pets.

Mark changed as well. "I realize now that she's not the Rock of Gibraltar, and that she does need taking care of sometimes," he said. When we met, he was more willing to act as protector when she was down, even though this role did not come naturally to him.

"We've both grown a lot," Nancy concluded. "We are really very different from what we were when we met." Undoubtedly their period of seeing other people helped bring these changes about.

Whether or not their marriage would have emerged wholly intact if they had crossed the line separating flirtation from infidelity we cannot say. Nancy and Mark avoided taking any actions that might have created lasting regret—actions they could not have "taken back."

Only one couple actually did cross that line without traumatizing their relationship. Married for sixteen years at age thirty-eight, Hannah and Keith Winslow met in their high school chemistry class when they were both sixteen. Keith was immediately drawn to Hannah, though Hannah, at the time, was more interested in "older" boys: she liked seniors, and she and Keith were only juniors at the time. Their relationship developed slowly. They dated each other casually at first, then exclusively for the last three or four months of high school. After graduation they enrolled in separate colleges, where they saw other people as well, continuing to write and see each other on holidays at home. Finally they became lovers at nineteen, three years after having met. Neither was in a hurry. "We always knew we'd get married," Hannah said. "We got along so well. It was better than any other relationship I'd ever seen, even on TV." They married just out of college when they were twenty-two.

After college they went to graduate school. Hannah pursued a Ph.D. in psychology; Keith was enrolled in medical school. Both programs unfolded in, as Hannah puts it, "a sexually charged atmosphere." Soon, in the sway of various psychological theories concerning sexuality and experimentation, Hannah pressed for the two of them to see other people, and Keith agreed. They were only twenty-six, in their generation a young age already to have been married for four years. Theirs was a planned infidelity; the two of them sat down together and consciously decided to be with other people.

This they did in an orderly fashion, each of them knowing the other's sexual partners before a tryst took place. No wounds were inflicted. "It became not very interesting," Hannah recalled, explaining how this phase of their marriage eventually drew to a close. "It became very clear to me that Keith was much better than any of the other men I saw. Other guys could be nice, but not magical." Keith agreed, and the two decided to become faithful once again. They have remained so ever since.

The Trauma of Infidelity

But for other couples infidelity was profoundly destructive. Ben and Kathleen Gross, both in their early seventies and married for forty-five years, still vividly recalled Kathleen's one lapse in 1947, three years after they were married. They had been attending graduate school at the time. Ben was working very hard, so hard that Kathleen seems to have felt neglected. She began an affair with another student. Her marriage was terribly shaken when, wanting to break off the affair, she told Ben that she had been seeing another man.

She chose to tell him, she said, because she believed that his knowing would make it impossible for her to continue. But her confession deeply wounded the young couple. "It was not at all clear that the marriage would survive," Ben offered circumspectly, remembering that period. Nevertheless, they held on, and a slow reconciliation took place. "In a sense we both just hung in there," Ben said; "You were forgiving," Kathleen added. Ben was willing to forgive because, as he said simply, "I wanted to be married to her."

Theirs was an interesting tale for a number of reasons, not least of which was the impression both gave even now, some forty years down the line, that Kathleen's one transgression lived on vividly in memory. It was not that the infidelity interfered with their daily lives; they were a happy and calm couple who rarely argued and who clearly enjoyed each other's company immensely. Ben *had* been forgiving, and the two had gone on.

It was more that there was something in the way they spoke of that period, something that said "This still matters." Neither had forgotten; neither seemed able to forget. Kathleen told me that she personally dealt with the fact of her one infidelity by trying to "block it out," a strategy that, she told me, "works *now*."

The story was fascinating, too, in what it seemed to reveal concerning infidelities and how and why they occur. Neither Ben nor Kathleen possessed much sense of why Kathleen had done what she had; Kathleen's reference to Ben's absorption in his work was made only in passing. Neither seemed particularly convinced by this as an explanation. For me, it was a striking gap in the conversation because most couples *could* explain themselves: happy couples invariably offered solid, *shared* explanations of even their own worst behavior. But confronting her long-ago infidelity, both Ben and Kathleen appeared to be at a loss.

This was all the more striking in that just moments earlier Kathleen had given what, to the outsider at least, seemed an obvious reason to want to hurt her new husband—which was that for many years before their marriage he had repeatedly hurt her. They met at age eighteen when both were student teachers in the elementary grades. Kathleen was "pretty fond of him right from the beginning," but Ben had conflicting emotions. He was Jewish, Kathleen Christian, and his family disapproved. The result was seven years of, in Kathleen's phrase, "whirlwind courtship"—whirlwind meaning seven years, for Kathleen, of being repeatedly abandoned by the man she loved. Each break would last two months or so after which Ben would call, or the two would run into each other on campus, and the relationship would resume. When they were seeing each other, Ben referred to her among his family only by her code name of "Jake."

For Kathleen, it was an extremely unhappy period. Worse yet, it was far less unhappy for Ben, who was calling the shots. "He didn't have as much *Sturm und Drang* as I did," Kathleen recalled. "I was alone, but he was surrounded by brothers to whom he was very close."

After seven years of this they finally married, away from Ben's family—raising the question of whether Kathleen's lone infidelity may actually have been an unconscious way of evening the score. But whatever the root of Kathleen's behavior, it certainly is fair to say that an infidelity *can* be a form of "acting out," a way of communicating with one's spouse through deed instead of word. And this was precisely the kind of communication that happy couples strictly avoided. Happily married couples stayed happy by knowing where the line was drawn; they took care not to cross it.

Infidelity and the Shared Identity of Marriage

The question of why Kathleen told her husband what she had done brings us to one of the most difficult aspects of infidelity, which is the corrosive effect upon a marriage of keeping a secret from one's mate. It is entirely possible that unconsciously Kathleen confessed in order to wound her husband as he had repeatedly wounded her, but it is also possible, likely even, that she told him for another, far more positive reason as well: her desire to feel close to him again. Certainly she could have chosen to end the affair silently and to keep its existence to herself. Certainly her husband would have suffered significantly less had she done so. However, an undeniable distance would have been opened up between the two. For the rest of her life Kathleen would have *known*. And her husband would have been in the dark.

The importance of the shared world to the happy marriage cannot be exaggerated. Secrets are profoundly divisive; two people cannot completely share a world when one person knows something significant the other does not. Many happily married couples had formulated this principle for themselves:

• **It is essential not to take any major action that you will <u>have</u> to keep secret from your mate.**

For Kathleen to have continued to share the secret of her affair with her lover, even though she had broken off the relationship, would have made her by definition closer to him than to her husband, at least on that score. We are closest to the people with whom we share intimacies. When Kathleen said she told her husband because she wanted to end the affair, she was right: to tell one's husband about an affair *does* end it in a sense. Beyond the obvious fact that it is difficult to carry on an affair your husband has demanded that you end, even if the affair continues it is no longer secret. It has become part of a shared marital world—an unhappily shared world, true, but a shared world nonetheless.

The divisive effect of secrets upon marriage explains why so many couples confess transgressions that, on the face of things, might better be left unsaid. It explains, too, why couples who had emerged from a period of infidelity unfazed were those couples who had pursued other people entirely in the open. Both the Walters and the Winslows had mutually decided to experiment, and neither couple had kept secrets from the other. Their shared worlds remained intact.

To a very real degree, the secrecy of an affair or attraction can be as threatening as the act itself. Lucas and Debra Lyon-Jones's situation is a crystalline example of this truth. Lucas's betrayal of his wife's faith was, as we have seen, factually speaking rather mild: it amounted to a single kiss and no more. The fact that the object of his momentary desire was his wife's younger sister made matters much worse, of course; nevertheless there were a great many mitigating factors. For one, the sister had essentially been raised by Lucas's wife, and her pursuit of her older sister's husband appeared to be clearly a case of pure sibling rivalry; the younger sister was no more serious in her attraction to her brother-in-law than her brother-in-law was in his attraction to her. In short, it would have been reasonable for Lucas simply to have shrugged the incident off, telling himself he had been momentarily caught up in a war that was actually being waged between two sisters—a struggle that in truth had relatively little to do with him.

That he could not do this is revealing. Within a thriving marriage, as Lucas's to Debra was, keeping a secret from one's mate is extremely uncomfortable. Though technically Lucas had not been unfaithful to his wife, the secrecy, the moment of desire for her sister: all this amounted to a larger, emotional infidelity—one so large that ultimately, a full two years later, he felt compelled to confess. And it was Debra's revelation, on the night of her thirty-second birthday, that she was willing to have the fourth child he wanted that sparked his admission. Her mention of a child dissolved Lucas's ability to keep the secret. Having children together is the ultimate form of sharing; it is a sharing of one's very genetic being. Lucas's guilty secret was forced out by his need to be as close to his wife as he possibly could be at that moment.

Still, one might ask, why confess *two years* after the fact? A secret is divisive only so long as it remains alive and vivid in the mind of the partner who is keeping it, and for most of us the passing of two years will fade even the most intense of memories. But this was precisely Lucas's problem. He could not leave the past behind because he was constantly reminded of it by the presence of his wife's sister. Every time he saw his sister-in-law, which was often, he shared an intimate secret with her from which his wife was excluded.

Making matters worse was the fact that both Lucas and Debra possessed remarkable memories for detail. They were quite possibly the best storytellers of all one hundred couples; speaking of their wedding eight years before, they could recall details down to the tap-tapping sound the female judge's heels had made on the granite floors of city hall. For Lucas, two years—even five or ten years—was not sufficient time to wash out a memory. Two years after the fact, that one night was still as vividly present for him as it had been the morning after. Confession is good for the soul, and Lucas needed to confess.

Staying the Course

Most couples consciously understood the corrosive nature of secrets; some gave this as one reason for their having remained faithful. And, because they saw infidelity as an irrevocable crossing of the line, they made conscious decisions to respect the line. Not that even the happiest of couples could not be tempted; they could. (Patterson and Kim report that 67 percent of their sample said they were tempted as often as once a week!) Joe Compton, the father of three whom we met in chapter four (it was he who learned a gentler form of discipline from his wife, Karen), was one of the more forthright of interviewees on the subject of infidelity. "I made a conscious decision after I got married," he told me. "Knowing I'm as horny as the next guy, and knowing most people will take it if they can get it, I consciously decided I would never get in a position where I had to say 'no' because by then it's too late." Over the years he had practiced what he preached. When a female colleague who was obviously interested in him had begun to ask for rides home, he had made sure someone else came along. His strategy being to head off potential affairs at the pass, he simply did not allow himself to be alone in an automobile with an attractive and willing female in the first place. "I just wouldn't ever want to be unfaithful," he said. "My kids would see me as a lesser person if I did that, and there isn't a piece of tail in the world that's worth giving up happiness for."

Sometimes, of course, situations did evolve to a dangerous point before a spouse quite realized what was happening. The one time Barbara Weinstein felt seriously tempted to be unfaithful involved precisely the sort of situation Joe Compton had long managed to avoid. Barbara had returned to school and was doing an internship under the direction of a man she found attractive. One Friday night they were working late, alone in the building, a circumstance that had arisen because Barbara had botched a report that was due. "He was making it all better," Barbara said, "and I felt vulnerable. I wanted to be hugged." Barbara was now being drawn to her boss in much the same way she had been drawn to her husband: as a strong male who could take care of things, who could take care of her. Unwittingly, her boss had tapped into an important fantasy of Barbara's, the founding fantasy of her marriage, in fact. It was a highly tempting situation.

Barbara soon recognized the danger, and acted on her recognition. "I called home at that moment," she said. "I needed to anchor myself in reality." Again, the shared reality of marriage is at stake in an infidelity. As Barbara felt a separate world springing into life around her and her colleague she understood that the reality of her marriage was being challenged. She called her husband in order to reconnect not only with him, but also with the world they had created together.

The ability to perceive danger before it was too late is crucial to the happy marriage. The happily married people with whom I spoke were all sufficiently self-aware that they could recognize where a flirtation was headed in time to call a halt. Also, happy couples possessed a sound understanding of the psychology of novelty. One woman, recounting a minor crush she had developed on a man at work, shared her strategy for nipping an incipient transgression in the bud. "I asked myself," she told me, "if I were meeting my husband and him for the first time on the same day, which would I choose? The answer was my husband, hands down. So I knew that the only thing I was responding to in the other man was just the newness of the situation."

Though a new love holds undeniable charm, she understood that love is new only once. The principle by which she and other thriving couples lived was this:

- **Happy couples follow a policy of talking themselves out of attractions to others long before they leave the stage of temptation.**

Sex in Mid-life

Most of us see the mid-life period as the danger zone when it comes to infidelity, and this proved to be largely true for the couples with whom I spoke. If a couple was going to have problems in the sexual realm—and many, many couples claimed never even to have been tempted to stray—this was a prime time for those problems to commence.

By sheer happenstance, I spoke with Maria Gonzalez and her husband, Carlos, at the very time when Maria's own mid-life crisis had shifted into high gear. Not that Maria was altogether willing to call it that: it was her husband, Carlos, who told me that his wife was experiencing a mid-life crisis. She herself was not sure how to describe her problem.

When I met them they were both thirty-nine years old and had been married for seventeen years, since the age of twenty-two. They met in junior high school when they were thirteen. "Carlos was always after me," Maria recalled, "drawing hearts on the board and pulling my pigtails." From the start, he protected her. Carlos, a bright and ambitious son of immigrants from Mexico (he and Maria both had been slotted into the accelerated part of their class), was always an intractable boy: "I was the kind of kid who would say 'white' if everyone else said 'black.' " When it came to Maria, this streak of rebellion translated into a strongly protective attitude. Once, when Maria heard that she was going to get a C for the semester in an English class, she broke into tears. Carlos, who had earned a B, told the teacher, "Let's switch." The teacher, who had never liked him because he always argued with her about the meaning of poems, went along, happy for the chance to lower his grade.

Both graduated from high school at the top of their class and enrolled in college. Carlos continued his ardent pursuit of Maria while working night and day to put himself through school. His life was a struggle; there were times when he did not have enough spare change to buy himself a cup of coffee. And, when he was not working at two jobs or studying for class, he threw himself full tilt into the courtship of Maria's parents. Knowing her parents would not like Carlos (he had adopted the "Elvis Presley look" in his high school years), Maria put off introducing them until they were eighteen and he had become a more acceptable suitor from the point of view of conservative Hispanic parents. Now Carlos worked overtime trying to make a good impression. "I would be *very* helpful to them," he said. "I laid tiles, I did the plumbing, I fixed their car. They had no other family in America, so I did everything."

By age twenty-one Carlos was planning a career in law. He had been accepted by the University of California at Berkeley law school when Maria's parents decided to move back to Mexico. An obedient Hispanic daughter, Maria would have to move with them. Carlos did not think twice. He proposed marriage and gave up his plans to study law so that he could work to support a wife. The immigrant culture to which he belonged demanded no less. Both sets of parents were against the union; Carlos had only one thousand dollars to his name. There was no money to support a marriage.

They married anyway, and spent three hundred of the thousand dollars on the wedding reception. Carlos began his adult life of work and, as he put it, "never looked back." In seventeen years he had never taken a vacation; by dint of constant, unrelenting effort he had built a solid financial base for his family, which now included two children. When we met he was working at not one but two jobs. By day he was a field manager for a major oil corporation; by night he taught adult education (a job he said was necessary for his "sanity"). Maria worked now, too, as a payroll clerk.

The past seventeen years together had been very intense. Hard work; long, stormy arguments in the early days; a traumatic stay in the hospital for Maria in her twenties: there had been scarcely a moment to breathe freely. Maria was clearly showing signs of strain.

As Carlos saw it, the true source of Maria's problem was that she did not have a chance to exist on her own before marriage; she was never allowed to establish her identity as a separate human being. Both Carlos and Maria were emotionally quite young at twenty-two, younger than many of their classmates. They had lived at home throughout their college years; Maria had never dated anyone but Carlos. Carlos's father was so strict that as a grown man of twenty-two Carlos was still observing a ten o'clock curfew.

"We grew up together," Carlos said. "Our first year of marriage we were like two kids let out of school. We bought junk food, we stayed up late, and we fought like little children, too. We would yell and scream and push each other. We were very immature." The result of their too-young marriage, Carlos believed, was that Maria now felt suffocated. "Marriage is like seventeen minutes underwater without an oxygen tank," Carlos offered, in one of the few negative images any interview subject was to put forth. "You're trying to be an individual and you can't. Maria is in my shadow too much. She needs to grow on her own."

Naturally enough, the question of whether growing on her own would include marital infidelities had arisen in both of their minds. On this score Maria's co-workers had exercised a highly disruptive influence. All single or divorced, they were, in Carlos's estimation (which Maria seconded), leading "pretty wild lives." Maria listened to the tales of their exploits with envy; having lived her entire life under the protection of first her parents and then her husband, she had never experienced adventures of any kind. Standing on the brink of middle age did not help her to fend off the temptations her co-workers held out; Carlos felt strongly, and Maria did not dispute it when he said so, that she was going through a period of questioning her sexuality. "I think a lot about the past," she said, "about not having had a youth." But she did not know what this meant she should do; she did not know what she wanted.

And so there they were: Carlos as much in the lead as ever, Maria mired in disarray; both of them clearly very much in love, very much involved. Everything, for them, was dialogue. Listening to them, it was clear to me why they agreed to meet for an interview; they loved to sit and talk! It was impossible for me to imagine the two of them divorced, if only because each so clearly reveled in discussing the *possibility* of divorce with the other. "We talk about divorce," Maria revealed, "but in our minds we would never do it. We always have that goal of staying together." Nevertheless, they may have been facing real danger. "I'm pushing it," Maria said, trying to explain their present dynamic. She offered as an example her behavior the morning before when she had suddenly, and summarily, ordered Carlos to prepare breakfast for the family before he went to work. He did.

This action, both said, was unjust. Carlos had always shared the housework equally with his wife; their problems did not stem from the classic wife's resentment toward a husband who had been waited upon hand and foot. Beyond housecleaning, Carlos did most of the cooking as well. In ordering Carlos to fix breakfast Maria was not striking a blow for equal rights; hers was an act of provocation pure and simple. She was trying to see how far she could go, how much she could get away with. "I think she is playing Russian roulette!" Carlos declared in his customarily animated fashion. These two clearly brought out the energy in each other; there was "chemistry" between them. Maria might be confused, but the pull was there. "I'll question him like crazy," she said with spirit. "How do you know you love me? You've never been with anyone else."

Carlos always answered that he simply *knew*. "I tell my students I am six thousand five hundred years old," he said, laughing. "I'm not having a mid-life crisis." He told her, too, that he would gladly do whatever will make her happy. If what she needed was a divorce, he would see it through.

But neither of them expected their story to end this way. "If we survive this," said Carlos, "it will be better for us in old age." Already, in their minds, they were turning a period of crisis into something more benign, into a time of growth and discovery. Perhaps it is this quality above all, this capacity not to panic, not to fear the worst, that will ultimately hold them together. That, and their clear love and respect for each other.

For some the passions and turmoil of mid-life could be cruel. The years following Paul Stein's fortieth birthday were anguished ones for him and his wife, Natascha. They had met, as discussed, in Germany during the war. Theirs had always been a tempestuous and dramatic relationship. Under the rule of the Nazi regime, their liaison was technically legal but in reality very dangerous. Were Paul to file for a marriage permit, they were warned by a friend of the family, he would be shot. As it was, his boss informed the authorities and Paul was beaten by a group of SS members who worked with him at the factory.

Fearing for his own life, Natascha's priest refused to marry them, but their bishop gave them leave to declare themselves husband and wife: "Do not consider yourself to be in a sinful situation," he told them. It was the most the Church would offer them.

Married at heart, they had their first daughter in 1943 when Natascha was just sixteen years old. Life was fraught with peril. Paul lived underground for a time, and was eventually sent to a forced-labor camp in 1944. "It was slave labor," he told me, "digging ditches for the troops. We were sent to the Battle of the Bulge where we were under fire from both sides." Paul escaped and made his way to the farm where Natascha and his infant daughter were staying. There he assumed Natascha's maiden name and successfully evaded capture for the remaining months of the war.

Life remained difficult after the war. Because Natascha's passport was Dutch, the two had enormous difficulty gaining permission to marry from the government; it would not be until 1947 that they could legitimize their relationship. Finally they were allowed to emigrate to the United States as "Displaced Persons" under a United Nations Relief program. It was to be the beginning of nearly fifteen years of constant, unrelenting labor for both. Arriving in America, they hired themselves out as a domestic couple. He was chauffeur and butler, she cook and upstairs maid. "The lady of the house said to me, 'Oh, you're German. You must be a wonderful cook,' " Natascha recalled. "Little did she know we hadn't had food for ten years."

The stress of trying to reestablish their lives in a new country was enormous. In Germany Paul had been trained as a pharmacist; in America his degrees were worthless. He was forced to attend, first, evening high school, then college and graduate school while working forty-eight hours a week in a pharmacy. For her part Natascha would leave home at 7 A.M. for work, returning fourteen hours later at 9 P.M. Their little daughter was shuffled about from nursery school to various day-care arrangements; all three made enormous sacrifices. Paul was thirty-four when he finally graduated.

Their life story bears telling because no mid-life crisis happens in a vacuum. A crisis occurs within the context of an individual life, a personal history. When Paul's crisis came it was shaped by the years of struggle he and Natascha had seen; the ferocity of his crisis mirrored the ferocity of his long struggle to survive. They were by now in their forties, and life had changed. They had lived the American dream;

Paul was a pharmacist with his own business in Southern California, and they owned a home in a nicely kept suburb. Two more children had been added to the family.

"With success came the attitude," Paul said, "that 'I deserve to indulge myself, I deserve to have some of the better things in life.' " He added, "It was a typical male menopause. I bought an Opel sports car, I stopped wearing undershirts, I began to sleep in the nude."

And he saw other women. "Natascha was home with the kids," Paul remembered, "and I ran my own way." He was only minimally present as a husband even when Natascha underwent a double mastectomy for breast cancer.

Paul's life exploded in his face when Natascha, who was working in the family pharmacy, found a letter to him from a girlfriend. She was devastated. She took Paul's car and drove to the beach, where a friend found her a motel room. She was suicidal.

It was to take them many years to recover. Even though Paul quickly realized that he "couldn't have my cake and eat it, too," Natascha could not move on so easily. "The sad part for me," she remembered, "was the rage I felt from all the years of being a doormat. My needs were never considered at all," she added, her husband nodding assent. "Everything centered on Paul's ambition. He didn't want me to participate in his college world, and I had no say in the household either. I couldn't even sign a check. He was very domineering, very macho, old country. And there was very little physical tenderness between us. We saw each other only on Sunday mornings."

Now, confronted with her husband's faithlessness, Natascha was overcome by rage for all her many years of submission. She tried to channel her anger productively; having decided that she needed to make her own way in life, she attended real estate classes and worked to earn her license. But nothing helped. "Once a week I had to erupt," she said. She lived in a state of chronic fury. "I kept up a good front," she said, "but I was just barely hanging together."

When we met, they were deeply committed to each other, deeply in love—a state given added poignancy by the fact of Paul's recent heart attack. Nearing old age, they were once again living in the shadow of death. The two joined hands frequently throughout our interview, and they spoke to each other as much as to me.

The source of their miracle was "Marriage Encounter," a weekend program originally developed by the Roman Catholic Church, whose emphasis is upon, in Paul's words, "finding avenues of deeper communication." It is not designed for couples in trouble but rather is intended to make good marriages better.

They went for a weekend when a friend—unaware of the difficulties they had been having—brought it up. The journey was revelatory for both. One of the "assignments" they were given was to write a love letter. "Paul wrote a college paper," Natascha said: "Why Do I Really Want to Stay Married?" In his essay he listed, objectively, all of his reasons for staying with her. The list was dry, cold, rational; Paul did not once mention love. Natascha was devastated. She had written a love letter to the husband who had caused her so much pain; she had received a term paper in return. "I filled a whole notebook," Paul said. "But I didn't have the words."

For Natascha, it was the end. She packed her bags and told her husband that their marriage was over.

Moved finally to say what was in his heart, Paul fell to his knees and recited the wedding vows, word for word, to his wife of thirty years. "That is how I feel about our marriage," he said when he had finished.

It was a moment of radical change for both. "It was a deep religious and spiritual experience," said Paul, who compared his awakening to Saul being struck blind. "It was momentous."

"Paul finally broke through my shell," Natascha told me. "He had changed radically, in one moment." It was the experience of witnessing her husband's heartfelt change that brought her back to the marriage.

Eight years later they were strong and united. Where before they were polarized in sex roles ("very German," Natascha said), now they shopped and cooked together. They rarely argued, but "when one of us doesn't like something coming down the pike," Paul said, "we say so." They are in love, and they will live out the rest of their lives in peace. Theirs is truly a happy ending.

9

ℰ

Work and Love

Although in many ways "happy families are all alike," happy couples found themselves dramatically divided by age on two crucial issues. Older couples by and large had lived their lives one way; younger couples were struggling to live theirs another.

The two issues, linked in so many ways both obvious and subtle, were those of divorce and work. Whereas older couples had been able to support a full-time mother in the home, a mother who felt secure in her role, younger couples had neither the money nor the confidence to duplicate their parents' lives. Younger wives, living in the shadow of divorce, simply could not assume, as their mothers had, that thirty years from now their marriages would still be intact.

The very real threat of divorce for the younger generation shaped their feelings and attitudes toward work. Elaine Stassen, a young wife who, in her late twenties, had left her job to care for her infant son, was typical of her generation: "I watch Donahue and Oprah, and I see it all the time: the men turn forty and leave for a younger woman." Fearing for her future, Elaine had returned to graduate school. "I got my degree so I could feel that if anything happened I could survive and take care of Jamie." Even though her marriage was strong and stable, Elaine seemed to feel very little confidence in the future: "Things aren't just under your control," she said, trying to explain her lack of trust. It was a presentiment of danger her husband did not share. "Oprah and Donahue are directed at women," he told me. "I never even think about it." As the working member of the couple Jason had the emotional luxury of being able simply to assume that his marriage would last. He felt strongly, and perhaps rightly, that Elaine would be far less menaced by the threat of divorce if she, too, were working outside the home.

For young couples, couples in their twenties and thirties, the brave new ideal of working motherhood had thrust upon wives an ironic dilemma. Young wives are no longer supported in marriage by a society that, through legislation and social precedent, makes divorce all but impossible. (As Sylvia Hewlett points out in her book *When the Bough Breaks*, the liberalization of divorce laws *preceded* the liberalization of attitudes toward divorce. Once divorce became a legal right, people came to see it as a valuable personal right, too.) Young wives today, unlike their mothers before them, must ask themselves what will become of them if they do not work and their husbands decide to leave. Not infrequently the younger women with whom I spoke were practicing a kind of "defensive" careerism, working not because they wanted to but because they were afraid not to. The realities of our contemporary culture of divorce had profoundly colored their choices concerning work.

Older Couples and the Division of Labor

Because older couples simply expected their marriages to last, older wives had enjoyed a significantly different experience of motherhood. By and large, older couples had arranged their lives according to the traditional assignment of breadwinning to the man, child rearing and homemaking to the woman. This division had worked very well for the couples with whom I spoke—far better than later generations of women have been led to believe. It worked because in happy couples the wife's contribution to the home and family was not seen as the unskilled and low-status occupation it is often viewed as today. (Ironically, before women could become lawyers and doctors en masse, motherhood as a life calling commanded far more respect.) Universally, happy couples—of all ages—regarded each other as equals, whether or not both were employed outside the home.

The sense of equality shared by older couples was sustained by a complete absence of power struggles. By the time they were in their late forties or older, happy couples simply were not vying with each other for dominance, if they ever had. It was not that they experienced no conflict; as we have seen, depending upon temperament and inclination, a happy couple might quarrel frequently and lustily. It was instead that their arguments were not, at any level, about power and status.

The equal standing of happily married couples revealed itself most clearly in their handling of family finances. Without exception, every happy couple reported that their money was *theirs*, not his or hers, that they experienced no power struggles at all over financial matters. These couples never gave the impression that one partner was controlling the money while the other was reduced to the position of supplicant; in fact, several older husbands volunteered, without prodding, that they found the image of a wife having to ask her husband for money profoundly humiliating to the woman. Frequently wives managed all of a couple's funds, thus reducing the husband's natural economic advantage as the sole employed member of the household.

Again, these couples could certainly experience conflict over money; especially when money was tight, they could grow angry with each other about how much of it they had, and how far it might be stretched. But every conflict, without exception, consisted of two entirely equal sparring partners. It is impossible to overemphasize this point:

• **Happy couples display a pervasive and fundamental equality on the question of money.**

What is more, the most brutally *unhappy* wife with whom I spoke was locked into a decade-long financial battle with her husband that had led her to retain an attorney to draw up a formal financial contract specifying precisely how much income he owed her, as his wife, each month. This was a couple who had lived together in the same home for nearly forty years; the financial contract was not part of a divorce or separation action on either side. This couple was very much married but were desperately unhappy. Their feelings of anger and despair had fueled an ongoing struggle over one of the most fundamental resources of any marriage, the family finances. If happy marriages revealed an utter absence of power issues surrounding economics, unhappy marriages were rife with them.

When partners are entirely equal in terms of control over family finances, the fact that one person is earning money while the other is not fades in significance. And, of course, the having of children often created a strong force for equality—once again, quite contrary to what many younger women have been led to believe. For many couples, for happy couples in particular, children are the great equalizer. The worry and the work, as well as the joys and excitement, that children bring to a marriage tend to eclipse any one partner's brilliant career or driving ambition. Once children are on the scene, they take center stage. Among my couples, even when a parent was highly successful at work, the focus was on the children—which meant that both parents' egos were equally eclipsed at home. It is difficult to be a godlike neurosurgeon at home when child number one is struggling with math, child number two is practicing for a piano recital, and the baby has the croup!

Perhaps surprisingly, for happy couples, the traditional sexual division of labor worked fairly well—although it could make unhappy couples miserable. Which is not to say that happy couples never found their allotted roles in life oppressive. A mother of small children could feel profoundly overwhelmed and burdened by her full-time motherhood; it was simply that this did not propel her and her husband into an all-out war between the sexes. For the happy wife, resenting her sex role simply did not automatically translate into resenting her husband.

Martha Juniper's experience was typical. For all of her innately cheerful nature, Martha had found her years at home with small children immensely stressful. She and Hugh had bought an enormous house with extensive grounds and Martha, a budding interior designer, was overwhelmed by the task of decorating and maintaining the house—this at the same time she was trying to raise two small children born less than a year apart. She was very dissatisfied and unhappy in those days, but her classic gilded-cage angst simply did not take the form of a power struggle between herself and her husband. Martha would wait eagerly for Hugh's return home, hungry for contact with a fellow adult—and when Hugh came in the door he did not disappoint. Hugh was fully sympathetic to her plight; he was there to talk with his wife every night into the wee hours no matter how early he was expected at work the next day. Her pain did not separate them. Hugh listened, and Martha appreciated his concern. That was enough. Neither saw the problem as the fault of the other; they saw it rather as the inevitable result of young family life. Eventually Martha decided to simplify her life by moving the family out of the grand home they had occupied to a town house a third the size with no grounds to tend. Hugh fully supported her in this decision, and the two have lived happily with this solution for twenty years.

Wives at Work

Although happy husbands and wives saw themselves as fundamentally equal, it is true that most husbands in the older generation had not had to deal with the issue of a wife's career ambitions. Nevertheless, the few men who *had* married ambitious women were, true to their commitment to equality, entirely happy with their wives' careers.

Larry Weissberg was typical. His wife, Jane, had always wanted to pursue a career. A black American who had been raised in poverty as one of ten children, she longed to succeed in the world of work. "First I wanted to be an actress," she told me, "then I wanted to be a newspaper reporter, and then I wanted to be a doctor. By the time I met Larry I wanted to do something in the area of human relations." Her first job was scrubbing kitchen floors at two dollars a shot.

By temperament Jane is an intense and driven person: "Jane is ebullient, effervescent, some people would say hyper," Larry offered. Jane described herself as "active, alive, and engaged." Possessed of boundless energy and a terror of poverty, Jane wanted only to work and succeed. She did *not* wish to give up her ambitions to become a wife and mother.

But fifteen months after their marriage, their son was born. "It wasn't planned," Larry said. "She wasn't ready, but on the other hand she knew it was very important to me and it was a real commitment on her part."

"I told Larry if we had a girl I would have one more baby, and if it was a boy I was going to quit." Larry accepted her wishes readily; each accommodated themselves lovingly to the other's needs—Larry's for a child, Jane's for a career. Jane worked up until two days before her baby's birth, and then left work to stay home for five years. "Being home was hard on her," Larry said. "There was some tension for her I'm sure. I have visions of her in that same shift she always wore. But it didn't produce any tension in the family. I think she was making a sacrifice for me. She did it with trepidation, but willingness. And she was a terrific mom."

When she was able to rejoin the work force she quickly landed a prestigious position working for the public-education bureaucracy, where she thrived. Larry supported her return to work fully—to the point where it was he who convinced her finally to complete the doctorate she had begun some years before. "Getting a Ph.D. was really a goal of hers, but she was not going to do it the way she was going," he told me. "She had this prestigious job that was great fun and brought in quite a bit of money, and she had to leave it if she was going to finish her education." Larry convinced her to make this second "sacrifice," a sacrifice she needed to make on her own behalf. She left the job and spent ten months without an income writing her dissertation and looking for a job. "It was a discouraging time," Jane remembered. Eventually she found a job teaching in the public school system at half the pay of her previous job.

It was a disappointment at the time, but the risk she had taken at her husband's urging quickly paid off. Within a year she had found a new position in administration and she was on her way. Today she is a high-ranking administrator at a major university.

The example of Larry and Jane Weissberg reveals a fundamental principle concerning the relation between work and love in the good marriage:

• **A good marriage supports each partner's development in every realm: in love, in family, and in work.**

This principle is so true that not infrequently partners offer crucial support the other does not even fully realize he or she needs. It is entirely possible that the dynamic Jane would never have found the wherewithal to leave a prestigious and engaging job in order to lock herself away with typewriter and dissertation proposal—a step she had to take if she was to move on to better things. Without her husband to push her, she might never have completed her Ph.D. and achieved the significant success she has.

Doubts That Do Not Undermine

Strong couples are so involved in each other's welfare that they are open to each other's aspirations even when they are not immediately convinced of the wisdom of their partner's decision. Ruth Sidel's experience is typical. She had begun her working life in the field of social work, spending fifteen years—from 1956 to 1971—in various part-time positions. During this period she and her husband, Vic, had two children, and all was well.

Then, in 1971, she had an epiphany. It was sparked by a trip to the optometrist. Having decided to purchase a new pair of frames, Ruth made an appointment to have her lens prescription checked. To her surprise she discovered that for some time she had needed a new prescription. When she put on the new glasses she was shocked: there was a whole world out there she had barely glimpsed. "There were tiny twigs and leaves on all the trees that I hadn't been able to see for years!" she told me, her voice still conveying the sense of wonder and discovery she had felt then.

This revelation sparked a life change: If there were twigs on the ends of branches, she reasoned, there was something more to life than social work. "It was the day of the feminist movement," Ruth recalled, "and there was this sense of *potential*, this sense that you didn't have to settle at forty for what you had started at twenty." Entering mid-life, Ruth decided abruptly, riding in a cab and looking at twigs, that she would quit her job.

Not surprisingly, Vic greeted this news with some concern. He was far less certain than his wife that a mid-life discovery of twigs on trees guaranteed the possibility of making a major career change at forty. After fifteen years in her field Ruth had reached an advanced position, he reminded her; he worried that if she did not soon find something just as significant and interesting to do with her life she would become depressed.

But within a month she had left her job, entirely unfazed by her husband's doubts. She was ready for a new adventure. "I left thinking,

'Oh, maybe I'll get a Ph.D. in anthropology,' " Ruth told me, recalling the sense of excitement she had felt at the time. Not two months later a group of four physicians—including Vic—and their wives were invited to visit China. If they accepted, they had to come within the next two weeks; Ruth could not have accompanied her husband had she still been working. It was the opportunity Ruth had known was out there: the trip to China was to launch her upon a highly successful second career. She wrote a book about what she had seen in China when she returned, and spent the decade of the 1970s becoming an authority on the Chinese system of health care while pursuing a Ph.D. in sociology. Today she is an established sociologist, with a position as full professor at Hunter College. It was that first book on China that helped earn her the job.

The principle that emerges from their story, and from the stories of nearly all happy couples, is this:

• **In the good marriage, partners have a great deal of faith in each other <u>even when they are concerned that the other may be wrong</u>.**

While the good marriage does involve a union of two minds, this does not mean that both partners experience simultaneous career epiphanies—far from it! Ruth's husband was worried that his wife might be making a mistake. But, and this is the crucial point concerning the working of a strong marriage, his skepticism was not destructive. There was no element of unconscious competitiveness in his reaction as there can be in the bad marriage. He was not trying unconsciously to undermine her confidence; he was simply concerned for her happiness.

Thus Ruth was entirely free to follow her own instincts, regardless of what her husband thought. And she knew, too, that her husband would support her fully on whatever path she chose. His love and respect for her were unconditional; he was not threatening to withdraw support if she chose to pursue something new and risky. He was simply expressing an opinion that Ruth was entirely free to reject—as she did, without hesitation. That is how, ideally, a marriage should work—much the way in which good parents work. Good parents do their best to support their children's final decisions, even when those choices cause them concern. Good wives and husbands do the same. Ruth knew Vic would back her no matter what she chose to do with the second half of her life. And he did.

Doing Well, Doing Good

Ruth's marriage also illustrates a second principle that emerged from many couples' life experiences: An apparent sacrifice on the part of one spouse often ends up bringing that spouse unforeseen rewards. This had happened for Ruth early on, when she followed her husband to New York. At the time it was an enormous sacrifice for Ruth, all of whose family and friends remained behind in her native Boston. "I was crying in the car as we drove down from Boston," she remembered. But as it turned out, the move brought her nothing but good. "His career moves were always dominant," she told me, "but I profited enormously. My career accelerated tremendously after we moved to New York City." Her loyalty to her husband, her willingness to make sacrifices to advance his career, had ended up advancing her own.

Other couples told similar tales—here we can remember John Kanter's choice, as a major concession to his wife's wishes, to forego a promotion that would have required another traumatic move for the family. It was this very decision to put family before self-interest that, both Rachel and John agree, helped finally to kick his career into high gear. He ended up doing better professionally when he sacrificed work to love.

It was Ruth Sidel who offered the most succinct summary of this principle:

• **Happily married people "do well by doing good."**

In the happy marriage altruism "pays"; doing something good for a loving spouse, even when it entails sacrifice on your part, can bring unexpected rewards in return. When we do something good for our partners, often we end up doing well in life—better than we might have had we doggedly pursued our own self-interest.

Feminism Redux

Of course, even very loving couples could run afoul of the cultural assumptions concerning the relative importance of men's work versus women's. Marcia and Stu Ross told the liveliest tale of their years-long struggle over whose ambitions would require what sacrifices from whom.

Stu fell in love with Marcia from across the room at a publishing cocktail party in Chicago in 1963. "It was the bolt of lightning," he said, "and I zeroed in and hit on her like I've never hit on anyone." An ambitious young investigative reporter for a local television channel, Stu, then twenty-six, did not expect to marry because he did not think he would ever find a woman who valued the things he did. "I had been dating women without brains who were purely accoutrements," he said. "I was thinking about asking a Playboy Bunny to the party, but I didn't." Marcia's seriousness of purpose (at twenty-two she was just having her first play produced) and intellect were a revelation to him.

The next day Marcia, then an editor at a university press, was scheduled to accompany a major author to a television interview at Stu's station. On her way she stopped in a hotel shop to buy the author a new shirt, and it was there that she learned President John F. Kennedy had been shot. When she and Stu met for the second time at the station, the assassination gave their meeting a gravity it might otherwise not have had.

"Everyone was traumatized," Stu remembered. "You wanted to keep talking about it, and getting to know someone under those circumstances swept all the usual trivialities aside. The emotions Kennedy's death triggered were so profound that you immediately spoke more deeply to each other than you would have normally."

Their relationship, begun in the shadow of a national tragedy, was intense from the beginning. On their first dinner date Stu asked Marcia about a charm on the bracelet she was wearing; it proved to be her Phi Beta Kappa key. He was impressed. He liked the fact that she was smart, he liked the fact that she was a writer.

"I was very surprised that he *liked* the idea of my writing," Marcia told me. "I went out a lot, and I found that my being serious about a career was a turnoff to the professional men I dated. I had decided not to focus on husbands because I didn't know whether anyone out there would want a woman who was serious about writing."

But Stu wanted her, and wanted her badly. They became passionately involved; they were married within a year, Stu having proposed to her so soon after they had begun to date that when he dropped to his knees one night to ask her for her hand she did not have a clue as to what he was doing. "He was acting very nervous and distracted that night, and I thought, 'Oh no, he's going to turn out to be weird,' " Marcia remembered. "But then I thought 'Oh, he's going to ask me for a contribution to the March of Dimes [an organization in which Stu was active] and he's nervous about it.' "

When Stu asked her not for a contribution to charity but for her agreement to marry him she started to cry. "I was devastated," Stu said. "But then she said, 'Yes, but we have to be engaged a really long time.' "

From the start the marriage involved a great deal of adjustment for Marcia. She had been planning to take a job in Paris for the next year; now she turned it down. Stu told her that it was fine with him if she accepted her second choice, a position as director of publications for a major university, as long as she could take a three-week honeymoon before starting work. Soon they were married.

When their first child was born Marcia stopped work to mother full-time. "The sex roles were *very* clear in our generation," Stu said.

"I'm not sure today whether I would have given up my job for the kids," Marcia added. "But then it didn't even come up as a question."

Nevertheless, within six months Marcia was, in her word, "bonkers." "I didn't drive, and I had cut myself off from the adult world," she said. When her daughter turned one, Marcia took a job with a small publishing company that was just starting up. Her mother took care of little Sally for the next year, and eventually Stu and Marcia hired a housekeeper who had been working for a cousin. But with her second and, then, third child Marcia returned home full-time.

Meanwhile Stu's career had taken several turns. His tenure as an investigative reporter was now threatened by network politics surrounding the Vietnam War; Stu's station was too liberal for the network's liking. And, too, he was interested in launching a print career. It was at this point that Marcia began to "emerge," as both put it. She had been immersed in a period of intensive mothering; now she longed to get back to her writing. This proved to be the beginning of a major change for the two of them because Stu, who had been drawn to Marcia precisely because of her intelligence and her commitment to writing, did not in fact take her particularly seriously. It was not that he dismissed her talent; he saw her as gifted and intelligent. It was more that he dismissed the notion that her gifts should translate themselves into a real career in the real world. "I believed her but I didn't believe her," Stu told me, trying to explain how he had thought about his wife's aspirations as a young man.

Unaware of how serious his wife was, Stu called a newspaper editor on her behalf and convinced him to give her an assignment. The resulting article was so good that it was widely reprinted, and the newspaper editor began to call Marcia instead of Stu. Her career as a journalist was under way.

The next wrinkle was to come from Stu. When it became clear that he would have to leave the network, he accepted a position at a major university. But this was not what he wanted to do with his life; more and more, he realized, he yearned to write, too. So one day Stu simply came home and announced that he had decided to stay home and write.

Marcia was stunned. "I kept saying, 'This is insane,' " she recalled. "Someone has to work." Stu, who longed to develop a deeper relationship with his children, told her in all seriousness that she should work, and he would take care of the kids. The chance to grow closer to his children was an opportunity Marcia could not deny her husband: "I asked myself, how can I keep him from getting to know and nurture the kids?" She could not.

She agreed to a three-month trial period during which both would work at home. This concession was, as Stu said, "basically just Marcia giving in." And so they embarked upon the second stage of their work lives. Marcia made Stu promise to do 50 percent of the housework and child rearing; "I said yes," Stu told me, "because I would have said yes to anything." He was true to his word.

Now Marcia and Stu began writing together, sharing a byline on columns and magazine articles. The work was plentiful, but for some time Marcia found their arrangement hair-raising. "I was having a panic attack once a week," she told me. "I would say, 'Sure we've got an assignment this month, but what about next month?' "

But the assignments continued to come in, and by the next year

Marcia had grown accustomed to their arrangement. And Stu had grown increasingly close to his children. "I loved picking them up after school," he said. "When I tell other men of my generation about how close I am to my kids, they always express envy." Life was on an even keel.

With the support of his wife, Stu was living out his dream of being a writer. He was happy. But Marcia, who had deferred her own dream of being a playwright for many years now, was growing increasingly restless. The more time she and Stu spent working on their journalism—and by now they were winning awards for their syndicated column—the more she longed to return to her first love, the writing of drama.

The problem was, Stu could not understand her longing at all. "I am very reality grounded," he told me, "and I didn't respect the theater." Those were the days of the journalistic greats, of David Halberstam and Norman Mailer, and Stu thought of journalism as a noble profession. He could not understand why his wife would want to waste her time making things up.

Increasingly, the two quarreled over her desire to write plays again. It was a question of money; in order to support the family both Stu and Marcia needed to be earning income, and Marcia was unlikely to earn much money writing plays. Then, to Stu's consternation, Marcia's first idea for a play was a quasi-Freudian, feminist drama that was none too friendly to the male sex. "I told him I had this idea for a play on women's sublimated hostility to men," Marcia said. Needless to say, few husbands would welcome the news that their wives were now going to leave work in order to write a play about women's anger! And Stu was no exception. Worse yet, Marcia conceived the idea for the play while Stu was away on a business trip. He returned home to find her filled with creative passion over a dramatic concept that he found frankly awful. "I patronized the shit out of her," Stu recalled.

Nevertheless, Marcia wrote the play. That she was able to do so even in the face of real opposition from her husband is a sign of how fundamentally sound their marriage was. As we have seen, in the good marriage partners are not destructive to each other *even when they cannot be immediately supportive*. The fact is, Stu could not respond enthusiastically to a feminist-Freudian farce; it just was not in him to do so. But because his doubts about the project were expressed in the context of an overriding respect for his wife's abilities, those doubts were not corrosive. In order to proceed, Marcia did not need her husband's approval of the play because she already had his full approval of *her*.

The play did well. She was signed by an important agent, and she was invited to join a play-writing development program. "Suddenly I was seeing that this wasn't just a diversion," Stu told me, "but a passion."

Even so, the conflict continued. The family needed the income Marcia could bring in from her journalism, and Stu simply thought journalism was a more important form of expression than theater. He wanted his wife to write nonfiction. Finally they resolved the conflict in much the same way that they had earlier decided Stu's work fate. They brought their problem informally to a marriage counselor whom they knew both personally and professionally. He asked Stu how he would feel if Marcia worked on plays "ten percent of the time."

It was the perfect way of framing the issue. "I couldn't say no," Stu told me. "The ten percent was just like when Marcia agreed that I could try free-lancing for three months."

Not surprisingly, the upshot was that Marcia and Stu both eventually earned much higher incomes than they had before; like Ruth Sidel and John Kanter, Stu and Marcia both "did well by doing good." Marcia, who, after all, was hardly trying to shirk her financial responsibilities, soon began to ask herself how she could use her developing skills as a playwright in order to earn money. She took a class in television writing and began a new career writing scripts for educational films. She also began to write popular fiction. At the time we spoke, she had published two novels.

And Stu, when the inflation of the Carter years began to burgeon out of control, returned to work outside the home. With the recession of the early Reagan years, he took a well-paying position as director of public affairs for a nearby university. By now Marcia really wanted the time to work on her plays—a desire that necessitated that, as Stu put it, "a portion of my creativity was put into deep freeze."

But he did not flinch. "I knew that what was fair was fair," he told me. "She had supported me a hundred and twenty-five percent, she needed to take her time and shine."

This is a lesson to us all: The good marriage does not operate by the principle of the fifty-fifty tit-for-tat. In the good marriage partners give much more than 50 percent. A husband who feels himself to have been supported 125 percent is a husband who freely makes it possible for his wife to pursue her dreams; a wife whose husband has shown her nothing but love will support his desire to work at home so that he can be the one to pick the children up from school. Marcia was willing to endure weekly panic attacks so that her husband could pursue his dream; Stu was willing to return to the world of full-time work and daily commutes so that she could pursue hers. Each signed on for the other's dream, and each helped the other to make the dream come true.

When I met them they were happy indeed. While they had made financial sacrifices in order to follow their dreams, they were putting three children through expensive private universities; they had certainly earned what they needed to earn. And by that time both had found ways to accommodate both reality and desire. Marcia was writing plays and novels, and Stu had managed to create a very well paying but part-time position as personal publicist for a major corporate head. His employer agreed that he could spend 75 percent of his work time on public relations, the remaining 25 percent on his own books and articles. It was ideal.

And, too, Stu had now come to thoroughly understand and appreciate Marcia's talents. Where once he had patronized her, now he felt only respect. All hint of a struggle over whose dream should prevail had vanished from their lives.

Jobs and Babies

Although members of an older generation, Marcia and Stu had wrestled with the same problems facing perhaps the majority of couples in their twenties and thirties today. With so many mothers in the work force, the question universally facing working couples is: Who takes care of the children?

When they were happy together, younger couples actually experienced far less conflict over this issue than the media would lead us to believe. Many couples happily divided the child-rearing chores evenly between them; in the case of a few couples, such as Carlos and Maria Gonzalez (who had been very happy in the past and hoped to be happy once again in the future), it seemed quite possible that the husband was actually doing more of the housework than was the wife. Other couples just as happily adhered to more traditional divisions of labor. Although assigning most of the homemaking chores to a working wife might seem unfair, this was not the way happy couples saw it. When wives were doing more of the work, often it was because they actually preferred to do more of the work; they wished to maintain the wife's traditional authority over house and home. As they understood, asking one's husband to assume 50 percent of the burden also means ceding to him 50 percent of the authority, something they did not want to do.

Again, such agreement between spouses as to what is fair is essential to making a marriage work. It is not the precise details of what each spouse is doing that matter, but how they *feel* about what they are doing. To a very real degree, "fairness" lies in the eye of the beholder. When a woman was strongly focused on her home, frequently she wanted a husband who would accept without question her say-so on how to raise the children and what color to paint the family room. And she was willing to put in the time to back up her authority. A "lopsided" arrangement that might seem very unfair to a woman who expects her husband to shoulder half of the work at home could seem perfectly fair to the woman who wished to be the dominant parent in the house. The principle:

• **If a marriage is to be happy, both partners must feel that their particular division of labor, <u>and</u> of authority, is fair.**

Working It Out

The process of reaching the point at which each partner felt the other was doing his or her fair share *could* take time and effort. Chris and Roger Howser experienced a by-now almost classically difficult transition from two-career couple without child to two-career couple with child. They met in college at Indiana University on an annual cycling trip across the state. Both active and athletic, they were soon happily in love; they married shortly after Chris graduated from college. Roger was then in graduate school, studying engineering. Chris taught high school for a couple of years and then went on to graduate school herself, studying for an M.A. in business administration. Intelligent and ambitious, neither wanted to have children. They were happy pursuing their careers, which moved along at a brisk-enough pace to satisfy both.

Roger would have been content to continue on this track for the rest of his life, but when Chris turned thirty she began to have doubts: Did she really want to go through life without children? She was in the extremely ambivalent position of not wanting children, but at the same time not wanting *not* to have children; within months she found that she was living in a state of chronic conflict. It did not help matters that Roger was prey to no such ambivalence. Going into their marriage, he had not wanted children and he did not want children now. His mind was clear.

The issue was finally resolved, irrationally perhaps but decisively, through a case of sibling competition: once her sisters began to have babies Chris simply could not bear to be left out. She and Roger settled their differences by telling each other that they would just go off birth control and see what happened.

Chris was pregnant within the month and, when their daughter Phoebe was born, they were overjoyed; they were so taken with parenthood that within months both knew they definitely wanted a second child as well. Nevertheless, their transition to parenthood, after thirteen years of a two-career marriage, did not come easily. Theirs was a classic conflict: They confronted the standard issue of Chris's feeling that she was carrying far more of the baby burden than her husband was. Her feelings of overload began well before Phoebe's birth. "The whole day-care thing did not seem to be a reality to him," Chris told me, "whereas it loomed larger than life for me from the moment I knew I was pregnant. I did all the plotting and planning, and every night I'd have a new strategy for finding someone perfect. All he would say was that it was premature."

As Chris realized in retrospect, her preoccupation with lining up day care months before the baby was due probably was premature. Nevertheless, the fact that she was concerned about child care from the first trimester on while for Roger it was at most a distant question set the stage for their relationship throughout the first year of Phoebe's life. During that period Chris felt constantly that she was doing all the work. She was doing the physical work of preparing all the meals and picking up after the baby; on Sundays she would cook all five of Phoebe's dinners for the week, freeze them, and leave a list for

Roger—who picked Phoebe up from day care—telling him which meal went with which night. At night Roger would come in with Phoebe and drop her things—diaper bag, whatever little toys they had sent with her to day care—by the door as he entered. Chris would pick them up when she got home from work an hour later.

Beyond this, Chris felt she was doing all the mental work, too. As she pointed out to Roger in one argument after another, he did not sit in his office during the day planning out the next grocery list; she did. She was doing all the worrying, all the planning, much of the physical picking up, bathing, and cooking. And she was constantly angry with her husband. Finally the three of them went for a weekend trip. In the motel room that night, lying awake in the dark, Chris brought up her list of grievances yet again, saying that Roger wasn't helping, wasn't doing his share, wasn't there for her and their child. Roger said quietly, "I'm doing everything I can. I can't do any more."

"It really hit me," Chris remembered. The finality in her husband's voice made her see that she was truly pushing him over an unseen line that she needed to respect. She forced herself to pull back.

Even so, their tension continued until sometime around Phoebe's first birthday. Suddenly, Chris experienced a sweeping change of heart. "It was like waking up out of a fog one day," she told me. "All of a sudden I just felt totally like the old Chris was back. No more weird overdriven, overburdened working mom stuff; the baby wasn't like a tumor in my head anymore. Suddenly I realized I didn't have to fix all her meals on Sunday and leave a schedule for Roger; suddenly I realized 'Daddy loves baby as much as Mommy does, and Daddy will feed baby.' I still, in the back of my mind, think I could do it better, but it's not this overwhelming, overpowering thing."

Chris believed that much of their problem that first year was her overanxiety about her new baby. "Women do carry the mental burden," she said. "At work I'd be worrying all day about whether there would be milk in the refrigerator when I got home, where Roger's attitude would be, 'Oh, there's no milk, I'll go get some.' I'd be down to a quarter can of formula and I'd be in a panic all day until I got to Target and bought more." Roger simply did not feel this level of anxiety about his child—an attitude that his exhausted wife read as a lack of concern.

Once Chris was able to calm down, she, Roger, and Phoebe coalesced into a smoothly run and happy—if frequently overwhelmed—

working family. Nevertheless, the old dynamic can crop up again as they confront new issues of parenthood. "Now that Phoebe is two we're dealing with discipline for the first time," Chris said. "I tend to be the bad guy. I was taking charge the minute there was something bad going on; I would think 'Roger won't handle it.' He'll occasionally chide me; he'll say, 'You know best.' And then I stop trying to interfere."

Summing up what has changed about her attitude, Chris said, "I'm not the boss of the baby anymore. It's a team effort at this point."

Theirs had become so much a team effort that Roger could envision himself as a full-time parent. Whenever the two of them sat down together and asked each other what they would really want most in life if money were no object, both agreed that they would want one of them to be home full-time—and Roger always observed that it would not necessarily have to be Chris. He was now as fully invested emotionally in their child's well-being as his wife; they were a team. The lesson:

- **Once a couple have children, they <u>must</u> function as a team in order to be happy.**

It is the sense of teamwork that is important, not the actual details of who-does-what. One of the calmer family households I visited was the home of Ken and Caroline Hanks. The parents of two boys, ages nine and five, they had been married for fifteen years when I met them. They were in their mid-thirties and well on their way toward realizing their goals.

Even though both had always intended to work, they had ended up following a classic division of labor with Caroline at home and Ken climbing the career ladder in the local police department. "I worked full-time for the first eight months after Danny was born," Caroline told me, "and then I quit because day care was the pits. He was in a family-care situation being taken care of by an ex-teacher. The woman's daughter would come and bring her boyfriend, who was violent. Danny's diapers weren't being changed, and he seemed depressed." Ken was just as worried as his wife. "I made a point of dropping in at the house at bizarre times," he told me. Both were deeply concerned.

Caroline left her job with the full support of her husband. "We don't live well," she told me, "but we are comfortable on Ken's income. Our goals don't require that we be rich."

Together the two offer a classic definition of teamwork. Ken's career progress has been incredibly demanding: at one point he was working full-time in an appliance store, studying for his police entrance examination, and pursuing a degree in criminology, all at the same time. Being accepted into the police academy was a highly competitive proposition in his city, and he had spent the past four years trying and failing. Finally he came home and told Caroline he'd had it. He was giving up.

She would not hear of it. "You love police work," she told him. "You can't quit."

"He sulked for a few days," Caroline remembered.

"I'd fought for four years and hadn't even come close," Ken said. "I just didn't want to expend the energy."

But he did and was rewarded at last. The academy granted him admission. His rise through the ranks since graduating had been rapid—although this, too, had taken its toll in the form of constant over-work and stress. One time he was so near the edge that Caroline unilaterally declared a vacation weekend. She made reservations at a lodge and announced to Ken that the four of them (there were two children by now) were taking a trip. He protested; he was studying once again for a promotion, and he needed the weekend to prepare. But Caroline told him, in essence, "You can go or not, but we're leaving." She gave him no choice. "I made her promise I could take my books," he told me.

They extended the same concern to their children. "We were doing constant commuting with the kids," Caroline told me. "We were putting 35,000 miles a year on the cars just driving them around. Finally we realized they were stressed, too." So they began to cut back. Instead of driving Danny twenty miles to a private school for soccer, Caroline pulled him out of the program and enrolled him in a gymnastics class close to home. Both partners were keeping a close watch on everyone's activities, making sure to cut back when life was getting out of hand. And they took "mandatory" out-of-town vacations. Even though at present they were living what will be the busiest years of their lives, they were keeping things under control. They were happy.

When Family Responsibilities Cannot Be Shared

Thus the notion that each member of a partnership must be doing precisely the same thing in order to ensure happiness and equality is simply wrong. What is essential to the success of a marriage and a spouse is not sameness but equality of effort and commitment. Both Ken and Caroline were working practically around the clock; every once in a while Caroline—who had almost twenty-four-hour-a-day responsibility for the house and children because of her husband's work hours—would call him at work and say she couldn't take it anymore. "I always tell her," Ken said, "don't say that, because if you break down I'm going to break down!" Both were working non-stop, and they knew it. Both could sympathize with the other's feelings of overload.

This ability to support each other in *different* capacities is essential, because very often the work of running a family simply does not readily lend itself to a fifty-fifty split. Here I think of Hannah and Keith Winslow, who, shortly before I spoke with Hannah, had learned of their daughter's dyslexia. This is the stark reality of child rearing that is so often overlooked in discussions of "liberated" marriage: children have problems, and some children have more problems than others. When a child enters any kind of "special" category—whether it is problems in development and learning, or problems in the emotional or medical areas—the demands placed upon parents soar. Somebody has to be there for the never-ending school conferences, the visits to the child psychiatrist, the appointments with the doctor.

When I met Hannah, she and her husband were doing a remarkable job of handling the highly distressing revelation of their daughter's learning disability. Their division of labor was nearly complete; Keith's sixty-hour-plus workweek as a surgeon at two different Los Angeles hospitals meant that he simply could not be there for the many and varied consultations with learning specialists and school psychologists that lay ahead. It was up to Hannah, who was working part-time out of their home, to attend all these meetings on her own, and to support her daughter emotionally as she underwent the multiple testing and assessment to which a normal child her age would not be subjected. A rough period for parents and child lay ahead.

Keith's responsibility was largely emotional. He gave Hannah the constant and ongoing support she needed; he was the one whose job it was not to panic. As Hannah told me with a smile, "He keeps me in the normal operating range."

Once again, theirs was a classic division of labor upon which many psychologists frown: the wife "carrying" all the emotions, the husband "suppressing" his. But for the Winslows, at this time in their lives, it was essential. Taking one's beloved daughter from one expert to the next in order to subject her to the clinical scrutiny of professionals is an extraordinarily stressful responsibility. Both Hannah and her daughter were going through a very painful process. What they needed at that point was *not* a husband and father who would be fully experiencing his own feelings of anxiety, but a husband and father who could be, quite simply, a rock. Once life settled down again; once a good teacher and classroom had been found for Molly; *then* Keith could get in touch with his fears and Hannah could be the strong one. But for now they needed one person, and one person only, to do the worrying. They needed a strong and stable division of the emotional labor of being a parent.

Working together, Hannah and Keith would pull their daughter through. And they would pull each other through. Judging by the experiences of an older generation, their ability to stand together in this crisis of their late thirties would bring them real happiness as their lives moved on. As we will see, there *is* light at the end of the tunnel.

10

C

Happy Ever After

In good marriages, the retirement years are golden indeed. Couples in their sixties, seventies, and eighties were so much happier than were couples in their twenties and thirties that I found myself envying them their lives. These were people who had raised their families and made their careers, people who now, finally, could relax and enjoy the fruits of their many years of labor.

To a very real degree, it was simply the absence of stress that had so raised the spirits of these couples. No matter how devoted we are to our children and our work, both family and career do create chronic stress in our daily lives. One of the richest rewards of the full and demanding lives that these couples had led in their youth was the peace and quiet that followed. (And, as many a grandparent has observed, grandchildren can be a great deal more fun than one's own children: grandparents experienced the joys of having the little ones around without the headaches of midnight feedings.)

But beyond the absence of career and family stress as a major source of contentment, the people I talked to had won happiness in the later years by means of their very high level of functioning as a couple. The notion of the "dysfunctional" family gained meaning for me as I spoke with couples whose marriages truly had worked. These couples had been able to join forces to make the dreams of both come true. Now, in old age, the happy results of their life partnership were evident for all to see.

Family Finances

The highly productive way in which these couples had managed their lives was perhaps most obvious in the financial realm. Obviously, peace and happiness are difficult states to come by when you don't know where the next paycheck or annuity is coming from—and none of these couples had ended up in such a precarious state. All were financially secure. For the wealthy, of course, the retirement years had not required extensive joint planning or effort; the husband (in every case but one) had made a great deal of money during his career, and he and his wife now enjoyed their ample savings in retirement.

But for most, achieving a secure retirement had required commitment and effort from both partners. One couple, Lars and Angela Seagram, had built a small upstairs apartment above their home and were now renting out the larger house below to provide a steady retirement income for them to live on. The rent was enough to allow them to take two trips a year. They further economized by driving only cars purchased secondhand from car-rental companies, and by closely monitoring small expenditures.

Lars had learned long ago to save money, and Angela had been a full partner in his thrifty ways, telling me, "I can make do on any amount of money." Lars had even instructed one of his young neighbors in the art of saving. The young man, a computer company representative, had been earning a healthy income in the vicinity of six figures, but even so was chronically short of cash. "I told him, save something every day," Lars said forcefully. "If you get a frozen yogurt every day, that's a dollar and seventy-five cents you could be saving." The younger man listened; a few years later, after he had moved away, he returned to show Lars his new savings passbook. Lars, a highly organized person when it came to finances, had passed the secret on.

Marjorie and Henry Williams had also taken steps to ensure a secure old age. When I met them, they were living in a small apartment in

Santa Monica. Although their surroundings were modest, they owned the other apartments in the complex and could look forward to rental income for the rest of their lives. They, too, had found ways to work around a limited retirement income. Unable to afford airplane tickets, they booked inexpensive passage to faraway lands on ocean freighters transporting manufactured goods.

Every couple I talked to, at this stage of their lives, was financially in synch. True, they might disagree slightly on what, precisely, they would spend their limited resources on. Paul and Natascha Stein, having just weathered Paul's heart attack, now had divided opinions on the subject of whether or not to renovate their kitchen. Facing the reality of death, Paul (who had fully recovered from the attack) wanted very much to go forward; "I deserve it," he said. But Natascha, confronting the specter of widowhood, was fearful. What would such an outlay of money mean for her if Paul were to die?

On a far less serious plane, Judy and Harry Jacobs were also dickering over their own kitchen. Judy wanted a new one; Harry took the attitude that, since their current kitchen was perfectly fine (it was), why not spend the money on travel? "Harry doesn't understand," Judy offered mildly, "that sometimes women need a change."

These were the only disagreements about finances that I encountered, and they were minor, to say the least. Older couples had reached a level of remarkable accord when it came to money. The most striking example of a couple's being in complete agreement was the case of George and Lois Midland. Theirs was a classic case of middle-class people who had become "house rich" in the real estate explosion of Los Angeles. Thirty years ago, in 1960, they had put together every penny they could find to purchase a small three-bedroom house overlooking the Pacific Ocean. At the time of this writing, the lot alone was worth more than a million dollars, and George and Lois had decided to sell. They had decided to move to a small and inexpensive condominium, they told me, and lead a merry life spending down their capital.

Their utter agreement as to the wisdom of this plan was striking. Lois would be leaving behind the most glorious flower garden I had seen anywhere—something many people would have difficulty parting with. But, she told me, it was costing her a small fortune to keep it up; it wasn't worth it. Moreover, their decision to spend one million dollars during their retirement years also grew out of a joint agreement not to leave anything behind for their heirs. This plan, too—which would have shocked most of the parents of grown children that I interviewed—commanded both partners' full allegiance. They were utterly united in the decision to do something of which the world at large would disapprove (even the attorney they retained to draw up the plans volunteered the observation that "I've never heard parents talk this way."). No matter how we may judge their plan (about which, more later), the point is that it could, in fact, work for them because both were committed to it.

Self-Direction

Couples could carry out well-laid financial plans because by the time they had reached the retirement years all had developed an active, "self-starting" capacity to function. All had been able to establish full lives for themselves without requiring either a job or children to create those lives for them. Not a single husband or wife regretted his or her retirement; no one had had any difficulty filling the time. Some, of course, took this opportunity simply to sit still at last. "I call myself a bum," Harry Jacobs said happily. Many others were highly active people who had promptly taken on myriad activities, travel, and friendships. Catching these couples between commitments, I sometimes felt breathless listening to their agendas for the day. The Junipers were typical. Over the past month, they told me, Hugh had spent an entire day conducting a bird census in a nearby wooded area, had helped a former colleague conduct an audition for an advertisement he was producing, gone shopping for a keyboard, taken a course in landscape photography, planted his daughter's rose garden, and prepared for a talk before the Garden Club.

Once a successful Hollywood executive, Hugh did not miss the world of work. In part he had Martha to thank for this; it was she who had made the decision that it was time for him to retire, and it was she who, it seemed, had guided him through the process. The accidental death of their daughter in a car accident had set things in motion; facing the loss of her child, Martha now told her husband that life is short. Hugh's career, a long and successful one, had peaked, and it was time to move on. Martha's strong feelings on the subject clearly helped Hugh to make this major change with a minimum of stress. In effect, Martha relieved Hugh of the need to wrestle with this momentous decision. Once again, their capacity to work together smoothed the way for both.

For his part, after having left work Hugh quickly discovered that his talents as an executive were just as useful in the world of garden clubs and condominium associations. As a professional, he had been an effective manager of people; in retirement, this continued. He had not lost his professional self, he had simply shifted his management skills to other venues.

Wives made the transition to the empty-nest years just as smoothly. None of the wives who were working had yet retired, but many had seen their children grow up and leave. Whereas once they had spent their days tending to house and family, now they created days just as full of friendship and interests. Not surprisingly, given how happy and united their marriages were, almost all were entirely content to move on to a stage of life in which their husbands did *not* leave the house each morning for work. The old saying, "For breakfast, for dinner, but not for lunch" applied to only a very few. The one wife who was genuinely unhappy with her husband's retirement seemed to be suffering more from his failing health than from his presence in the house. Because he was not well, she felt an obligation to stay home all day to care for him. Sadly, for this couple, retirement of necessity amounted to a withdrawal from the world.

Children and Grandchildren

It was heartening to discover how many of these couples now enjoyed entirely happy and benign relationships with their grown children. One of the closest families was that of Marjorie and Henry Williams —testimony, I believe, to how far an innately cheerful temperament such as Marjorie's can take a person in life. After the long, hard years of struggle with Henry's gambling habit and with nightmarish day-care arrangements, their family life had turned out very well indeed. Their two daughters, now ages fifty and fifty-one, had both gone to Berkeley, and had married their husbands in a double wedding attended by 400 guests. Henry and Marjorie proudly told me that two of their grandchildren had earned a Ph.D. and that all were accomplished and doing well in life. In their eighties, the Williamses were experiencing the profound satisfaction of having realized the immigrant's dream of hard work and social mobility across the generations. "We are a happy family, and very close," Marjorie told me. Although neither of the daughters and none of the grandchildren lived in Los Angeles, they were constantly in touch. "We phone and write and visit," Marjorie said happily.

This was a common outcome. I think my favorite family of all, when it came to the subject of children, was the Richmonds of suburban Chicago whom we first met in chapter two. Married for thirty-nine years and the parents of ten children, they radiated pride in their brood. They had raised their family of five girls and five boys in a small two-bedroom house; one bedroom was the girls' room, one was the boys', and Joan and Kevin slept on a fold-out couch in the living room. They had not experienced this as any kind of sacrifice, they had never felt crowded; their children were their life. As we have seen, whenever a child was in trouble, they were there. Even while we spoke their youngest and never-married daughter, Sharon, was living there with her own child—a situation that might have thrown another family into turmoil. But Joan and Kevin lovingly accepted their daughter's unwed motherhood. Joan took care of the little girl while Sharon worked and saved; Sharon's fiancé lived with them as well. Thanks to her parents, there was to be no descent into welfare motherhood in Sharon's young life.

At this point every child was happy and well employed. One son had managed to become the firefighter his father had always wanted to be; another daughter was earning a six-figure income in Washington, D.C. Kevin proudly showed me her business card, which he carried with him in his wallet. There was a strong sense of the American dream come true in this small and happy household, of children, with their parents' strong backing, moving forward in the world.

Grown children could be a source of pride, pleasure, and even strength. The lives of Harvey and Marian Spicher richly illustrate the old-fashioned, and today largely forgotten, virtues of the large family. Their three healthy sons had, of course, offered enormous emotional support throughout their parents' struggles with their brain-damaged son. And they had taken steps to ease their parents' financial tensions as well. The fierce arguments Harvey and Marian once had over her use of the family credit card had now become a thing of the past, thanks in part to help from their boys. One grown son, still living at home, paid rent to his mother, giving her the chance to have some money that was hers alone. Another son lent her his charge card. Their agreement, which Marian strictly respected, was that she could charge up to two hundred dollars on the card, after which she would pay him back. "My boys are terrific," Marian said, and they are. The lives of Marian and her husband Harvey reveal how very supportive grown children can be of their parents' marriage, how much children can and do give back to their parents at some point in time.

For his part, Harvey was unriled by his wife's use of his *son's* credit card—even though this arrangement ran directly counter to everything he had been taught to believe as far as family finances are concerned. The reason Harvey could be tolerant of Marian's credit arrangement with his son is precisely the fact that it *was* his son who was extending the credit. He could take pride in a son who would want to help his mother out, and he felt confident that Marian loved her boy so much that she would not do anything to harm his economic standing. In short, the effect of their son's "mixing into" their conflicts over money had been to resolve that conflict.

We hear so much about grown children in trouble: forty-year-olds on drugs being bailed out by their parents, divorced mothers returning home with grandchildren for their parents to raise . . . These stories are familiar to us all. But in the drama of the failed adult child we miss the splendor of the adult child who has become a responsible human being, strong and sure. Such a grown child can have a profoundly positive effect upon his parents' marriage. We miss the fact that the adult child has just as much an investment in his parents' marriage as does the small child; few adults would wish their parents to separate. And unlike the grade-schooler, an adult child can be— perhaps often is—in a position to help. Harvey and Marian Spicher are one couple whose marriage was a great deal stronger because of the children they invested their lives in raising.

The principle that emerged from their story and others':

- **If the small child puts stress on his parents' marriage, the healthy grown child can just as surely support their marriage.**

The Child Who Is Always a Child

Other couples, of course, were not so lucky. Irene and Jerry Kolb continued to struggle with the turmoil caused by their grown son's homosexuality; Bill and Eva Whitman faced a lifetime of problems associated with their son's drug use; Mary and Lou Hawkins were living with chronic worry over what would become of their brain-damaged son when they were gone. This was one of the lessons to be learned from couples in their sixties and older: Your child is always your child. When an adult child suffers, so, too, do his parents. (One older wife told me that her own father, who was still living, was very concerned about the trip she and her husband were planning to take to Russia. Here was an eighty-five-year-old man fretting about his sixty-one-year-old daughter's safety in Moscow.)

A. J. and Marta Long turned wry when we shifted from the topic of their marital difficulties (caused by A. J.'s obsessive work habits) to the troubles their grown children had encountered. Life had dealt the Longs a cruel irony; just as they had finally resolved their own painful and long-standing difficulties over his obsession with his business, each of their three children met with hard times. "We went through about five years of trouble with our grown children," Marta said. During this period both sons experienced serious emotional problems, and their daughter lost her firstborn child to a serious illness. "We had to go into double harness to get through it all," Marta said. "It was like, Hang in there, baby. Do the best you can do."

Today both sons had recovered, but their daughter continued to founder. Her first marriage had ended in divorce, and when the next marriage also failed her second husband retained custody of the children. "She's not capable of keeping the children," Marta said. "She hasn't gotten over her first child's death." And she added: "When I compare my daughter to me I just pray one day she'll get as tough as me. Because otherwise you're a victim."

Forgiveness

Toughness was an important quality, indeed, for older couples; most had developed enormous strength of character and conviction over the years. In the final stage of their lives and marriages, these couples were possessed of remarkable stamina; all seemed to have drawn a second wind somewhere around age fifty.

Many achieved this through a process of self-forgiveness, a term raised by several couples. As Martha and Hugh Juniper told me, "One of the problems among older people is they can't forgive themselves and so they can't love others. We are accepting of ourselves and forgiving of ourselves for past wrongs." It was striking to hear this sentiment coming from the Junipers who seemed, to me at least, to have done very little for which either needed to atone. Yet it was so; this innately cheerful and successful couple had in fact felt a need to forgive themselves.

As one enters the sixties and seventies, it seems, an accounting comes due. Now a couple was compelled to confront whatever they had or had not accomplished. This was an essential process:

• **Those couples who thrive in their older years have made peace with the past.**

No couple offered to spell out precisely what they felt they needed to forgive themselves for; self-forgiveness seemed to be more a generalized feeling about the total sum of one's life rather than a specific accounting for specific wrongs. Nevertheless, the fate of a couple's children was clearly one major issue. These couples had lived out their younger years in a profound state of responsibility for the lives of their young; now that their children were grown, a reckoning was at hand. This was obviously true for those whose grown children were faltering, but it seemed to hold true even for those people whose children were sailing through life. Apparently, easing out from under that enormous burden of responsibility was not a simple matter.

In all, it seemed that one of the requirements of a happy old age was a capacity to "let go" of one's children—or, at least, to let go of the profound sense of responsibility parents assumed while their children were young. A corollary principle emerged:

• **Just as the adolescent must separate from his parents in order to lead a healthy adult life, so the parent must separate from the child in order to enjoy a healthy old age.**

Beyond the fates of their children, the specter of a couple's own approaching deaths prompted a time of taking stock. For most, the reality of death affected them largely at an unconscious level. The people I talked to varied enormously in the degree to which they acknowledged the coming end of their lives; as you would expect, those who had faced the most traumatic deaths already (of a child, or of a parent at a young age) were also most consciously aware of their own mortality. On the other hand, many older people seemed to spend no more time thinking about death than did younger couples. It was only in their often-stated need for self-forgiveness, a concern almost never mentioned by younger people, that we can sense the presence of death. The famous psychoanalyst Erik Erikson, one of the few writers to develop a theory of old age as a distinct developmental stage, wrote eloquently of this time in life: "It is the acceptance of one's one and only life cycle as something that had to be and that, by necessity, permitted of no substitutions. . . . The lack or loss of this [acceptance] . . . is signified by fear of death. . . . Despair expresses the feeling that the time is now short, too short for the attempt to start another life and to try out alternate roads. . . ."

Erikson's wisdom was borne out in the lives of happy couples. These wives and husbands saw their one and only life as something that had to be; they were not living out their retirement years crippled by regret. They did not despair.

And it was this lack of despair, this feeling that one's life was supposed to have been lived as it had been lived, that allowed older couples to remain firmly rooted in the land of the living. Because they felt no need to start over again, they did not see death as the end of hope or opportunity. They did not wish to rewrite their lives; hence they had far less to fear from death.

In short, the presence of death in these couples' lives seemed to work almost entirely as a positive source of motivation. They did not see it as a punishment for sins past:

• **When spouses are proud of their life together, they are not preoccupied with life's end.**

When happy couples consciously did consider their own mortality they saw death positively as a warning that they should live life to its fullest, and give their best, to each other and to the world. Small wonder that so many found this stage of life so fulfilling; so many were living as we all would live if we only knew how.

Investing in the Future

Erikson believed that a person can reach this state of grace only through the process he called *generativity*. Generativity, he wrote, is "the concern in establishing and guiding the next generation." Happiness in old age, he told us, comes from an active involvement, whether through one's own children, through the children of others, or through creative work, in the generations to come.

The experiences of most of the couples with whom I spoke bore this out. Harry Jacobs was so fully engaged with the future that at one point in our interview he brought out a magazine article on just that subject and began to talk about what the future of our country was going to be. Here was a man of seventy-five, actively concerned about the next 100 years of American life!

For most couples, of course, this investment in the future took the form of a profound involvement with their grandchildren. "Grandchildren are the treasures of a long life," Marta Long told me, offering the anonymous quotation she had once read and often reflected upon now. It was emblematic of how profoundly involved in life these couples were that all of them felt deeply invested in the generations following them. And, clearly, their involvement in the lives of young people was good for them. In the words of Erikson once again: "Mature man needs to be needed, and maturity needs guidance as well as encouragement from what has been produced and must be taken care of." The spirit and acts of generativity, Erikson wrote, enrich the soul.

When older people divorce themselves from the younger, Erikson said, stagnation results. "[Such] individuals . . . often begin to indulge themselves," he wrote, "as if they were their own—or one another's—one and only child; and where conditions favor it, early invalidism . . . becomes the vehicle of self-concern."

And indeed, early invalidism was a fate many of my couples had managed to avoid. Most were remarkably healthy; none were preoccupied with the failing body—not even those whose bodies actually were failing. Those who had suffered or were now suffering health problems did so with admirable strength and resolve. These older couples, nearly twenty-five in all, were thriving, living, moving forward with energy and enthusiasm—in spite of the fact that they no longer had the things of youth to look forward to.

For most, grandchildren were the future upon which their vision was trained. Almost all were actively involved in the bringing up of a new generation. Joan Richmond was running an informal day-care center populated entirely by her own grandchildren; the summer before she had daily taken care of five of her grandchildren while their parents worked. When I asked the obvious question as to whether this wasn't a great deal of work she answered absolutely not, she loved caring for her grandchildren. She neither foresaw, nor looked forward to, a time when she would not be involved in the care of children.

The nurturing of grandchildren kept couples connected to the current of life, kept them psychologically "generative" long after their own families had been raised and their careers concluded. And, as Erikson wrote, generativity can take many forms. Couples who did not have grandchildren found other ways to contribute; Judy and Harry Jacobs, one of whose sons had died of AIDS while the other had not yet had children, invested themselves generously in the lives of their son's friends, becoming surrogate parents to the battered group of young men and women living out their own young lives in the shadow of AIDS. They also gave time and energy to volunteer work at their temple and at the local public school. "People who have a lot to offer as retirees should give what they can," Judy said firmly.

The truth of Erikson's observations was at least partially borne out by the one couple who parted ways with all of the others on the subject of their grown children: George and Lois Midland. Their desire to leave nothing behind for their children was a radical departure from the spirit of generativity Erikson sees in healthy older people. "We don't owe the kids anything," they told me frankly, explaining their position. They quoted an embroidered pillow they had seen among the belongings of another retired couple: "Go first class," the pillow said. "Your heirs will."

"Our children have all done very well," Lois added, "so they don't need the money."

It was not that they were on bad terms with their children; they weren't. Their house was filled with beautiful professional photographs of their grandchildren, photographs they had commissioned and paid for. Nevertheless, theirs were not the usual emotions associated with "generativity." And, as Erikson would predict, this couple was considerably more preoccupied by thoughts of their own eventual deaths than were others. "I don't want my ride on the ferris wheel to end," George told me. Then, saying he was in good shape at seventy-four he asked me, "But how many people do you know who are worth spit at eighty?" The Midlands' resolve to "take it with them" coincided with a strong focus upon, an ongoing awareness of, the imminence of death. It seems fair to say that Erikson is right: the old need the young as much as the young need the old. In their older years couples who invested themselves in the future lives of the young were happiest of all. And they were the least haunted by death.

Coda

Ultimately, what the couples in this book give us is a sense of possibility. Happy families, they teach us, are as commonplace as the unhappy ones; being happily married for a lifetime is a real possibility. The couples in this book, most of them, were not extraordinarily gifted in the expression of love (though some certainly were)—they were simply faithful, committed, and able to learn. Above all they were governed by an enduring sense of respect, for themselves and for their mates. If they can do it, we can, too. That is the lesson.

This sense of possibility is essential because, at heart, it is a form of *confidence.* We hear so much about the importance of self-confidence to every other undertaking in life, and yet we neglect this factor when it comes to the major undertaking that is marriage. People need to feel a basic confidence that marriage is possible—if only to weather the storms a fifty-year union will bring. We need to feel confident that the storms will pass. People who believe that they *can* create a strong marriage if they set their minds to it do not give up.

In times gone by, before the divorce revolution of the 1970s, this crucial sense of possibility was supplied by society at large: people simply expected their marriages, and those of their friends and relatives, to last. Couples in their fifties and older universally told me this. Whenever I asked them why they thought their marriages were so much more stable than marriages today they answered that for their generation divorce was simply unthinkable. Clearly, while the unthinkability of divorce may have kept a great many bad marriages together, it also preserved a great many good marriages when times were hard.

The unthinkability of divorce for older generations was, of course, also a form of confidence, an unquestioning belief that any marriage, whether brilliantly happy or not, would certainly last a lifetime. When we say that people used to "believe" in marriage this is what we mean. It is not just that in the 1950s people believed in the sanctity of wedlock—rather that they took it for granted. When we attend a wedding today we do so carrying the 50 percent failure rate in our minds; after twenty years of liberal divorce laws the church pews and temple aisles are filled with cynics. (Remember Patterson and Kim's discovery that more than half of their sample felt there was no reason to marry at all!)

In sharp contrast, before divorce became an accepted institution wedding guests routinely expected the young couple exchanging vows before them to stay together for good. In those days lifelong marriage seemed a natural state, not the minor miracle it has come to seem since the 1970s. Thus what our culture can no longer give us—a fundamental faith that marriage is possible—we must now find within ourselves, and within others. This book is intended to help.

The lesson to be learned from the long and happily married is that bad times can pass, and good times return. In the course of a decades-long marriage, partners quite simply get better at being married. Here I remember Frank and Rebecca Sullivan. The Sullivans were possibly the one couple who most inspired me, who made me feel most powerfully that happy endings are possible. In their eighties, they were still palpably in love, so much so that it was Rebecca herself who broached the topic of sex (a subject I had hesitated to bring up to a couple old enough to be my grandparents!). "I guess I should mention," she said sweetly as she talked about her marriage, "that we've always had a very nice time together in bed." Frank nodded agreement happily: "If it isn't as often now, it's better."

Their life story was all the more inspiring in that they had weathered very hard times indeed. They spoke to me of the tumultuous years during which they had struggled with four children, with financial problems, with the constant disruption of living in the half-built family home to which Frank devoted every passing moment not already claimed by work and a long Southern California commute. Sitting with them in their living room, listening to their stories, I perceived their early years together as one long saga of chronic, unrelieved "stress," to use the terminology so favored by my own generation.

But now, forty years down the line, all was calm. The house was long built and lovely, the children were grown and doing well, the retirement trips to Europe had commenced. Trying to put into words what had changed between them, Frank said, "I think we were always happy, we just didn't know how to express it."

It is possible, the Sullivans told me, to be happy and yet not know it—it is possible for joy to emerge from pain. At the very least we owe it to ourselves and our children to try; we owe it to ourselves and our children to keep the faith. To *believe.*

Bibliography

ℭ

Barringer, Felicity. "Doubt on 'Trial Marriage' Raised by Divorce Rate." *New York Times*, 9 June 1989, A1, B5.

Bateson, Mary Catherine. *Composing a Life*. New York: A Plume Book, 1990.

Beck, Aaron T. *Love Is Never Enough: How Couples Can Overcome Misunderstandings, Resolve Conflicts and Solve Relationship Problems Through Cognitive Therapy*. New York: Harper & Row, 1988.

Berger, Peter L., and Thomas Luckmann. *The Social Construction of Reality*. Garden City, New York: Anchor Books, 1967.

Bernard, Jessie. *The Future of Marriage*. New York: Bantam Books, 1978.

Blau, Melinda. "In It Together." *New York*, 4 September 1989, 44–54.

Blumstein, Philip, and Pepper Schwartz. *American Couples: Money Work Sex*. New York: William Morrow and Company, 1983.

The Book of Common Prayer. New York: The Church Hymnal Corporation, 1979.

Bradsher, Keith. "Young Men Pressed to Wed for Success." *New York Times*, 13 December 1989, B1, B8.

Buchanan, Robert. "Eau de Lifestyle." *7 Days*, 20 July 1988, 7–8.

Burgess, Ernest W., and Paul Wallin. *Engagement and Marriage*. New York: J. B. Lippincott Company, 1953.

Caplow, Theodore, Howard M. Bahr, Bruce A. Chadwick, Reuben Hill, and Margaret Holmes Williamson. *Middletown Families: Fifty Years of Change and Continuity.* Minneapolis: University of Minnesota Press, 1982.

Cooper, David. *The Death of the Family.* New York: Pantheon Books, 1970.

Cuber, John F., and Peggy B. Harroff. *Sex and the Significant Americans: A Study of Sexual Behavior Among the Affluent.* New York: Penguin Books, 1965.

Davitz, Lois Leiderman. "7 Secrets of a Super (Solid) Marriage." *New Woman,* August 1988, 40, 42–43.

Dean, Paul. "I Do, I Don't." *Los Angeles Times,* 14 February 1990, E1, E5.

D'Emilio, John, and Estelle B. Freedman. *Intimate Matters: A History of Sexuality in America.* New York: Harper & Row, 1988.

de Rougement, Denis. *Love in the Western World.* New York: Harper & Row, 1956.

Dyer, Everett D. *Courtship, Marriage, and Family: American Style.* Homewood, Illinois: The Dorsey Press, 1983.

Erikson, Erik H. *Childhood and Society.* 2d ed. New York: W. W. Norton & Company, 1963.

Facklam, Margery. "The Secrets of Strong Families." *American Baby,* June 1987, 70–73.

Figley, Charles R., and Hamilton I. McCubbin, eds. *Stress and the Family.* Vol. 2, *Coping with Catastrophe.* New York: Brunner/Mazel Publishers, 1983.

Gabriel, Trip. "Why Wed? The Ambivalent American Bachelor." *New York Times Magazine,* 15 November 1987, 24–34, 60.

Gillis, John R. *For Better, For Worse.* New York: Oxford University Press, 1985.

Glenn, Norval D. "Marriage on the Rocks." *Psychology Today,* October 1987, 20, 21.

Goldbart, Stephen, and David Wallin. "Mapping the Terrain of the Heart: Passion, Tenderness, and the Capacity to Love." *Tikkun* 5 (March/April 1990): 44–47, 126–28.

Goleman, Daniel. "Chemistry of Sexual Desire Yields Its Elusive Secrets." *New York Times,* 18 October 1988, C1, C15.

———. "Feelings: Gender Gap Lingers." *International Herald Tribune,* 25 August 1988, 7.

———. "Scientists Pinpoint Brain Irregularities in Drug Addicts." *New York Times,* 26 June 1990, B5, B9.

———. "The Lonely Crowd: Study Finds Isolation Raises Health Risk." *International Herald Tribune,* 5 August 1988, 1.

———. "Want a Happy Marriage? Learn to Fight a Good Fight." *New York Times,* 21 February 1989, C1, C6.

———. "What Bothers Women About Men, and Vice Versa." *New York Times*, 13 June 1989, B1, B10.

———. "When Rage Explodes, Brain Damage May Be the Cause." *New York Times*, 7 August 1990, B1, B8.

Graves, Ginny. "From Spit-Up to Split-Up." *Parenting*, May 1990, 21, 22.

Hall, Holly. "Wedded Faces." *Psychology Today*, December 1987, 10.

Harris, Louis. Inside America. New York: Vintage Books, 1987.

Hertz, Rosanna. *More Equal Than Others: Women and Men in Dual-Career Marriages.* Berkeley: University of California Press, 1986.

Hewlett, Sylvia Ann. *A Lesser Life: The Myth of Women's Liberation in America.* New York: William Morrow and Co., 1986.

Hochschild, Arlie, with Anne Machung. *The Second Shift*. New York: Viking, 1989.

Kaprio, Jaakko, Markku Koskenvuo, and Heli Rita. "Mortality After Bereavement: A Prospective Study of 95,647 Widowed Persons. *American Journal of Public Health* 77 (March 1987): 283–87.

Jacobson, Neil S., and Alan S. Gurman. *Clinical Handbook of Marital Therapy.* New York: The Guilford Press, 1986.

Johnson, George. *In the Palaces of Memory: How We Build the Worlds Inside Our Heads.* New York: Alfred A. Knopf, 1991.

Johnston, Jill. "Liar! Liar! Liar!" Review of *Daddy, We Hardly Knew You*, by Germaine Greer. *New York Times Book Review*, 28 January 1990, 7.

Klagsbrun, Francine. *Married People: Staying Together in the Age of Divorce.* New York: Bantam Books, 1985.

Kohn, Alfie. "Making the Most of Marriage." *Psychology Today*, December 1987, 6, 8.

Larsen, David. "Late Finale: When Long Marriages End." *Los Angeles Times*, 25 January 1990, E1, E9.

Lasch, Christopher. *The Culture of Narcissism: American Life in an Age of Diminishing Expectations.* New York: Warner Books, 1979.

Lauer, Jeanette C., and Robert H. Lauer. *'Til Death Do Us Part: How Couples Stay Together.* New York: The Haworth Press, 1986.

Lear, Martha. "The Pain of Loneliness." *New York Times Magazine*, 20 December 1987, 47, 48.

Lear, Martha Weinman. "The New Marital Therapy." *New York Times Magazine*, 6 March 1988, 63–64.

Leibowitz, Michael R. *The Chemistry of Love*. New York: Berkley Books, 1984.

L'Engle, Madeleine. *Two-Part Invention: The Story of a Marriage*. New York: Farrar, Straus & Giroux, 1988.

Libman, Joan. "Therapists Begin Taking a Dim View of Divorce." *Los Angeles Times*, 28 November 1989, E1, E3.

Lynch, James J. *The Broken Heart: The Medical Consequences of Loneliness*. New York: Harper Colophon Books, 1977.

————. *The Language of the Heart: The Body's Response to Human Dialogue*. New York: Basic Books, 1985.

Maugh, Thomas H., II. "Sex, American Style: Trend to the Traditional." *Los Angeles Times*, 19 February 1990, A1, A22.

McCubbin, Hamilton I., and Charles R. Figley. *Stress and the Family*. Vol. 1, *Coping with Normative Transitions*. New York: Brunner/Mazel, 1983.

Mehren, Elizabeth. "Hite Report Plagued by Controversy." *Los Angeles Times*, 29 October 1987, E1, E3.

————. "The War Over Love Heats Up Again." *Los Angeles Times*, 29 October 1987, 1, 20.

Morgan, S. Philip, Diane N. Lye, and Gretchen Condran. "Sons, Daughters, and the Risk of Marital Disruption." *American Journal of Sociology* 94 (July 1988): 110–29.

Otten, Alan L. "Deceptive Picture: If You See Families Staging a Comeback, It's Probably a Mirage." *The Wall Street Journal*, 25 September 1986, 1, 22.

Paddock, John R., and Karen M. Schwartz. "Rituals for Dual-Career Couples." *Psychotherapy* 23 (Fall 1986), 453–59.

Patterson, James, and Peter Kim. *The Day America Told the Truth: What People Really Believe About Everything That Really Matters*. New York: Prentice Hall Press, 1991.

Person, Ethel Spector. *Dreams of Love and Fateful Encounters: The Power of Romantic Passion*. New York: W. W. Norton and Company, 1988.

Raskin, Bruce, and Bill Shapiro. "More Sex, Please, We're Fathers." *Parenting*, March 1990, 78, 80–85.

Rubenstein, Carin. "The Baby Bomb." *New York Times Magazine/Part 2: Good Health Magazine*, 8 October 1989, 34, 36, 38, 40–41.

Russel, Cheryl. *100 Predictions for the Baby Boom: The Next 50 Years*. New York: Plenum Press, 1987.

Scarf, Maggie. *Intimate Partners: Patterns in Love and Marriage*. New York: Random House, 1987.

Schmidt, William E. "Valentine in a Survey: Fidelity Is Thriving." *New York Times*, 12 February 1990, B1, B2.

Schreiberg, Stu. "Behind Every Great Woman . . ." *Los Angeles Magazine*, July 1985, 150–53, 188–89, 191.

Schwartz, Roslyn, and Leonard J. Schwartz. *Becoming a Couple*. New York: University Press of America, 1986.

Simon, Cheryl. "Instant Intimacy." *Psychology Today*, February 1988, 13.

Skolnick, Arlene S. *The Intimate Environment: Exploring Marriage and the Family*. 4th ed. Boston: Little, Brown and Company, 1987.

Skynner, Robin, and John Cleese. *Families and How to Survive Them*. New York: Oxford University Press, 1983.

Solway, Diane. "Creative Couples: Is Love Blind?" *New York Times*, 19 July 1987, B1, B14.

Sternberg, Robert J. *The Triangle of Love: Intimacy, Passion, Commitment*. New York: Basic Books, 1987.

Taylor, Shelley E. *Positive Illusions: Creative Self-Deception and the Healthy Mind*. New York: Basic Books, 1989.

Terman, Lewis M., assisted by Paul Buttenwieser, Leonard W. Ferguson, Winifred Bent Johnson, and Donald P. Wilson. *Psychological Factors in Marital Happiness*. New York: McGraw-Hill Book Company, 1938.

Vaughan, Diane. *Uncoupling: Turning Points in Intimate Relationships*. New York: Oxford University Press, 1986.

Wallerstein, Judith S., and Sandra Blakeslee. *Second Chances: Men, Women, and Children a Decade After Divorce*. New York: Ticknor & Fields, 1989.

Walster, Elaine, V. Aronson, and L. Rottman. "The Importance of Physical Attractiveness in Dating Behavior." *Journal of Personality and Social Psychology* 4 (1966): 508–16.

Welch, Dawn. "Married, with Problems." *Self*, August 1991, 40.

Wiener, Leonora. "No Sex, Please, We're Mothers." *Parenting*, August 1989, 45–49, 111–12.

"Wives Take Lead on Divorce." *Los Angeles Times*, 12 June 1989, Metro, 3.